Forty Ways
Think About
Architecture

This edition first published 2014
Copyright © 2014 John Wiley & Sons Ltd

Registered office
John Wiley & Sons Ltd, The Atrium, Southern Gate, Chichester, West Sussex, PO19 8SQ,
United Kingdom

For details of our global editorial offices, for customer services and for information about how to apply
for permission to reuse the copyright material in this book please see our website at www.wiley.com.

Wiley publishes in a variety of print and electronic formats and by print-on-demand. Some material
included with standard print versions of this book may not be included in e-books or in print-on-demand.
If this book refers to media such as a CD or DVD that is not included in the version you purchased,
you may download this material at http://booksupport.wiley.com. For more information about Wiley
products, visit www.wiley.com.

Designations used by companies to distinguish their products are often claimed as trademarks.
All brand names and product names used in this book are trade names, service marks, trademarks or
registered trademarks of their respective owners. The publisher is not associated with any product or
vendor mentioned in this book.

Limit of Liability/Disclaimer of Warranty: while the publisher and author have used their best efforts
in preparing this book, they make no representations or warranties with respect to the accuracy
or completeness of the contents of this book and specifically disclaim any implied warranties of
merchantability or fitness for a particular purpose. It is sold on the understanding that the publisher is
not engaged in rendering professional services and neither the publisher nor the author shall be liable
for damages arising herefrom. If professional advice or other expert assistance is required, the services
of a competent professional should be sought.

978-1-118-82261-6 (paperback)
978-1-118-82257-9 (ebook)
978-1-118-82258-6 (ebook)
978-1-118-82256-2 (ebook)
978-1-118-82253-1 (ebook)

Executive Commissioning Editor: Helen Castle
Project Editor: Miriam Murphy
Assistant Editor: Calver Lezama
Senior Production Editor: Samantha Hartley
Cover design, page design and layouts by Jeremy Tilston, The Oak Studio Ltd
Printed and bound in Italy by Printer Trento

Forty Ways To Think About Architecture

Architectural history and theory today

Edited by
Iain Borden
Murray Fraser
Barbara Penner

To Adrian

A brilliant and generous teacher, writer, colleague and friend.

Table of Contents

Acknowledgements

When, in June 2013, we first began this volume to celebrate Adrian's career, we set ourselves two very ambitious goals: first, to produce the volume *before* Adrian's official retirement (in September 2014); and second – and even more optimistic – to keep the volume a secret from Adrian until publication. We gave our project the code name 'Quaranta', and swore everyone – all 40 contributors and the many others who were involved in editing and production – to secrecy.

Miraculously, to our knowledge, nobody slipped up. We are most grateful for the amazing efficiency, enthusiasm and, above all, discretion displayed on the part of everyone who made this volume possible. It is hard to believe that a collection of essays like this one can be produced in such a short space of time – surely there is no better testimony to the regard and affection in which Adrian is held than this.

In particular, we would like to gratefully acknowledge the help and support of Briony Fer. From digging out images from Adrian's slide and photo collections to giving us by-proxy permission to reprint 'Future Imperfect', this would have been a much poorer collection without Briony as our co-conspirator.

This project has benefited greatly from excellent administrative and editorial support. Danielle Willkens did a truly exceptional job at keeping on top of contributions and coordinating the submissions – she acted with real skill, patience and tact. Helen Castle and the editorial team at Wiley (especially Calver Lezama and Miriam Murphy) provided outstandingly efficient support in terms of editing and production. We thank them most sincerely for their efforts.

While not being a 'Bartlett' book per se, it never could have happened without the generous financial support from the Bartlett School of Architecture and its then Director, Marcos Cruz, who wished to recognise Adrian's outstanding contribution to the school over forty years in a suitably substantial and lasting way.

Thanks also, of course, to all of the many contributors, who responded so magnificently to our request for ideas, texts and images in a ridiculously short time frame. Without you, it never would have happened.

Introduction

IAIN BORDEN, MURRAY FRASER, BARBARA PENNER

Adrian Forty started teaching at the Bartlett School of Architecture in autumn 1973. At the same time he was taken on as a doctoral student by Reyner Banham, and soon became regarded as a protégé of that renowned British architectural historian and critic. Banham left The Bartlett for the State University of New York at Buffalo in summer 1976, at which juncture Mark Swenarton, another of Banham's doctoral students, joined The Bartlett's history and theory staff. Together, Forty and Swenarton founded a new master's programme which ran for the very first time in the 1981–2 academic year. At that point the course was called the MSc History of Modern Architecture; later on it would become the MA Architectural History. Adrian continued to teach the first-year undergraduate programme in architectural history and theory while co-running the MSc course, first with Murray Fraser, then with Iain Borden, and then with a group of colleagues that included Ben Campkin, Barbara Penner, Peg Rawes and Jane Rendell. Adrian has also been a revered doctoral supervisor, world-famous scholar and a much-valued mentor and colleague. Finally, he retired from the Bartlett in summer 2014, fittingly 40 academic years since he first began there.

This book is not intended as a simple festschrift to celebrate Adrian's retirement. Rather, we see it as an opportunity for a wide spectrum of scholars and architects – again, 40 in total – to use the opportunity to write about what has happened to architectural history and theory in the four decades that Adrian was at The Bartlett. Some of the contributors refer to Adrian's ideas and writings, while others choose to write on themes which might be inspired from having read his books and essays, or which they simply feel he might enjoy. The essays look at the many scales of architecture from its urban manifestations to how buildings are conceived, built and occupied, then down to a closer look at construction materials and details. We have invited art historians and design historians as well as those who are more directly engaged in designing or teaching architecture. The net result is a rich mix of contemporary thinking about architecture, summed up in readable and lively essays rather than scholarly prose.

'FUTURE IMPERFECT'

The essays in this book bear testament to the richness, diversity and influence of Adrian's thinking, teaching and writing about architecture. Indeed, we are delighted to be able to include here, in the opening essay, the text of Adrian's inaugural professorial lecture at UCL, which he delivered in December 2000 (see Chapter One). Entitled 'Future Imperfect', this lecture provides a valuable insight into some of the main ingredients of Adrian's approach to architecture, including his reflections on how these relate to Reyner Banham's own inaugural professorial lecture at UCL which had been delivered exactly – to the day – 30 years previously. 'Future Imperfect' thus takes us through a remarkable range of considerations, including the value of studying actual works of architecture as well as their representations, the significance of everyday buildings as well as the canonical works of famous architects, and the dialogue which the historian can construct between 'theory' and architectural objects.

Adrian photographing the Salk Institute in La Jolla, California, closely watched by his younger daughter, Olivia.

But this lecture was also far more than a reflective consideration on methods and principles. Typically, and essentially for Adrian, it is also a reflection on both an unusual theme – imperfection – and a series of actual objects. So in his talk Adrian takes us on at once a conceptual journey, guiding us through notions of perfection and imperfection from Aristotle and Alberti to Ruskin and Godard, and also a tour of architecture as buildings and objects, from the medieval Abbeville Cathedral to 20th-century works by Perret, Le Corbusier, Price, Gehry and Koolhaas, as well as to much less well-known buildings such as a social housing estate on the edge of Paris.

Equally typical of Adrian is the fact that none of this is 'difficult' to follow: although he studiously takes apart the abstract term of imperfection, he does so in a manner which is always clearly comprehensible and accessible to all. He also does so with a wit and occasional idiosyncratic flourish (the ending line is pure delight) which maintains a sense of his own personal charm and eloquence – we are always aware that this is Adrian, a real person, who is speaking, and that we are not just hearing an enunciated text.

There is one further aspect of this lecture which gives another insight into Adrian's working and intentions, as signified by the first word of its title: 'future'. Despite having written one of the seminal books on design history (*Objects of Desire: Design and Society since 1750*, 1986), and having recently completed another equally influential book on architectural theory (*Words and Buildings: A Vocabulary of Modern Architecture*, 2000), Adrian leaves these largely in the background of his talk. This is not a grandiose display of previous successes and achievements. Instead, the lecture is about the future – a future that is of Adrian's own work – and in particular on his then-just-beginning research into the culture of concrete in relation to architecture. And this, perhaps, signifies above all else a quality which is always evident in Adrian's work, namely a restlessness to move on, in this case from design to words to materials, and so always to consider new aspects of architecture and the world in which it operates. The 'Future Imperfect' lecture is therefore not just a reflection on the past, or a consideration of where we are, but of where we might be heading in the years to come.

EXPANDING THE FIELD

Before turning to 'Future Imperfect', however, as well as to all the other essays in this collection, we would like to outline briefly how Adrian has contributed in significant ways not only to architectural history and theory teaching at The Bartlett, but also to its development as a discipline in the UK and internationally. As Adrian himself has noted, architectural history in the UK has only relatively recently come to occupy a more secure and settled place within academe – a situation that Adrian's own efforts at The Bartlett have helped to bring about.[1] Prior to the 1960s, many of the most noteworthy scholarship and architectural history initiatives were produced independently of universities and architectural schools. To cite just two examples: the *Survey of London* series, begun in 1894, has been, until very recently, an independent initiative (and in 2013 left the auspices of English Heritage to join The Bartlett); and the RIBA Drawings Collection was assembled by John Harris, who had no affiliation with any institution of higher education. Architectural history was pursued largely by scholars who were based at museums (for instance, Sir John Summerson at Sir John Soane's Museum) or were of independent means. Voluntary associations from the Georgian Group to the Victorian Society and learned societies such as the Society of Architectural Historians of Great Britain played crucial roles in supporting the discipline through conferences and publications. Certain journals, such as the *Architectural Review*, also emerged as important platforms for the dissemination of architectural history.

Of course, there were a few important exceptions to this rule. By the time Adrian entered the scene, architectural history in the UK was already in the midst of change. Some opportunities for doctoral training did exist by the 1950s and 1960s, thanks largely to the influx of European émigrés fleeing from Nazism in the 1930s. Located just down the road from The Bartlett, the Warburg Institute had been transplanted to London from Hamburg in 1933 and Rudolf Wittkower was employed there between 1934 and 1956. Wittkower's educational impact was notable, as he trained Colin Rowe among others. Equally – if not more – critical was the arrival in London in 1935 of Nikolaus Pevsner, who then in 1941 began to work at Birkbeck College (also very near to The Bartlett), and whose *An Outline of European Architecture* (1942), *Buildings of England* publications (begun in 1951), and co-editorship of the *Architectural Review* were all so crucial to establishing a popular understanding of what architectural history should be – that is, the story of the aesthetic and spatial intentions of architects. Pevsner also began to take on doctoral students at Birkbeck and also at the University of Cambridge (where he was Slade Professor of Art), including Reyner Banham and Robin Middleton.

The general expansion of higher education in Britain in the 1960s was significant for the fortunes of architectural history. This period, for instance, saw the establishment of the University of Essex's Master's course in Architectural History and Theory, under the leadership of Joseph Rykwert, which, from 1968, trained a large number of well-known historians and theorists, from Robin Evans to Mohsen Mostafavi. (Rykwert, with Dalibor Vesely, then went on to establish the research programme at the School of Architecture at the University of Cambridge in 1980.) Overall, however, it is notable that architectural history training in the 1960s was still largely taking place within art or art history departments rather than in schools of architecture; following an undergraduate degree in History at Brasenose College, Oxford, Adrian's own master's was in Art History at the Courtauld Institute and his first teaching position was at Bristol School of Art (1971–3). This situation slowly began to change in the wake of the 1958 'Oxford Conference', which decreed that schools of architecture should not only train architects but also conduct architectural research – a decision which was to have far-reaching consequences for architectural education. At The Bartlett, it led to the appointment of Richard Llewelyn Davies in 1960 who renamed the School of Architecture the School of Environmental Studies – a tale expertly summarised in Peter Hall's contribution to this volume (see Chapter 32) – and committed it to an ambitious multidisciplinary programme of research that saw architects working alongside psychologists, economists, planners and physicists. Llewelyn Davies also decided that an architectural historian should have a place at the table.

Enter Reyner Banham, who was appointed to a senior lectureship at the Bartlett School of Environmental Studies in 1964, and who produced some of his best-known studies during his 12-year tenure at the university.[2] Banham also took on doctoral students including Charles Jencks, Mark Swenarton and Adrian himself. While Banham rebelled against many of the aesthetic tenets of Pevsnerian architectural history (a questioning that is more quietly continued by Adrian too), he never wavered from Pevsner's belief that architectural history should not be the preserve of an elite, but that it should be something very

Adrian in the Chilean desert.

active and alive within a culture. This anti-elitist commitment has been carried through into Adrian's famously lucid lectures and writings on architecture, which have been enjoyed by Bartlett students since he began to teach at the school in 1973, and may also help to explain why Adrian has never disdained teaching undergraduates. Indeed, one of Adrian's most important contributions to The Bartlett has been his Year One introduction to architectural history, a course which he has run for several decades, and is now something of a legend, being massively popular with students and tutors alike. As with all of Adrian's teaching, the course places a firm emphasis upon looking: students are required to visit buildings and then to write about them, drawing upon their own first-hand observations and experience.

In terms of entrenching architectural history as a subject of academic research within architecture schools in Britain, however, probably the most significant move on Adrian's part was to establish in 1981, with Mark Swenarton, the aforementioned MSc History of Modern Architecture (now the MA Architectural History). This was among the earliest of its kind in Britain, or indeed anywhere in the world. A large number of the scholars who are now teaching architectural history and theory in British schools of architecture, as well as in many schools abroad, have taken this course over the years, and so it can claim to have had an incredible impact on the field. Many alumni of the course are also contributors to this volume.

EVERYDAY AND EMPIRICAL, STRUCTURAL AND SOCIAL

What, then, has been Adrian's contribution to the teaching of architectural history and theory, as exemplified by the Master's course? Perhaps the first aspect to mention is its openly socialist stance, or what is often labelled neo-Marxist (who can possibly be classified as a real Marxist these days?). Certainly the key founding principle of the MSc History of Modern Architecture was its polemical introduction of political analysis into architectural history and theory – something which was simply not being done elsewhere in 1970s and 1980s British architectural academia. Perhaps the closest parallel elsewhere was Manfredo Tafuri and others at the Venice School, which was defiantly hard-line Italian Marxist, and happened to fire up many of those of a left-wing disposition at that time. In essence what Adrian did – as a PhD student of Banham – was to adopt his own version of the Tafurian sense of politics as a means of displacing Banham's training in German Idealist history (something which Banham had acquired from Pevsner). And influenced in turn by Banham, Adrian went on to cross-fertilise his highly political approach by mixing it with the best traits of the British tradition of empirically based history writing.

Another important difference in the new approaches was that while Tafuri and his colleagues were deeply interested in critical theory from the Frankfurt School et al, in Britain the political approach to history was always more infused with what is usually described as cultural studies. To understand what Adrian was trying to do with the new Master's programme, one has to see it as emulating British left-wing social historians such as Raymond Williams, EP Thompson, Raphael Samuel and Stuart Hall. As well as being much more interested in conditions of everyday life and actual lived social processes, as opposed to the more abstract concepts favoured by critical theory, it also meant that the British historians were never really seen as being such overt or hard-line Marxists as were their continental European counterparts. Yet with the subsequent collapse of the Soviet Bloc, and the near eclipse of Communist parties in most European nations, it is the culturally driven approach which has served the passage of time the best.

A further key point is that Adrian was always consciously open-minded about ways to expand his politically and culturally driven approach to architectural history and theory, and so he too has since the 1980s willingly incorporated a great deal of critical theory into his thinking and teaching – yet without ever becoming what is referred to as a 'theory merchant', which is the sort of scholar who by inclination doesn't want to look at empirical examples based in real life. His penchant is more for French structuralism, especially of the Barthesian mode which uncovers deeper cultural meanings behind everyday artefacts and activities. Adrian was always painfully aware that Reyner Banham was militantly anti-theoretical, this being part of Banham's character to the extent of having been a real chip-on-his-shoulder. Adrian thus instead has consciously kept abreast of new theoretical developments, while taking care never to overstate that side of things or to turn into a cheerleader for a particular theoretical approach. This degree of openness, and lack of any dogmatism, also meant that Adrian has always been very keen for students to try to expand the field of architectural history and theory, embracing postcolonial theory, gender studies, feminist theory, psychoanalytical theory, etc. A mark of the Master's programme is that it has been so open to new approaches and different views, which helps understanding of why it has lasted for so long and been able to take on board such very different kinds of students over the decades. As Adrian memorably remarked to colleagues not long ago, 'The Bartlett is not a seminary'; referring to the fact that it has never been, and hopefully never will be, doctrinaire in its approach.

Also crucial is the interest in the practices of architectural design and construction which characterises The Bartlett's Master's course, something which has helped to bridge the link to practising architects. Adrian is one of those few architectural historians who can talk equally passionately and intelligently about old buildings and the latest designs today. Something to realise, and which also links him in a sense to Tafuri, is that Adrian absolutely loves the architecture of the Italian Renaissance. He might not ever write a lot on that subject, but he is immensely knowledgeable about the period. He shared with Tafuri, and many others of course, the belief that the modern conception of what we have come to understand as architecture – both for better and for worse – began in the Renaissance. Adrian is of course best known as a historian of 19th-century British architecture and also 20th-century modernism in many countries, but as his book on concrete shows, he is just as much at ease when looking at contemporary developments as well. When teaching students, what interests Adrian are the reasons why architecture has changed – and will continue to change – over time as a consequence of social, economic and political factors. And if one is genuinely interested in such processes, then one is by definition interested in all periods of history so as to be able to trace how these sweeps of historical change occur. In terms of the kinds of architectural examples that Adrian teaches about, while he talks extensively about the canonical works, he has also always been strongly interested in the more quotidian, even banal, architecture of our cities.

A final and concluding thought on all this. In his first book, *Objects of Desire*, Adrian took it upon himself to read a very long book about the history of soap, which it is doubtful if any other architectural historian has ever done before or since. This first book, with its interest in everyday design history, was an obvious sign of the scope of his intellectual concerns. His broad range of interests and encyclopaedic knowledge are also evident in the range of doctoral students he has supervised at The Bartlett over the last four decades, who among them have tackled subjects from Irish state housing to the impact of the profits of the slave trade on British aesthetic culture in the 18th century to Portuguese vernacular modernism. Above all, then, Adrian remains the opposite of an elitist historian. In his teaching, in his talks and in his writings on architecture, he constantly seeks to draw in everyday cultural understandings of buildings and cities, while also appreciating the more specialised and rarefied design processes and intellectual discourses which tend to shape the field of architecture. The world of architectural history, and indeed of architecture, is much indebted to his work.

Notes

1   This account of the development of architectural history training in the UK is greatly indebted to Adrian's own account of it. See Adrian Forty, 'Architectural History Research and the Universities in the UK', *Rassegna di Architettura e Urbanistica*, Vol 139, 2013, pp 7–20. See also Helen Thomas, 'Joseph Rykwert and the Use of History', AA Files, Issue 66 (2013), pp 54–8, and Peter Hall's contribution to this volume (Chapter 32).

2   The extraordinarily prolific Banham published eight sole-authored or edited books in total during his time at The Bartlett (1964–76), including: *The New Brutalism: Ethic or Aesthetic?*, Architectural Press (London), 1966; *The Architecture of the Well-Tempered Environment?*, Architectural Press (London), 1969; and *Los Angeles: The Architecture of Four Ecologies*, Allen Lane (London), 1971.

Future Imperfect

ADRIAN FORTY

Adrian Forty's Inaugural Professorial Lecture, delivered at UCL in December 2000

The last time there was an inaugural lecture in architectural history at The Bartlett was thirty years ago – in fact it was exactly 30 years ago, to the day. It was held on this same day in December 1970, in this room, and it was given by Reyner Banham, and the title was 'At Shoo Fly Landing'. I wasn't there – I missed it – but I know what he said, and I'll tell you quickly. Shoo Fly Landing was the name originally given to the spot on which the Santa Monica pier stood – 'shoo-fly' because the stench of the local tar pits made this the instinctive gesture of anyone in the vicinity. The Santa Monica pier, which was the real topic of the lecture, appealed to Banham because it wasn't the sort of thing architectural historians normally took any notice of. Although it was such an obvious, familiar feature of the Santa Monica coastal landscape, it turned out to lack any documentary records whatsoever, but, with a certain amount of poking about underneath the pier, Banham managed to piece together its origins and successive transformations. If part of the purpose of the lecture was to show that architectural historians usually failed to notice what was under their noses, the other point of it was to show that it was the pier that had triggered the entire subsequent development of Santa Monica, and that without knowing the history of the pier you could not grasp the rest of the history of Santa Monica's urbanisation. In other words, no pier, no Santa Monica.

Besides telling the story of Santa Monica pier, Banham in his lecture made three general remarks about architectural history as a discipline, which, thirty years on, it would be worth considering again. The first of these was that architectural historians spent too much time looking at photographs of works of architecture, and not enough time crawling about on, in or under the built works themselves. Works of architecture, Banham pointed out, are fixed to the ground, and this fixity is a necessary feature of their property as works – but a feature that photographs always obliterate. Now one of Banham's more useful pieces of advice I remember as a young lecturer was 'never talk about anything you haven't been to see, because there'll probably be somebody in the audience who has'. I would endorse this advice – although I'm going to lapse from it once or twice in this lecture – but there's a sense in which it can now be qualified. A growing familiarity with semiotics and structuralism in the last 30 years has allowed us to see that – to paraphrase Roland Barthes – the reality of an object is not exhausted by its phenomenal existence, but extends into each and every representation of it. In other words, we have works, and we have photographs, and it is not that the photograph is simply a poor substitute for the work, but rather that it is another facet of the work's being, and one that can be thought about in its own right; as a result, of course, the work is never 'finished' – as long as images of it continue to go on being produced, it will, so to speak, always still be in development. No-one has done more to show us how to think about all this and to develop our understanding of photographs as part of the system of modern architecture than Beatriz Colomina. We might take as an example a fashion advertisement from last October's *Vogue*. The sharp-eyed among you will already have spotted that the background scenery is provided by Case Study House #22 in Los Angeles, designed by Pierre Koenig; this same building happens to have been the object of what must be one of the most famous architectural photographs of all time, taken by Julius Shulman. Now to consider the building *without* these images would be absurd – they have become part of the work; and I think I can say that architectural history has become reasonably sophisticated at dealing with built objects *and* their representations without confusing one with the other. It is no longer so necessary to make the distinction that Banham emphasised between the 'hands-on' historian and the library-bound scholar who only experienced the work through images.

Banham's second observation was that architectural historians spent too much time looking at 'canonic' works, at acknowledged masterpieces, and not enough time looking at what was staring them in the face or under their noses – in other words, the everyday and the ordinary. Banham presented this very much as an 'either/or' scenario, and it is certainly true that as a historian you tend to develop a reputation either as a 'high art' person, or as a 'popular culture' freak; as someone who has paddled in both ponds, I don't really see why one should have to stay in one or the other, and indeed I'd prefer to see the two ponds not as two but just as one big one. If we take this pair of buildings, one might say that the corrugated iron affair longs to be the 15th-century parish church; or so too that the railway carriage in an orchard dreams of becoming Palladio's Villa Barbaro – but on the other hand, there is a sense too in which the Villa Barbaro longs for the primitive Arcadian simplicity of the railway carriage. In other words, there is something to be gained by thinking about each in terms of the other; to grasp the significance of any particular object, it is an advantage to think of the entire system in which it belongs. Architecture is unusual among the arts in that it has a very large significant 'other', usually called 'building' – architecture is a relatively small and specialised sector within the general field of building. This isn't a situation that arises with the other arts – in literature we have high art and popular fiction, and although people certainly distinguish between the two, it isn't that one is an art, and the other isn't – they are simply different genres within the same practice, and it is perfectly possible for an author to produce works in both genres. The same is true of cinema, painting and any other art you can think of. But in our field we have a situation where, while all things fixed to the ground are 'buildings', only a few of them are 'architecture'. Now, for architects, this distinction is very important, in fact it's a matter of life or death – their entire occupation depends on preserving it and one can understand why so much is invested in the upkeep of the defences; on the other hand, for everyone else outside the construction industry, the distinction doesn't really matter. In so far as buildings provide the setting for everyday life, it's not of great importance whether you call some of these 'architecture' and some 'building'. And though it may well be that some works will make us more conscious of who we are and what our relations with our fellow beings are than others – and on that account might be said to be better, or more interesting – considered from the point of view of the recuperation of social consciousness, the distinction between architecture and building isn't all that important. So again, I'd like to suggest that we can afford to be more relaxed about the rather categorical distinction that Banham made between the study of high architecture and 'ordinary' stuff than he felt able to be in 1970.

The third of Banham's distinctions was between historians who got their material from investigating built works, and those who got their material from other sources, from 'theory'. Banham was very blunt about this: 'The strength of architectural history is that it is fundamentally about physical objects and physical systems, not about abstract categories or academic disciplines. It will always rejuvenate itself by going back to those objects and systems in order to ask new questions about them.' Now here Banham described a distinction that has become normative in architectural history – and put himself very firmly on one side. You know the scene – on the one hand there are the theorists, for whom works of architecture are just a means of illustrating a theoretical discourse; and on the other hand we have the train-spotters. Both types will be familiar to you, but I don't think they cannot mix – and indeed I would suggest that part of the pleasure of architectural history comes on the one hand from examining the work, and using that experience to test out theoretical propositions; and on the other hand from bringing theories to interrogate the work. It's a two-way process, as a result of which both works and theories are enriched. And certainly the best of our students' work has been very successful at this, at moving from object to theory, and back again from theory to object, thinking through objects, and seeing through theory.

I am going to leave Banham's inaugural lecture now, but I want to say a little about Banham's work as a critic of architecture. Banham's reputation as a critic of architecture rests in part on the analogy that he drew between architecture and non-architectural objects of all kinds. Simply put, the argument was that if architecture were to be judged by the criteria applied to consumer goods, and if the techniques and values found in, say, automobile or aircraft production were applied to architecture, we would have some significantly different results. Although Banham seems to have changed his mind about this analogy at the end of his life, there's no doubt that it has been extremely influential in the architecture of the last forty years. The main features of the consumer goods industries that Banham drew attention to were, first of all obsolescence – Banham argued that architects who designed their buildings to last for ever were behaving unrealistically and tended to produce an inappropriate monumentality. In the consumer goods industries, on the other hand, where limited life expectancy was taken for granted, there was far greater freedom to experiment; in particular, consumer goods industries seemed to be much better at making things that people wanted and that corresponded to popular desires than architecture, which generally seemed to be rather remote from everyday tastes and desires. Now there is a further aspect of consumer goods where there is an analogous relation to architecture that I would like to talk about – and this isn't something that Banham was especially concerned with – and this is 'perfection'. 'Perfection' is an extremely familiar, well-known feature of commodity aesthetics. Goods are sold to us as 'perfect' – if the plate has a chip in it, you reject it; if your new car has a squeak or a rattle, you take it back to the dealer. Quality in consumer goods is largely synonymous with this kind of technical seamlessness. Take a recent Mercedes advertisement – 'the perfect vehicle for life without compromises'. Commodity aesthetics are to a large extent dependent upon making something that is necessarily imperfect appear perfect. It is only very occasionally that someone comes along and does something that doesn't conform to this – such as Ron Arad's 'Concrete Sound' stereo – and tampers with the rules about perfection. Now this kind of expectation of the perfect object that we have of consumer goods transfers very easily to architecture, and this has happened to a considerable extent in the last fifty years. Our experience of the standards of finish, and of smooth operation that we have become familiar with from often quite inexpensive pieces of electrical and mechanical equipment, have become the norm for what we expect of buildings. At the same time some architects have approached the design of buildings as if they were consumer goods, whose manifest appeal is on the basis of their technical perfection. This isn't always such a good thing, it has to be said, for when something goes wrong, as it has at the Waterloo Eurostar terminal, it goes doubly wrong: when the glass in the roof started cracking it wasn't just a matter of repairing it, the whole aesthetic needed fixing too.

When the analogy of the perfection of consumer goods was introduced into architecture, it of course merged with an already existing, much older notion of perfection that was well embedded in architecture. This is an idea that goes back a very long way, indeed to Aristotle and to the theories of art that come out of classical philosophy. Aristotle, to distinguish between art and nature, had written that 'art generally completes what nature cannot bring to a finish'; in the 17th century, this idea became a major article of faith amongst baroque architects. The most obvious results were to be seen in landscape gardening – at Versailles, all the straight lines and clipped hedges of the central part contrast with the chaos of the outlying parts where nature has been left to her own devices. 'Nature intends that everything should be perfect but is frustrated by accidents,' wrote the ideologue of late 17th-century French art, André Félibien. The artist's task was to come and finish off what nature on its own could not achieve. One way or another, the belief that it is one of the purposes of art to create order out of the inherent disorder of the world has been fairly fundamental to Western notions of art in the last five hundred years, and has certainly been productive of some of the more remarkable results achieved by architecture. It has been an extremely important article in the belief system of architects, and continues to be so, but not, it has to be said, always to architects' advantage. Colin Davies gave a nice example of this in his inaugural lecture last month – during the Second World War, the German architect Konrad Wachsmann collaborated with Walter Gropius on the development of a prefabricated house for mass production, called 'the packaged house'. Despite several years of development, the investment of over $6 million, a factory set up in California, and a planned production of 10,000 houses a year, only a few dozen were ever actually made. Why? Because Wachsmann, true to type, kept on refining and improving the design, trying to get it perfect, and by the time he was satisfied with it, the market opportunity was over. This might be said to have been a case of too much perfection for its own good.

Given that perfection has been such a strong fixture in the architectural belief system for so long, it is hardly to be expected that it should have got away without being challenged. And of course it has been. The best-known critic of perfection, and exponent of imperfection, was the 19th-century English writer John Ruskin. Looking at medieval buildings, Ruskin was struck by their frequent imperfections, and in these imperfections Ruskin saw the signs of intense impatience, of a struggle to attain something that it was beyond the mason's means to attain. One of Ruskin's examples was this pair of openings on the tower of Abbeville cathedral: the mason couldn't work out how to reconcile the double-time of the rhythm of the arches with the triple-time of the rhythm of the billets, and so to get round the problem he simply bent the ogee arches inwards so that their tips joined up with the inner billets. Ruskin was impressed by the way medieval craftsmen could show contempt for exact symmetry and measurement, and could be careless with the details, because they were so determined to pull off the whole thing. To Ruskin's eyes, incompleteness was a means of expression, it revealed life, the energy of someone so preoccupied with the achievement of the end result, that they were prepared to bend the dimensions here, and miss out a bit there.

As Mark Swenarton has pointed out, Ruskin's ideas didn't finish with the Arts & Crafts and Jugendstil movements, but continued to be an important, if unacknowledged, component of early modernism. Le Corbusier, one of whose earliest formative experiences was his reading of Ruskin, never forgot what he had learnt from him, and indeed later in his life reverted to a position which was a good deal closer to Ruskin than has generally been recognised. Imperfection is a particularly interesting case here, because the finishes of Le Corbusier's 1950s buildings were notoriously awful. Le Corbusier didn't want the workmanship on these buildings to be bad – at the Unité in Marseilles he had no choice because there was no skilled labour. At La Tourette, the client didn't have much money. The roughness of these buildings was subsequently interpreted as an artistic gesture, a demonstration of the *facture*, but I don't think this was what Le Corbusier intended – he would have had better finishes if he had the means to do so – as he did on the later Unité at Firminy, where the construction is of much higher quality. Rather, it seems that he just accepted that if the work was not to be left incomplete, the construction would have to be poor quality. That he was able to accept this, and to be indifferent to the finish, would seem to be due in part to his knowledge of Ruskin. What, of course, excused the imperfection of the Unité and of La Tourette was that the works themselves were so strong, and that if the execution was crude, it didn't matter, because of the force of the whole building.

In these examples, it's not the work itself that is imperfect, it is only the means. Now it is one thing to allow imperfection in the way the work is made, which is really what Ruskin sanctioned, but it is quite another thing to conceive of the entire work itself as imperfect. This really does go against the grain of the whole Western tradition of architecture, from Alberti's *concinnitas* to the flawlessness of the digital architecture of the moment. But there are examples where people have tried to produce something that was inherently imperfect – candidates for this might include Gehry's work from the late 1970s, such as his own house in Santa Monica. A better example, to my mind, would be Cedric Price's InterAction Centre, where Price succeeded in making questions of 'perfection' or 'imperfection' largely irrelevant. Now what these various experiments in imperfect architecture, or architecture that is indifferent to perfection, all have in common, it will be noticed, is that they are all made out of either steel or timber. It is as if these materials, somehow more provisional, more open-ended, lent themselves better to the achievement of imperfection.

If, on the other hand, we turn to another material, to concrete, then it suddenly seems to become a lot more difficult to achieve the kind of imperfection that we have seen in these works. Notwithstanding what I have said about La Tourette – where you'll recall that it was the execution, not the work that was imperfect – concrete seems to be a material that simply won't allow of imperfection. Or if we take another scheme with an air of imperfection, Rem Koolhaas's Grand Palais at Lille, although the general effect is of something that has been fabricated with a can-opener, in fact the imperfections – irregularly leaning columns, odd transitions from one cladding material to another – are largely to be found in the steel or polycarbonate bits of the building; the concrete parts are reasonably normal, and provide an armature for all the liberties that are taken with the other materials. Now it is a curious feature of concrete that it manages to throw into confusion almost all the conventional assumptions about architectural aesthetics – and the case of imperfection is no exception. All the great works that make a virtue of being made out of concrete, works that would be inconceivable in another material – the Whitney Museum, the South Bank – are definitively complete and conform to all the accepted norms of perfection. Now why should this be, why should concrete tend so strongly to the perfect, and be so exclusive of imperfection? I am not sure that I can give a wholly satisfactory answer to this, but I'll have a go.

The core of the argument is that no-one wants to create imperfection out of concrete because it is already an imperfect material. So much effort has gone into trying to cure concrete of its imperfections, that to use it to produce imperfection would be to threaten the whole belief system to which millions of pounds of investment and fifty years of architectural effort have been dedicated. The person who really started on the pursuit of perfection in concrete was Auguste Perret, who developed techniques intended to make concrete seem superior to stone. At Perret's Musée des Travaux Publics of 1937, the aggregates of the structural elements are a carefully chosen mix of small and large particles, with some coloured elements in them all coming from one region of France; Perret developed a technique in which the surface of the concrete was carefully chiselled away by hand, except at the arrises, where smooth cement from the mould is left to form a raised fillet. This is done with extraordinary precision – one slip with the chisel, and the whole thing would be spoiled. The same happens on the columns. The amount of labour that went into producing this is unbelievable – not only did the formwork for the concrete have to be built with enormous accuracy, but then the entire surface of the building had to be worked over by hand. And the same effects are continued on the interior, where Perret boasted that no plaster was used at all. Since Perret's day, the efforts to perfect concrete have continued in all sorts of directions: finer aggregates, techniques of obtaining smoother and smoother finishes, the addition of resins to harden the surface so it can be ground and polished, and so on. Producing the perfect concrete has become a kind of philosopher's stone of the late 20th century. In more recent times, a major motive for all this has come from the bad reputation that concrete acquired in the late 1960s, and a desire to reverse this; in my view a lot of this effort has been misguided, because what it has been doing is to make concrete look less like concrete, and more like something else, usually stone. But to try to improve the public image of concrete by making it less like concrete seems rather absurd. Yet nonetheless, despite all these attempts to make concrete more perfect, there is the unavoidable fact that concrete is not a perfect material. In spite of the fantastic labour involved in Perret's building, the surface still turned out blotchy. The strategies adopted to disguise the imperfections of concrete are ingenious – but they are still disguises: take for example the stainless steel socks that cover the bottoms of the concrete columns of Canary Wharf station, which protect the columns from the scrapes, chips and grease marks that they would quickly accumulate otherwise. They're an elegant device, but their purpose is to allow us to see concrete as something other, something more perfect than it is.

Now I should at this point say that concrete is one of the most myth-attracting substances around: myths just stick to it like flies to fly-paper. One of these myths is that concrete is a mute, non-signifying material – and this I think has been part of its appeal to the so-called minimalist school of architects. Needless to say, I'm not convinced by this, and part of the point of the work I am engaged in at the moment is to take myths like these and 'to brush them against the grain', and find beneath the commonsensical smoothness of their surface whatever flaws and contradictions there may be. Another of these myths, and one directly related to the question we are looking at here, is that concrete is an artificial material. Now of course it is artificial, in the sense that it is a compound. But all those very considerable efforts to naturalise it – usually by rendering it as stone or wood – seem by their over-insistence contrived to convince us of its artificiality. And if it is an artificial substance, it has of course to be perfect, because synthetic substances – polyester, silicon chips – always are; if they weren't there would be no point in having them. But as well as being artificial, concrete is also a natural material – it's a gloopy substance that conforms to the natural laws of fluid mechanics, so that if you don't do something to contain it, it will spread out into a shapeless mess; in other words, it behaves just like those 17th-century artists thought nature behaved – it can never get it right on its own, it has to be controlled, coaxed, vibrated and so on for it to be brought to perfection. Now to think of concrete as both natural *and* artificial demands a greater degree of mental agility than most of us can manage. So much is invested in the absoluteness of this distinction between natural and artificial, so necessary is it to our whole cosmology, that to admit that something can be both of these would be just too anxiety-inducing. To avoid this, we habitually operate on the assumption that concrete is just artificial, or alternatively, just natural, but never both. Whichever myth we subscribe to, whether we say that it is artificial, and therefore in common with all synthetic things, perfect, or whether we say it is natural, it would risk upsetting the whole precariously balanced superstructure for it to be allowed to be used for results that could be characterised as 'imperfect'. For these reasons, I would suggest, experiments with 'imperfect' architecture have largely avoided using concrete.

Nevertheless, experiments there have been, and I want to look at one of them. On the outskirts of Paris, at Créteil, at the end of one of the métro lines, there is a housing estate called 'Les Bleuets'. The landscape of Créteil, like that of most of the suburbs of Paris, is characterised by a superabundance of cement, and this estate looks much like many other housing estates in the periphery – except for the thing you have probably immediately noticed about it, the enormous slabs of stone set randomly into the concrete, making it look as if Asterix had had a hand in the construction. The name 'Les Bleuets' means blue-flowering cornflowers, and the inappropriateness of this charmingly romantic name alerts one to some of the ironies to come. Les Bleuets was built between 1959 and 1962, designed by a then very young architect called Paul Bossard.

Les Bleuets housing estate in Créteil, Paris (1959), designed by Paul Bossard and featured by Adrian Forty in *Concrete and Culture* (2012).

What's interesting for my purposes about this scheme is that it set out to criticise what was happening in the suburbs not only of Paris but of most European cities in the late 1950s. Moreover, it carried out this criticism through the use of the very same medium as it was criticising – the precast concrete panel. I should at this point explain that if in the 1990s, it looked as if the end of architecture was spelt by the spread of design-and-build contracting, in the 1950s it was the precast concrete panel that looked as if it was going to push architecture into extinction. At this distance of time, it is hard to appreciate the passions that could be aroused by the precast concrete panel; to give an example, we can take the case of the Hayward Gallery and Queen Elizabeth Hall: the design for this was developed in the late 1950s by a group in the LCC Architects Department led by Norman Engleback and including several future Archigram members. For various reasons, among them acoustic insulation against the noise of helicopters flying up and down the Thames to the projected Battersea heliport, they designed it to be made from in-situ concrete. But the chief architect of the LCC, Hubert Bennett, didn't like

The Hayward Gallery and Queen Elizabeth Hall as part of the Southbank Centre, London (1961–9), designed by the LCC (later GLC) Architects Department, and featured by Adrian Forty in *Concrete and Culture* (2012).

the scheme, and he rejected it, designing a scheme of his own, using precast concrete panels. At this point, in 1960, the entire original team resigned from the LCC; the affair was blown up in the press, and eventually, after strong support for the Engleback team's design, Bennett backed down and allowed them to go ahead with it – on the condition that they used a certain proportion of precast concrete panels: hence the compromise result you see today. In the 1950s, the precast concrete panel had been developed as the most rational, the most economical way of producing buildings of a uniformly consistent quality. It was a method of construction that seemed to offer economies of scale, and by applying the same principles of standardisation and quality control as had been developed in other industries, notably car production, it looked as if it could make building construction as efficient, and as modern, as those industries. With the development of the perfect panel – a complex sandwich of concrete, Styrofoam and plasterboard – all that time that architects spent fiddling about on the design of details would cease to be necessary.

From the architects' point of view, the precast concrete panel reduced their job to that of a technician, whose main task became the arrangement of the components of the system according to the requirements of the brief. Apart from, if he or she was lucky, having some say in the choice of the material facing the panel, the architect's control over the aesthetic aspects of the project was reduced to zero. From a more general point of view, the universal use of concrete panel construction had the effect of making everywhere look the same – a feature all too noticeable in the suburbs of Paris – and of producing that general flattening and homogenisation of space that was remarked upon by Marxist critics as a phenomenon of capitalism. Moreover, the results, lacking any irregularity, any residue of irrationality, seemed to threaten the capacity of cities, urbanism, to act any longer as an expressive medium. This is how the main character played by Marina Vlady, in Jean-Luc Godard's film *Two or Three Things I Know about Her*, describes the effect. Made in 1966 and released in 1967, this was a film about Paris, and much of the action takes place in, or in relation to, a particularly bleak specimen of precast concrete panel construction in the periphery; at the end of the film Godard makes a city out of boxes of toothpaste, cigarette packets and soap powder cartons – the city of precast concrete panels is just packaging, and its significatory possibilities diminished to those of a cereal packet.

These are the materials – physical and ideological – with which Bossard found himself working at Les Bleuets. Precast concrete panels were being developed and refined by concrete contractors into technically perfect objects. Bossard, while still using precast concrete panels, was to go in the opposite direction, and to make of it an object of manifest imperfection. Unusually, rather than selecting an already developed system and using it, Bossard designed his own system; moreover, and even more unusually, he produced the technical specification and all the detail drawings of the system and of the scheme himself, instead of, as was and still is normal in France, leaving this to the contractor's bureau d'études. Bossard, moreover, undertook all the site work and supervision himself, again very unusual for a scheme like this. All the precast concrete sections were made on site, and were designed with very large gaps between them: they leak, and were designed to leak. The arrangement of the large pieces of shale in the concrete was left to the workmen on the site. The sections on the upper parts were cast, with the concrete poured around the stones; in sections at the bases of the buildings, the pieces of shale have been pushed into the still-wet concrete, so it oozes out around the edges. Bossard tells the story of how one day, a labourer asked if he could have a go at making one of the pieces. Bossard said 'okay, go on, but do it fast: you've got to do it in three minutes, you're doing a Picasso, not a Dürer'. The labourer stuffed the stones into the casting box, and poured the concrete, and then, when it was taken out, Bossard asked him what he thought of the result. 'Lousy,' said the labourer. 'Well,' said Bossard, 'it doesn't matter, we don't throw anything away.' So it was fixed in place, and Bossard again asked the labourer what he thought of it, and the labourer said it wasn't the same as the others. Bossard replied that none of the pieces were the same, and that if some were beautiful and some were ugly, well that was like the human race. The moral of the story for Bossard was that the right to mistakes was the first step to liberty.

Now if the crudeness and variations of the concrete components fulfil a Ruskinian theme, it was at the same time directed against the technical perfection and rationality of the precast concrete panel construction as it was being developed throughout France and Europe. Bossard used the same object, but imperfectly made, to criticise the whole practice. This is particularly evident in his treatment of the joints. The question of how you join one piece of concrete to another is one of the more revealing moments in the mythological structure of concrete. With in-situ concrete, elaborate lengths are gone to to preserve the seamlessness of the whole; we have recessed joints between each lift of the shutter – as at Ernö Goldfinger's Trellick Tower; or joints filled with lead, as at Louis Kahn's Kimbell Museum; or at the Brion tomb, Carlo Scarpa accentuates the joint so much as to make it seem that the two sections have moved apart. Occasionally, as with this building near Dresden, designed by the artist Gerhard Merz, the whole problem is ignored, so that although the overall effect is of a crisp white minimalist box, in fact the concrete has been poured without any attempt to mask the different stages of construction; nor are there any expansion joints, so cracks will develop in the surface. This is a rare case of concrete construction carried out with deliberate imperfection. With precast panels, the goal of construction is narrow tolerances, fine, close-fitting joints between the panels, that can be sealed with a thin bead of mastic. But at Les Bleuets, Bossard adopted a completely different approach: the joints are very wide, up to 4 centimetres [1⅝ inches], and are not sealed with anything at all, but left open, so that they leak. Before the development of rain-screen walls – and Les Bleuets predates this – leaky construction wasn't acceptable – precast concrete panels were meant to make a perfect, watertight fit. Bossard ignored this, and left gaping joints – a result which in the etiquette of the concrete constructor was roughly the equivalent of going around with your flies open. It's offensive. As an experiment in calculated imperfection, but carried out within what was the then normal, progressive mode of perfectible construction, the result at Les Bleuets seems to me rather impressive.

What I have tried to do here is to sketch out what a history of architectural imperfection might look like – and I have suggested some reasons why it hasn't been written. I'm certainly not the first person to have thought about imperfection in architecture – it was Robert Maxwell who drew our attention to the 17th-century poem *Delight in Disorder* by Robert Herrick:

> A sweet disorder in the dress
> Kindles in clothes a wantonness
> [...]
> A careless shoe-string, in whose tie
> I see a wild civility:

Do more bewitch me than when art
Is too precise in every part.

Nonetheless, though, architects have to cast their work in the future, and generally they do so with some sort of notion of perfectibility. It's hard not to. 'The future is but the obsolete in reverse,' wrote Vladimir Nabokov, and this being the case all our instincts are towards its perfectibility. But some of the experiments that I have outlined here suggest that powerful, irresistible though the goal of perfection might be, it can be seen as being mythological, as a part of a defence against the collapse of some of our conventional belief systems. Could we have a future *imperfect*? Now of course the future imperfect doesn't exist as a tense: we have the past imperfect – 'we used to go to the cinema', and we have the future perfect, 'in a few moments this lecture will have ended'; but the future imperfect is impossible – 'we will have been going to the cinema' – it doesn't make a lot of sense. But if the future imperfect is a non-existent tense, that shouldn't put us off. The future imperfect could be the architect's tense – and while only architects would be allowed to speak it, maybe the historian should be left to figure out the grammar and the syntax. But enough of that for now, we can go back to the comfortable security of the past perfect – 'you have finished listening to this lecture' – it's over.

CHAPTER 1
How To Write About Buildings?

ANDREW SAINT

The chatter about architecture goes on and on. Adrian Forty was perhaps the first person to propose that the surprise answer to the missing term in the old equation, architecture = buildings + x, was *words*. If that's right, as I am increasingly persuaded, it explains why so much talk and writing envelops the practice of design. The theory of architecture is a species of moral rhetoric, there for architects to convince clients, the public at large and most of all one another that lives will be enriched and beneficially altered by placing bricks in this direction rather than that. And Frank Lloyd Wright and Le Corbusier are really the Demosthenes and Cicero of architectural modernism, not its Plato and Aristotle. The dumber the building – and most buildings are mercifully silent – the more it seems to cry out for an accompaniment of words.

Suppose that is as much as half-true, another question arises. If words matter to architecture, how come they are so often poorly put together? To express it another way, why is there so little persuasive and beautiful writing about architecture these days? That is what I found myself asking recently when contributing to an anthology on a critic who is perhaps as far from Adrian's enthusiasms as you could get: Ian Nairn. There has been a revival of interest in Nairn recently, and for good reason: he writes so well and at his best (as in the well-known guidebook *Nairn's London* (1966)) for a compelling missionary purpose. His words still make people look and reflect and react, they propel them out of their seats and into the streets in search of *architecture*. How few writers writing in English can do that, I thought. Ruskin, perhaps? It is not what Pevsner does, nor the vast preponderance of scholars and theorists. They offer fact and comparison, and perhaps they prod the grey matter. Meanwhile the reader stays fixed in his chair.

Writing and jawing about buildings is of course infinite in variety, and so it should be. A lot of the talking, in architecture schools particularly, is of the preaching type, there to engender confidence in those who are daring to design. Later comes the enormous complexity and exchange of data necessary to get a building up and on its feet. There is little reason for either type of discourse to be coherent or beautiful. The most seductive of architectural theories have often taken the form of vatic, staccato or metaphorical utterances (Pugin, Le Corbusier, Loos, Buckminster Fuller). As for the plethoric information surrounding the business of building, there is seldom the time or luxury to render it better than clear and effective; people would look askance if you tried to make it otherwise.

All the same, a great deal that is written about architecture these days has, so far as one can see, no fixed or ulterior purpose. About much, perhaps most of this, I want to ask: why is it not better written? The unfortunate answer seems to be: because the audience for such writing is unclear, and so its manner of expression does not really matter. Academic journals, for instance, feed off the self-perpetuating system whereby their authors justify themselves by publishing in them. For architecture-as-science that may be fine, since the accumulation and analysis of information can be regarded as progressive and useful. But for architecture-as-art the case is otherwise. An audience, a listener beyond some picky and prosaic peer-reviewing committee, ought always to be in the author's mind.

It may fairly be urged that most writing about the history and theory of architecture should be as modest in language and recessive in tone as the writing about its science. You can after all draw effective attention to something special or beautiful without making a song and dance about it. Nor should you try to edge it out of the picture you are drawing. But if Adrian's notion is true, and buildings and words are complementary, there must be occasions when the writing rises to meet the architecture and does not stand too abjectly in its shadow. The reason why Ruskin and Nairn at their best or, to take two other examples at random, Goethe on Strasbourg Cathedral and Wordsworth on King's College Chapel, Cambridge, are so exciting and moving is because they have the guts to try and respond to, even emulate, what they are talking about.[1] That is architectural criticism at its best and highest. When it really comes off, it achieves an exalted harmony, as in the famous Rilke poem that begins *Wie soll ich meine Seele halten* ... [How shall I contain my soul ...]:

> *nimmt uns zusammen wie ein Bogenstrich,*
> *der aus zwei Saiten eine Stimme zieht ...*
> [drawing us together like a bow-stroke
> that lifts a single voice from twofold strings ...][2]

This doesn't have to be as arrogant or ambitious as it may sound. It can come over as well by attending lovingly to a detail as by attempting the rhetorical description of a cathedral. But it is certainly difficult, rare and precious.

One reason this level of criticism is getting even rarer these days may be the inversion of the relationship between writing and architectural imagery. Pictures cost less than words to publish nowadays on the whole, and are much more rapidly exchanged and absorbed. Architectural scribblers have become wallpaper providers. And if no-one is looking at the interstices between the images, why bother about the quality of the writing? Isn't architecture a visual subject anyway? A single picture can obviate a thousand descriptive words, takes less time to digest, and gives greater passing pleasure to all but a few.

Undeniable though that may be, it actually makes the choice and quality of the words more important. The heresy that architectural value resides in the image or concept of a building rather than in its creation, experience and use has been around since the rise of printing and the subsequent diffusion of treatises by Palladio and other architects. Never have its attractions been so easy, so superficial, and so corrupting as they are today. We can best combat that heresy not with more images but with more imagination – by means of the honourable rhetoric which only well-chosen words can supply. Architecture = building + *good* words.

Notes

1   Goethe's essay *Von deutscher Baukunst* [On German Architecture], first published in 1773; Wordsworth's untitled sonnet of 1820–1, beginning 'Tax not the royal Saint with vain expense', which is often referred to in collections as 'Inside of King's College Chapel, Cambridge'.

2   Rainer Marie Rilke, *Liebeslied* [Love Song], first published in 1907. The translation is my own.

CHAPTER 2

Pevsner vs Colomina: Word and Image on the Page

ANNE HULTZSCH

Under Adrian Forty's guidance, I was introduced to two very different approaches in architectural writing, each of which in their own way has acted as a spur and a challenge to my own interest in the physical experience of building: Beatriz Colomina's *Privacy and Publicity: Modern Architecture as Mass Media* (1994) and Nikolaus Pevsner's *The Buildings of England* series (first editions 1951–74). Now, years later, I find myself going back to these writings, pondering how the physical experience of the building expressed in the writing and reading of architectural history. Is Colomina justified in arguing that architecture can equally be understood through the building itself as well as through any form of representation, be it written, drawn or photographed?[1] Or is Pevsner – who, as critic Jonathan Meades noted, 'describes and leaves us to do the on-site ocular work'[2] – more correct in his approach? Few people would probably contest that both Pevsner's guidebooks and his historical writings should be considered as a guide to, rather than a substitute for, the direct encounter with the described building. Yet, if we believe Colomina, and many people do, we can likewise experience – even 'enter' – a building through a text, drawing or photograph. This is the way she constructs her histories of modern architecture: by looking, immersing and living in the archival traces of the past lives of buildings.

Until recently, it had been predominantly the words of both Pevsner and Colomina that had fascinated me and that I had – to exhaustion – taken apart. I had never in much depth considered what effect images had on the writing of both and how graphic design reflects, strengthens or even undermines underlying methods of historiography. And yet, it is the interplay between word and image that reveals the historian's attitude to architectural experience. Curiously, it was an earlier series of articles by Pevsner, predating the *Buildings of England*, that made me realise this. In his 'Treasure Hunts', written for the *Architectural Review* in 1942 – when he had just taken on the wartime editorship of the magazine – Pevsner explained how the layperson could date specimens of mainly nondescript historicist London buildings.[3] Intriguingly, and unprecedented in the otherwise rigorous layout of Hubert de Cronin Hastings's *Review*, Pevsner showed these buildings in bubble-shaped photographs placed often uncomfortably close to the text. The only apparent reason for this odd shape seems to have been to mark them as details in contrast to the rectangular views of whole buildings that were presented alongside. Without aiming at a precise reasoning for the existence of this layout scheme – possibly devised by Pevsner himself, a novice of magazine editing at the time – these images serve here to trigger some thoughts on the role of photography and layout in the writing – and reading – of architectural history.[4]

Pevsner never wrote extensively about photography and is even ascribed with a certain nonchalance towards the quality of images used in his teaching; his lecture slides are renowned for having been of remarkably bad quality.[5] He did however state that photography's main contribution to the historiography of architecture lay in the capacity to 'bring out a detail so forcefully that it carries more conviction on the plate than in the original'. The photographer thus became, he writes, a 'mentor' who could 'stop you to concentrate on something which the eye roving over the whole of a wall or a statue may miss completely'.[6] In a way, this is exactly what I have claimed his words do in the *Buildings of England*, but that is another matter.[7]

Pevsner's and Colomina's approaches mingle rather uncomfortably mainly because Colomina's assertion seems to diminish the importance of the material building – and the physical experience of the same – for the writing of its history. As Adrian Forty has acknowledged in a review:

To have written a book, *Privacy and Publicity*, that discusses the work of two of the most sensuous of twentieth-century architects entirely in terms of photographs of their buildings, without any reference whatsoever to the actual physical properties of the buildings, has so irritated some architects I know that they cannot bear even to utter her name.[8]

And yet, Colomina's distinct approach could not be more phenomenological – but it is so in a metaphorical way. While there is little explicit importance placed on her having visited the discussed buildings – but plenty of implicit

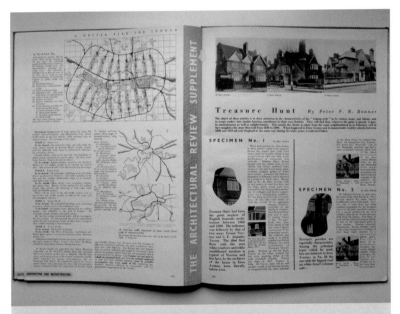

'Treasure Hunt', *Architectural Review*, Vol 91, May 1942, pp 151–3.
One of Nikolaus Pevsner's 'Treasure Hunt' articles, written under the pseudonym of Peter FR Donner, showing three architectural 'specimens' in Eton Avenue, northwest London (numbers 13, 15 and 26). Characteristic is the combination of a large front view of the specimen in the top strip on the first page, with details in bubble shapes set in an otherwise blank column and small rectangular reference pictures of more canonical buildings within the main text. Each image type is accompanied by captions that are short and informative for front views and reference pictures but extensive and printed in bold large typeface for the detail bubbles.

evidence of her having spent hours in the various archives – she applies, again and again, the same verb to illustrate the required mode of approaching any object: *to enter*. As she is narratively *entering* Le Corbusier's building in square du Docteur Blanche in Paris, she is equally *entering* a text, a drawing and a photograph.[9] While *to enter* literally refers to the moment of passing a physical threshold into an enclosed space – the quintessential architectural experience – Colomina uses it to indicate the process of understanding as well as sensing an object, claiming that to '*enter* is to *see*'.[10] Underlying this is the modern understanding that seeing is a process of reproduction, implying that each viewer sees, looks and *enters* differently.

Pevsner, on the contrary, seems to suggest that there is only one valid way to 'enter', understand and thus enjoy a building: whether on site or through photography, the viewer and photographer should follow the 'legitimate presentation of the architect's or sculptor's intentions'.[11] Rather than accepting an open-endedness of architectural meaning, as Colomina does, Pevsner insists that to know the intentions of the architect means to know *the* correct angle

Beatriz Colomina, *Privacy and Publicity*,
The MIT Press (Cambridge, Massachusetts), 1994, pp 112–13.
A double-page spread in Colomina's book *Privacy and Publicity*, in which historical photographs are centred on blank pages with short informative captions, disjointed from the main text but adding up to a fluid archive. Colomina's captions are pure information, giving little indication how the image sits in her argument. Illustrations are not numbered and thus not cross-referenced in the main text. This layout contains two images of Le Corbusier's Villa Schwob (1916) in La Chaux-de-Fonds, Switzerland, one of which is manipulated – a fact only made clear in the main text, not in the caption.

from which the building will make unambiguous sense to the initiated viewer. How would the uninitiated find this? By reading Pevsner's books, of course.

So how do images reflect these opposing positions? While the often small black-and-white illustrations in *Privacy and Publicity* are enigmatically centred each on a single page, framed by a thin black line and surrounded by the vast white of the page, Pevsner covers the spreads of the *Architectural Review* with differently sized and shaped images providing multiple scales of the same views. His are close to the text and accompanied by stand-alone captions that are full enough for the casual reader; hers regularly follow the associated text only after turning the page, inviting (or forcing) each reader to *enter* them, as she herself did. While in Pevsner's case they clearly serve to focus, identify and describe, to date through architectural detail by closely following his words on the depicted building, Colomina's photographs go beyond this but at the same time fail to clearly pinpoint the architect's 'intention', in Pevsner's sense. Of course, this would go against Colomina's argument – her pictures are archival material, historical evidence rather than substitutes for the direct experience of the building. Pevsner's photographs are equivalent to photographic snapshots; it is even possible to re-create them almost exactly in the same way today (in cases where buildings still stand and ignoring period evidence such as satellite dishes). Colomina's illustrations work best when seen as a series, consistently arranged on the printed page. Pevsner's are stand-alone substitutes for the represented object, the building. In this sense, while it is not entirely fair to compare a book with a series of short two-page articles (written during the War, no less), the comparison still allows to identify two approaches to the use of photography in architectural history that are consistent with the method employed in the writing of these pieces: Pevsner's object-centred identification and 'mentoring' of an experience on the one hand, and Colomina's fluid archive of additive fragments on the other.

More than identifying these two modes of imaging, the point I am trying to make here is that the work of the architectural historian should be regarded as, most often, consisting of images and words making up an argument *together*. Even if illustrations are purely illustrative, seemingly not adding to the argument, they by being so underline a certain historical method. There is a tendency in the reading, quoting and, at times, writing of architectural history to consider images apart from words or even ignore their inseparable interplay in its production. We write, but more often we do this while imaging, sorting slides on virtual desktops, hanging up photocopies from archives on a wall or cross-checking illustrations in books, as I have just done while writing this piece. Only rarely, I venture to say, do we write while in physical contact with the building whose history we construct (if you do – please get in touch). There is a maxim among many contemporary architectural historians to write only on what one has seen first-hand, as the experience of the physical building is largely regarded as crucial for the construction of its architectural history. This might have its roots also in the foundations of the *Wissenschaft* of academic art history, expressed in Heinrich Wölfflin's leitmotif to describe only what the eye can see.[12] Adrian Forty, in his most recent book *Concrete and Culture: A Material History*, credits his teacher Reyner Banham with having taught him to write, wherever feasible, only on buildings he had seen himself.[13] Forty's dedication to personal experience as a foundation of architectural history formed the basis of many of his courses at The Bartlett – and is also manifested in his own photographs used in his books, articles and lectures.

Rather than considering this simply as good practice (which it is in most cases) and dismissing any other approaches, one should look at this exactly as what it is: a method of constructing the history of architecture by means of words and images that, if printed, are always part of a physical artefact. Even if historians are most often constrained in questions of layout and print production, the choice of images and layout frequently remains in their hands. More importantly, it is publishers and graphic designers that become the anonymous co-authors of histories and theories and it is their contribution that remains to be acknowledged and studied.

Notes

1   Beatriz Colomina, *Privacy and Publicity: Modern Architecture as Mass Media*, The MIT Press (Cambridge, Massachusetts), 1994, pp 13–15.

2   Jonathan Meades, 'Pevsner at 50', *Building*, Vol 266, No 8187 (22), June 2001, p 31.

3   Peter FR Donner [Pevsner's pseudonym], 'Treasure Hunt', *Architectural Review*, Vol 91, 1942, pp 23–5, 47–9, 75–7, 123–4, 151–2; Vol 92, 1942, pp 19–21, 49–51, 75–6, 97–9, 125–6, 151–3.

4   Of course, this is not new territory. A good overview of current trends in, and theoretical ramifications of, illustrating architectural history has been provided by Iain Borden, 'Imaging Architecture: The Uses of Photography in the Practice of Architectural History', *The Journal of Architecture*, Vol 12, 2007, pp 57–77.

5   See Susie Harries, *Nikolaus Pevsner: The Life*, Chatto & Windus (London), 2011, pp 423–5.

6   Nikolaus Pevsner, 'Foreword', in Helmut Gernsheim, *Focus on Architecture and Sculpture: An Original Approach to the Photography of Architecture and Sculpture*, Fountain Press (London), 1949, pp 9–13 (p 12).

7   See Anne Hultzsch, *Architecture, Travellers and Writers: Constructing Histories of Perception 1640–1950*, Legenda (Oxford), 2014, pp 14–29.

8   Adrian Forty, 'Book Reviews: Domesticity at War, by Beatriz Colomina, Actar, Barcelona, 2006', *The Journal of Architecture*, Vol 13, 2008, pp 520–28 (p 522).

9   Colomina, *Privacy and Publicity*, pp 5, 46, 91, 234.

10 Ibid, p 5.

11 Pevsner, 'Foreword', in Gernsheim, *Focus on Architecture and Sculpture*, p 12.

12 This is most exhaustively expressed in Wölfflin's *Kunstgeschichtliche Grundbegriffe*, first published in 1915 and translated into English as *Principles of Art History* (1932).

13 Adrian Forty, *Concrete and Culture: A Material History*, Reaktion (London), 2012, p 11.

CHAPTER 3

Smooth and Rough: Tactile Brutalism

ANTHONY VIDLER

'Also in architecture there are indispensable themes of smooth and rough ...'

— ADRIAN STOKES, *SMOOTH AND ROUGH* (1951)[1]

Four years before Reyner Banham's celebrated article announcing the 'New Brutalism',[2] and soon before the completion of Le Corbusier's '*béton brut*' masterpiece, the Unité d'Habitation at Marseilles (1951), Adrian Stokes published a reflection on the architectural surface entitled *Smooth and Rough*. Concentrating, as Peggy Deamer has noted,[3] more on the visual effects of *apparent* tactility than on the effect of touch itself, Stokes transformed Melanie Klein's theory on opticality to describe the sensations provoked by a building. His metaphor was that of *stroking* (the smooth 'shining breast') and *biting* (the 'feeding nipple of that breast'). The aspect of smooth and rough surfaces of the building conceived as a body stimulated analogies with hunger, the openings 'torn' by 'vengeful teeth', attacked sadistically, yet healed and smoothed over as an 'indispensable' shelter.[4]

While referring more generally to the rusticated and polished surfaces of the Renaissance, Stokes inadvertently opened the way to a veritable aesthetic for the Corbusian *béton brut* that seemed so shocking to new modernists after the smooth white surfaces and glass curtain walls of the modernist and International Style era.

It is significant that Colin Rowe, when faced with the impenetrable (in

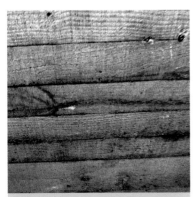

Marcel Breuer and Hamilton P Smith, Whitney Museum of American Art, New York, 1966. A photograph of the interior surface treatment: example #1.

Marcel Breuer and Hamilton P Smith, Whitney Museum of American Art, New York, 1966. A photograph of the interior surface treatment: example #2.

all senses) side wall of the chapel at Le Corbusier's monastery of La Tourette, fell into a quasi-Stokesian reverie on the qualities of the wood-formed concrete, reading the lines of the *brut* surface as so many perspectival traces leading the eye and the body to turn around the apparently implacable corner to the monastery entrance.[5] Indeed only Stokes could have inspired Rowe's soliloquy on the terrifying absence of a facade/face to the complex seen as a monstrous body perched threateningly on the steep hillside, with eyes at the front that looked only toward raw nature – God's territory, untouchable by the architect and to be viewed exclusively by the monks.

While Rowe, faced with the lack of a face at La Tourette, initially cites José Ortega y Gasset on the idea of 'surface', it is to Stokes that his shocked response is obviously indebted. The building, he finds, turns a cold shoulder toward the visitor who is confronted with its 'flank': 'A vertical surface gashed by horizontal slots and relieved by a bastion supporting gesticulating entrails; an enigmatic plane which bears, like the injuries of time, the multiple scars which its maker has chosen to inflict upon it.'[6]

The surfaces of Brutalism have rarely received so empathetic and disturbing an interpretation as in Rowe's meditation, anticipated by Stokes's characterisation of architecture as affairs of childhood regression, or rather repetition, where the 'inevitable abstraction, the plain geometry of building, the

 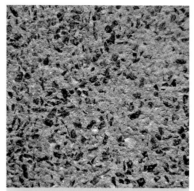

Marcel Breuer and Hamilton P Smith, Whitney Museum of American Art, New York, 1966. A photograph of the interior surface treatment: example #3.

Marcel Breuer and Hamilton P Smith, Whitney Museum of American Art, New York, 1966. A photograph of the interior surface treatment: example #4.

simple volumes, the prime shapes are so charged with feeling', that they feed the 'hunger of the eyes', together with 'some permeation of the visual sense, as of touch, by the once all-embracing oral impulse'.[7]

Indeed, distancing ourselves from the personal eccentricities of Stoke's Kleinian view, we might extend his insights on the abstract forms of architecture to Brutalist work, its delight in the transformations of concrete surfaces, polished smooth, roughened with aggregate, coloured with sands, bush-hammered, striated, marked with the grains of multiple woods, pressed by the cold flanks of steel sheets, and always striving to match the impeccable calculated effects of Stokes's own beloved exemplars of smooth and rough – the polished marbles and deeply carved rough edges that 'bite' the eyes, and grate the teeth of the observer, if not physically grazing his skin.[8]

In this context one might contrast Vincent Scully's assessment of Paul Rudolph's bush-hammered concrete surfaces at the Yale Art and Architecture Building three years after Rowe's Corbusian analysis of surface.[9] For Scully, the 'pre-weathered' vertical striations, contrived with ribbed forms that 'pushed forward' the aggregate, while it emulated Rudolph's drafting style, nevertheless produced a 'slotted and bashed surface' that was 'one of the most inhospitable, indeed physically dangerous, ever devised by man'. In a bravado Stokesian crescendo to his critique, Scully proclaimed: 'Brushing against it can induce injuries roughly comparable, one supposes, to those suffered in keel-hauling'. Wrapped in such a surface, Scully concluded, 'the building thus repels touch; it hurts if you try'. 'The sense,' he concluded, 'is of bitter pride, acrid acerbity rising perhaps to a kind of tragic gloom, since the light falls across the gashed ridges in long dusky veils, all brightness eaten by the broken surfaces, no reflection possible.'

Scully was quick to contrast Rudolph's dangerous surfaces with those of Le Corbusier, where 'the placement of the planks in the forms imparts to the concrete a surface which expresses the loving care with which it was received in the pour. One might say that it was cradled there.'[10] Here Scully returns to the motif that runs through Ruskin, Stokes and Rowe – the building as mother, standing in for the womb, and the surface as the result of the attacks, sometimes violent, sometimes smoothing, of the child.

Out of this combination of popular psychoanalysis and phenomenology (we can imagine Heidegger's hammer wielded by the child whose teeth were insufficient to overcome the anxiety of birth[11]) was born a strange aesthetic convergence that – named prematurely by Alison and Peter Smithson and Banham as 'Brutalism' – would also create almost at the very same moment something that Nikolaus Pevsner, opening the Paul Rudolph-designed Yale Art and Architecture Building in 1963, called 'brutal'.[12]

Le Corbusier, who was credited with inventing the Brutalist surface, was rightly annoyed when the Harvard administration described the Carpenter Center for the Visual Arts (1962) that he had designed for the University as 'Brutalist'. He wrote to José Luis Sert:

> '*Béton brut*' was born at the Unité d'Habitation, Marseilles, where there were eighty contractors and such a massacre of concrete that there was no way of imagining how to construct useful relationships through rendering. I had decided: leave everything '*brut*.' I called it '*béton brut*.' The English immediately jumped on the band wagon and dubbed me (Ronchamp and the convent of La Tourette) 'Brutal',— '*béton brutal*';—and at the end of the day, the brute is Corbu. They called it 'the new brutality.' My friends and admirers thinking of me as the 'brute' of 'brutal concrete' (*béton brutal*)![13]

Here Le Corbusier, recalling his origins in the Swiss town of La Chaux-de-Fonds, and Stokes striving to associate architecture with Klein's vision of childhood traumas, and Rowe licking his lips and sucking his teeth appalled at the absence of a facade but intrigued by the complexities of surface, and Scully terrified of being keel-hauled, each tried to come to terms with the beast of Late Modernism, itself ambiguously torn between the craft ideology of Ruskin and the abstract form-making of Heroic Modernism. For better or for worse, the Brutalist surface had, by 1965, come of age aesthetically.

Notes

1   Adrian Stokes, *The Critical Writings of Adrian Stokes* (3 vols), Vol 2: *Smooth and Rough* [1951], Thames & Hudson (London), 1978, pp 213–56 (p 241).

2   Reyner Banham, 'The New Brutalism', *Architectural Review*, December 1955, pp 354–61.

3   Peggy Deamer, 'Adrian Stokes: The Architecture of Phantasy and the Phantasy of Architecture', *Annual of Psychoanalysis: Architecture and Psychoanalysis*, forthcoming. Viewable at http://www.peggydeamer.com/images/adrianstokes_phantasy.pdf, Peggy Deamer website (accessed 9 October 2013).

4   Stokes, *Smooth and Rough*, pp 240–41.

5   Colin Rowe, 'La Tourette' [first published in *Architectural Review*, June 1961], in *The Mathematics of the Ideal Villa and Other Essays*, The MIT Press (Cambridge, Massachusetts), 1976, p 187.

6   Ibid, pp 240–41.

7   Rowe, 'La Tourette', p 187.

8   Stokes, *Smooth and Rough*, p 243.

9   Vincent Scully, 'Art and Architecture Building, Yale University', *Architectural Review*, Vol 325, May 1964, p 332.

10 Ibid.

11 Martin Heidegger, *Being and Time*, translated by John Macquarrie and Edward Robinson, Blackwell (Oxford), 1962, Section 15.

12 Alison and Peter Smithson first used the word 'Brutalism' in print in 1953 ('House in Soho', *Architectural Design*, December (No 12), 1953, p 342. Nikolaus Pevsner referred to Paul Rudolph's Arts and Architecture Building at Yale as 'brutal', in 'Architecture in Our Time: the Anti-Pioneers', *The Listener*, 26 December 1966.

13 Le Corbusier to José Luis Sert, May 1962. Quoted in Eduard F Sekler and William Curtis, *Le Corbusier at Work: The Genesis of the Carpenter Center for the Visual Arts*, Harvard University Press (Cambridge, Massachusetts), 1978, p 302.

CHAPTER 4
Homely Affinities

BARBARA PENNER

One of the richest and most productive of Adrian Forty's contributions to the fields of architectural and design history was made early in his career. In *Objects of Desire: Design and Society since 1750* (1986), Forty drew on social anthropologist Mary Douglas's remarks about dirt in *Purity and Danger* (1966) to help explain the appearance of a wide variety of modern objects and spaces.[1] Forty worked from Douglas's definition of dirt as 'matter out of place'[2] – something in our environment that we perceive as disorderly and seek to separate out and tidy up – and showed that product design played an especially important role in purifying efforts in the home. Manufacturers imbued domestic appliances from vacuum cleaners to refrigerators with an aesthetic of cleanliness; the gleaming surfaces of these products symbolically reassured housekeepers that standards of hygiene were being upheld.

Forty's observations about the impact of hygiene on domestic design and architecture have been broadly cited and have helped to generate fruitful new insights of their own – my own work on bathrooms is very much indebted to them.[3] And *Objects of Desire* generally remains an important work for design history. It is a model of how theory – mostly Marxist and structural theory in this case – can help to systematically make sense of objects and buildings of all kinds. (Besides Douglas, the other structuralist whom Forty prominently cites is Roland Barthes, whose 1957 book *Mythologies* continues to have an impact on his thinking.) In its use of a range of scholarship from other disciplines, including anthropology and cultural studies, the book is committed to the idea that architecture and design should be addressed as part of an 'expanded field' of human activity.[4] And although feminism is not explicitly foregrounded, Forty's feminist sympathies are obvious. For instance, he demonstrates the way in which emotive arguments surrounding dirt have been gendered, persuading women that protecting the family from dirt and pollution is supposedly their particular responsibility.

Any work of scholarship is the product of a particular time, place and intellectual milieu, and *Objects of Desire*, as this brief survey indicates, is no exception. In the 1970s, when Forty was at work on *Objects of Desire*, London's scholarly scene was being galvanised by many influences – Marxism, feminism, Lacanian psychoanalysis, French structuralism – that particularly impacted upon the new generation of art and architectural historians with which Forty associated. Although Reyner Banham did not embrace these new theories, he was also an important and very direct influence on Forty's work (the two shared an office at the Bartlett School of Architecture at University College London).[5] The way in which Mary Douglas, another UCL professor, fits into this picture is less obvious and deserves some attention.[6]

This essay will consider how Douglas's work relates to Forty's. The relationship was not a personal one: even though Douglas was something of a legend when Forty was at UCL, he never actually met her or heard her lecture. Indeed, when one goes back to *Objects of Desire* to search out Forty's references to Douglas, they are surprisingly slight given their impact.[7] In this sense, this essay speaks less about influences and more about affinities, for what is most interesting about reading Douglas's and Forty's books today is how they resonate with each other. There is a kind of shared sensibility: both books are 'homely', in that their authors discuss home – though they mention non-domestic spaces as well – and express ideas in a plain and unvarnished way.[8] Perhaps most strikingly, both authors draw on everyday domestic examples, anecdotes and metaphors to build full and coherent explanations for the way humans behave and environments are shaped.

In the wake of Douglas's death in 2007, her biographer, Richard Fardon, noted: 'If [Douglas] had to be recalled for a single achievement, it would be as the anthropologist who took the techniques of a particularly vibrant period of research into non-western societies and applied them to her own western milieu.'[9] We might be more specific than this: Douglas did not just bring her observations back to her Western milieu, she brought them back into her friends' homes and into her own.

Consider, for instance, the way in which Douglas introduced the symbolic nature of dirt at the beginning of *Purity and Danger*. She described her discomfort upon entering a friend's bathroom that was perfectly clean, but occupied a corridor space. Contemplating the gardening tools and gumboots that occupied it, Douglas noted: 'It all made good sense as the scene of a back corridor, but as a bathroom – the impression destroyed repose.'[10] Dissecting her own reaction, Douglas realised that her discomfort did not come from dirt (and in any case, she stressed, dirt is not necessarily dangerous), but was connected to the bathroom's appearance. Quite simply, it didn't *look* like a bathroom. This led her to make one of her best-known insights: 'In chasing dirt, in papering, decorating, tidying we are not governed by anxiety to escape disease, but are positively re-ordering our environment, making it conform to an idea'[11] – in the case of the bathroom, that of hygiene.

It is hard to think of a more stimulating prompt for a design historian than this anecdote, which implicitly assigns home décor with a serious social and symbolic importance, and Forty does not miss the opportunity. In *Objects of Desire*, he approvingly quotes Douglas's observation. He also follows her lead in treating home not merely as a shelter, but as an 'icon' which projects a unified image. Forty states:

> Ideas about the home vary between cultures and between periods, but at any one time and in any one place, there is likely to be a consensus about what a home should be like, what is right and proper there, and what is out of place.[12]

From the 19th century, Forty argues, the prevailing consensus was that a home should be a temple of cleanliness: hygiene fetishism emerged as the centrepiece of a highly gendered middle-class domestic ideology.

Forty draws on another argument in *Purity and Danger* to speculate as to why hygiene became such a defining preoccupation. Noting that, in Douglas's account, pollution occurs when a culture's internal relationships and social boundaries are threatened, he suggests that Victorian middle-class efforts to reform the working classes – to instil in them ideas of cleanliness and order

– were a bulwark against social upheaval. When Forty describes the various channels by which the reform movement attempted to reach the working classes, he also makes his strongest claims for the power of design. 'Only when advertisers, designers, and manufacturers began to make use of the imagery of hygiene,' he argues, 'did the general public fully assimilate the lessons which the hygienists had been teaching.'[13]

Forty's demonstration of design's role in making visible and communicating dominant social ideas and how these change over time is a valuable extension of Douglas's work. (Douglas herself had little to say about design in any formal sense.) In Forty's account, ideas are deliberately 'implanted' into products to serve various ends. It is the design historian's job to understand this process – how are ideas implanted and why? While Forty claims the way design embodies myths is universal, his insistence that products are always shaped by the available means of production ensures that his examples remain rooted in specific social and material relations. These are often in conflict: for instance, the class conflict that Forty uses to explain Victorian sanitary reform. Towards the end of Chapter 7, however, Forty takes a step back from this conflictual model, noting that it is not simply the case that ideas were implanted by manufacturers and other parties; rather, consumers wanted hygienic imagery in products because cleanliness had come to be equated with beauty. Hence, products imbued with the 'aesthetic of cleanliness' also became 'objects of desire'.[14]

Even with this final nod to the consumer, there still remains a large gap between Forty's emphasis on the calculated, even coercive, nature of design and Douglas's more natural and intuitive concept of dirt and responses to it. Would Forty regard decorating as 'positive re-ordering' as Douglas does? Though the consumer is mentioned and there is a broad interest in the social impact of design in his account, specific user behaviour is not his focus per se. In fact, one might easily be left with a strong sense of the differences rather than the similarities between the two authors: Forty's empirical collection of archival materials and case studies often seems very far away from Douglas's first-person cross-cultural trawl of ethnographic examples. Yet the affinities are striking too, notably the shared interest in everyday materiality and 'emphatically ordinary' places, best exemplified by the fact that the bathroom – that most humble of spaces – appears as a star witness in both of their books.[15]

In a new introduction to *Purity and Danger* written in 2002, Douglas notes that she began writing the book after she'd been confined to her bed with the measles. 'The background of daily life in nursery and kitchen may explain why the metaphors are homely,' she muses.[16] While Forty did not discuss the conditions under which he wrote *Objects of Desire*, and does not draw on personal experience as Douglas does, his language is no less homely. Although Reyner Banham grumbled about design historians who wrote in 'Barthes-Marx' and complained that it was unlikely to be understood, Forty deployed theory in a notably unfussy way and always took care to avoid obfuscation.[17] Forty's writing, incidentally, was also a world away from the expressive pop pyrotechnics of Banham's own design criticism.

Apart from his use of plain language, Forty's clarity derives from his use of concrete metaphors to explain scholarly attitudes.[18] For instance, this is his rather wonderful critique of architectural historians who connect design to social context without precisely explaining how they are related:

> Such cursory references to the social context are like weeds and gravel around a stuffed fish in a glass case: however realistic these may be, they are only furnishings, and taking them away would have little effect on our perception of the fish.[19]

The stuffed-fish-in-glass metaphor summons to mind an overcrowded Victorian parlour, no doubt as it is meant to do. Forty here signals that his parlour is a sparser, less fussy affair, with no stuffed fish, weeds or gravel – that is, no vague or unsupported contentions. And with the broom of Barthes's and Douglas's theories, he sweeps the fustian furnishings of academe away in one of modern design history's neatest acts of scholarly housekeeping.[20]

Notes

1   Comments on Mary Douglas, *Purity and Danger*, Routledge & Kegan Paul (London), 1966, in Adrian Forty, *Objects of Desire: Design and Society since 1750*, Thames & Hudson (London), 1986, Chapters 5 and 7. Douglas's influence is most strongly felt in Chapter 7, 'Hygiene and Dirt', but Chapter 5 on 'The Home' bears her mark too.

2   The origins of this phrase (which is not Douglas's own) have recently been painstakingly uncovered by Richard

Fardon, 'Citations out of Place: Or, Lord Palmerston goes viral in the nineteenth century but gets lost in the twentieth', *Anthropology Today*, Vol 29, No 1, February 2013, pp 25–6.

3   Barbara Penner, *Bathroom*, Reaktion (London), 2013.

4   The phrase, the 'expanded field', was first used by art historian Rosalind Krauss in relation to sculptural practices of the 1960s and 1970s. As historian Nigel Whiteley points out, this phrase also aptly describes Reyner Banham's broad approach to architecture in the same period. See Nigel Whiteley, *Reyner Banham: Historian of the Immediate Future*, The MIT Press (Cambridge, Massachusetts), 2002, Chapter 4, 'The Expanded Field: Fit Environments for Human Activities'.

5   Banham was at UCL between 1964 and 1976 when he moved to the State University of New York at Buffalo.

6   Douglas was at UCL for nearly half a century from the early 1950s with some breaks when she took up academic appointments in America.

7   Forty cites Douglas just twice, in Chapter 7 on pp 157 and 159.

8   The term 'homely' was used by Douglas herself in the preface to the 2002 edition of *Purity and Danger*. Mary Douglas, *Purity and Danger: An Analysis of the Concepts of Pollution and Taboo*, Routledge (London), 2002, p xi.

9   Richard Fardon, 'Dame Mary Douglas', *The Guardian*, Friday 18 May 2007.

10   Douglas, *Purity and Danger*, 2002, p 3.

11   Ibid.

12   Forty, *Objects of Desire*, p 94.

13   Ibid, p 161.

14   Ibid, p 180.

15   Ben Campkin, 'Placing "Matter out of Place": Purity and Danger as Evidence for Architecture and Urbanism', *Architectural Theory Review*, Vol 18, No 1, 2013, p 49.

16   Douglas, *Purity and Danger*, 2002, p xi.

17   Banham quote (from 1983) in Whiteley, *Reyner Banham: Historian of the Immediate Future*, p 358.

18   Indeed, Forty still recommends to students Sir Ernest Gowers's style guide, *The Complete Plain Words*, originally issued in 1954, which elegantly lays out the elements of clear writing, under headings such as 'Do you know, say and convey what you mean?' and 'Use few, familiar and precise words'.

19   Forty is referring specifically here to the historian Mark Girouard, writing about Queen Anne architecture. Forty, *Objects of Desire*, p 8.

20   This train of thought was partially prompted by a remark made to me by Adrian some years ago: 'Good scholarship,' he said, 'should be like good housekeeping: the labour that goes into it [i.e. the theory] should be largely invisible.'

CHAPTER 5

On Regeneration

BEN CAMPKIN

With its prefix 're', the word 'regeneration' contains a creative moment, a small addition to the stem, making a new word and meaning. It therefore both defines and embodies an iterative, incremental act of building on what is there, imagining and making anew. Noble and natural as the spiritual and biological connotations of regenerative growth and repair might seem – even, and perhaps especially, in a secular age, and one heightened to biophysical processes because of concerns about environmental catastrophe – as a grand narrative and metaphor for changing cities, 'urban regeneration' has recently come under intense critical scrutiny in places such as London, and is suffering a crisis of meaning as a result. Its referents have become clouded and it is often used misleadingly to describe practices that many argue to be *de*generate, in social and environmental terms.[1]

In the rhetoric of planners and politicians, current aspirations for regeneration oscillate between the social and economic, emphasising the need for economic growth, and identifying 'opportunity areas' for more intensive use of land and real estate. The Mayor of London's *London Plan* (July 2011) defines regeneration areas as those 'in greatest socioeconomic need', on the basis of the UK's 'Index of Multiple Deprivation', a statistical dataset published by the Government and focused on income, employment, health deprivation, disability, education, skills and training, barriers to housing and services, and crime.[2] There is an assumption that business- and property-led redevelopment and the housing market will cause a 'trickle down' effect, ultimately raising the quality of life and income levels of communities living in such areas. In practice, however, in London and elsewhere, the neoliberal strategies the Plan promotes have been widely criticised for working directly against such objectives: increasing inequality, reducing the amount of genuinely affordable housing, instigating the demolition of estates rather than their renewal, alienating communities instead of engaging with them, and so on. Since the financial crisis of 2008, and the end of the era of the New Labour government (1997–2010), in which achieving an 'urban renaissance' was a central policy objective, regeneration has therefore been exposed more sharply to scrutiny. There is a growing scepticism about the broad range of processes – including gentrification and property development – subsumed under this metaphor.

The contradictions and displacements concealed when the term is used are evident when we consider that, although regeneration is frequently justified in terms of fostering 'mixed use', 'diverse', 'creative' and 'biodiverse' neighbourhoods and 'sustainable communities', it often appears to remove precisely these qualities and activities and settled groups of people. Instead we see attempts to engineer creativity, sanitise biodiversity and disperse communities. Similarly, even within a regeneration drive that purportedly attempts to reverse decline and eliminate degradation, these conditions are often heightened, commodified or exacerbated in the process, in order to justify particular kinds of change.

In this context one positive counter strategy must be to keep returning to the roots of the word itself, and to examine its metaphorical uses. It has Latin origins, referring to re-creation, and an interesting etymology whereby in the 12th century it refers to spiritual rebirth, and in the 13th and 14th it is also used to refer to the formation of new cells in the repair of animal tissue.[3] Its use in reference to place can be traced back to the mid-16th century, but it is not until the late 19th century that 'urban regeneration' begins to feature, referring to reconstruction in cities such as London.[4] 'Regeneration' also appears in the 20th century in the repertoire of sociobiological metaphors through which the renewal of postwar London was conceived. In that context there was a sense that properly functioning neighbourhoods would self-regenerate, meaning that radical reconstruction was necessary where regenerative growth and repair did not occur spontaneously. Even considering these historical usages, however, it is striking that this word and concept have such widespread currency in present-day urban debate, and particularly in London, where the discourse and practice of regeneration gained intense momentum from the 1980s to the 2000s.

The trajectory of the *fin-de-siècle* Western neoliberal regeneration imaginary finds its logical destiny in the banality and hyperbole that typify contemporary local-government 'global city' place-marketing strategies. To continue with the example of London, in 2010 Newham Council – the authority responsible for the London Borough of Newham, with neighbourhoods that are high up on the UK's Index of Multiple Deprivation – used a film and brochure to project the image of a 'regeneration supernova' exploding across the borough, part of an area conceived as an 'arc of opportunity'.[5] The brief for the film and brochure prioritised a 'glamorous and sexy' presentation 'to tell people instantly about the scale of Newham's regeneration'. Interviewed when the film was released, Newham's Executive Director of Regeneration, Property and Planning remarked that Newham is 'literally a platform waiting for things to happen'.[6] As the giant washing machines lining the edges of the Olympic Park began to spin into action to decontaminate the industrial carbons in its soil – a very literal biophysical process by which the land could be re-exploited for its development potential – here was one of the host boroughs marketing the post-Olympic site as real estate to investors in the Far East at the Shanghai Expo. These two equally excessive yet contrasting grounded and celestial images encapsulate the post-industrial regeneration drive.

Newham briefed the external agency that produced the film that it should not be corporate, and yet they ended up using a highly corporate (or watered-down and corporate) graphic style. Its visual mode is perhaps the one that best sums up the empty rhetoric and tabula rasa approach of 21st-century neoliberal urban regeneration. It uses excitable editing to bombard spectators with word clouds and image grids: logos, hierarchically organised texts and tables of quantitative information; photographs with graphics superimposed; specially drawn maps and diagrams; computer-generated imagery; and 'photo-real' renderings. Some are from commercial 'stock' image libraries, others from architectural offices: visualisations of possible new buildings, a cast of diverse citizens, tourist icons, heritage buildings, green spaces and images of benevolent urban nature.

These artefacts of Newham's and London's regeneration strategies emphasise that here the role of local government in regeneration is primarily one of facilitating private-sector investment to instigate urban change. Its function is to market the potential of land and labour in order to attract global capital. It is easy to understand the desperate tone of the marketing effort when one considers that Newham is a borough that faced extraordinary challenges in 2010, and still does after the 2012 Games: poverty, unemployment, overcrowding of poor-quality private rented housing, a transient population. In this area, which was bypassed by the wealth that flowed through London in the boom years of the 2000s, local politicians and planners have to manage the borough's high levels of debt and its massive housing waiting list within the context of government welfare cuts. In response, a gentrification strategy is only very thinly veiled as regeneration strategy, focused on raising land values, opening new markets and attracting the 'right' kinds of businesses and residents to settle – with the assumption of a trickle-down effect in which this new wealth will benefit at least some of the existing communities. Developing a regeneration imaginary at the global scale, Newham's strategy inevitably became detached from any sense of the everyday environments and people the Council represented. The film was originally published on Newham's website, but it was really only intended for a limited audience of Expo visitors, and it was subsequently taken down, withdrawn from citizens' view.

The idea of a regeneration supernova – a catastrophic explosion forming a new star – is a projection of London that neatly encapsulates urbanisation proceeding at a rapacious rate. It unintentionally emphasises the inevitable dynamic between degradation and regeneration. As a spectacular metaphor it mixes the spiritual, celestial and biological, evoking an exciting scale and moment, but also a violent one. As a pitch for redevelopment it works because it is sufficiently abstract and preposterously grand, both full and empty of meaning, leaving potential investors to imagine what could be there in the future. Apart from its definition in astrophysics, there is a long tradition of using 'supernova' figuratively – for example, in science fiction. It can suggest brilliance, explosiveness, collapse, success or excess (a supernova ego).

Our figures and models of urban transformation disclose much about the kinds of societies we are and imagine we are or want to be. In attending to this we are faced with fundamental and always ideological questions of what we want to hold on to, develop, let go of. With this in mind, if an important metaphor through which we can imagine positive change has been broken, appearing to work violently against its original spirit, how can it be reappropriated? In other words, can we, or should we, regenerate 'regeneration'? What would a more radical and responsible regeneration imaginary look like? Adrian Forty has remarked that 'metaphors are experiments with the possible likenesses of unlike things'.[7] In contrast with many of the problematic sociobiological metaphors – such as images of blight and disease – that have been used to stigmatise low-income neighbourhoods, there is a great deal of potential for regeneration to productively articulate positive reconfigurations of urban nature towards improved public health and environmental conditions. In doing so it would need to refocus on the needs of the communities and individuals in whose name it is carried out, improving public health, and the provision of decent housing, recalibrating an understanding of growth as incremental, contextual and focused on achieving social value. Instead of being conceived as helpless and 'deprived', and feeling alienated from discourses and projections of change, communities affected by regeneration would need to be given the power to realise their own imaginaries of change.

Notes

1 See, for example, Claire Colomb, 'Unpacking New Labour's "Urban Renaissance" Agenda: Towards a Socially Sustainable Reurbanisation of British Cities?', *Planning Practice & Research*, Vol 22, No 1, 2007, pp 1–24; Mark Davidson, 'Love thy Neighbour? Social Mixing in London's Gentrification Frontiers', *Environment and Planning A*, Vol 42, No 3, 2010, pp 524–44; Michael Edwards, 'King's Cross: Renaissance for Whom?', in John Punter (ed), *Urban Design, Urban Renaissance and British Cities*, Routledge (London), 2010, pp 189–205; Rob Imrie, Loretta Lees and Mike Raco (eds), *Regenerating London: Governance, Sustainability and Community in a Global City*, Routledge (London), 2009; Libby Porter and Kate Shaw (eds), *Whose Urban Renaissance? An International Comparison of Urban Regeneration Strategies*, Routledge (London), 2009.

2 Mayor of London, *The London Plan: Spatial Development Strategy for Greater London*, Greater London Authority (London), July 2011. The dataset is produced by the Social Disadvantage Research Centre, University of Oxford. The first index was produced in 2000, covering 33 variables for 8,414 wards in England. It was championed by the New Labour government for the purpose of identifying areas most in need, so that resources could be targeted towards them. Further indices were published in 2004 and 2007, with increasing specificity to particular locales: HM Government, *Index of Multiple Deprivation*. See: http://data.gov.uk/dataset/index-of-multiple-deprivation (accessed 20 July 2012); Communities and Local Government, *The English Indices of Deprivation 2007*. See: http://www.communities.gov.uk/documents/communities/pdf/733520.pdf (accessed 20 July 2012).

3 *Oxford English Dictionary*. See: http://www.oed.com (accessed 1 March 2012). For an excellent discussion of the uses of regeneration as a metaphor in urban policy, see Robert Furbey, 'Urban "Regeneration": Reflections on a Metaphor', *Critical Social Policy*, Vol 19, No 4, 1999, pp 419–45.

4 The *Oxford English Dictionary* cites the following early example of 'regeneration' in reference to place: 'Regeneration, *n.*, 1 b. In extended use: renaissance; renewal, spec. of a geographical area by the improvement of its economic and social conditions, 1567, W Painter, *Palace of Pleasure* II. xxij. f. 166v, "The further he went, the greater he saw the increase, & almost a regeneration, or as I may say, a new birth of rare things, which made y littlenesse of the place more stately and wonderfull".' See: http://www.oed.com (accessed 1 March 2012).

5   London Borough of Newham, *Newham London: Investment Prospectus* (undated). See: http://www.newham.gov. uk/NR/rdonlyres/8AF0D6BC-7A8E-4625-85D1-2083502CB3D5/0/InvestmentProspectus.pdf (accessed 19 June 2012). The film was available online but has subsequently been taken down from Newham's website.

6   Andrea Klettner, 'Regeneration Olympian', *Regeneration and Renewal*, 30 July 2010. See: http://www.regen.net/ news/1018972/Regeneration-Olympian/?DCMP=ILC-SEARCH (accessed 19 June 2012).

7   Adrian Forty, *Words and Buildings: A Vocabulary of Modern Architecture*, Thames & Hudson (London), 2000, p 101.

CHAPTER 6

Fresh Reactions to St Paul's Cathedral

BRIAN STATER

On the morning of Margaret Thatcher's funeral, the architectural historian Marcus Binney wrote in *The Times*: 'Today, as the coffin is borne into St Paul's, it will be into a Cathedral that has never looked finer since it was completed in 1711.'[1]

This was a reminder that St Paul's is unique among English cathedrals, certainly those built prior to the 20th century. It has not been significantly added to, or subtracted from, in 300 years and a recent restoration has removed almost every trace of the passage of those three centuries.

But while the fabric of the Cathedral is unchanging, its wider cultural meaning has proved much more transitory. It may be said to have found recent new identities following the revolution of economic activity in the City of London and the appropriation of the Cathedral by both Left and Right, as a setting for significant political events.

Andrew Saint traced many earlier meanings in a 2004 essay 'The Reputation of St Paul's'.[2] His account closed with a discussion of the significance of the Cathedral during and after the Second World War. Despite terrible destruction by bombing nearby, St Paul's escaped serious damage and came to be regarded as an embodiment of British fortitude and defiance. Saint wrote: 'The metamorphosis of St Paul's into a symbol of togetherness, survival and suffering was best articulated in photographs, not words: above all in a snapshot taken by Herbert Mason, on 29 December 1940 from the roof of the Daily Mail, showing the dome transfigured against white cloud, lit by invisible fires behind a screen of smoke.' Saint concluded that what followed was a period of anti-climax. 'St Paul's,' he wrote, 'had now reached the limits of its capacity for meaning.' 'In these post-War years,' he added, 'fresh reactions to the Cathedral are rare.'

Mason's photograph certainly had a long and deep-rooted legacy. On 12 July 2000, almost 60 years after the image first appeared, it was evoked in the unlikely form of a quarter-page cartoon in the London *Evening Standard*. The occasion was the 100th birthday of the Queen Mother and the drawing was split in two. On one side, a sketch of the royal centenarian; on the other a precise rendition of Mason's view of St Paul's. The pair were linked by a simple caption: 'Great Survivors'.

Later still, in June 2012, a debate took place in the House of Lords on the future care of English cathedrals. Lord Cormack, the former Conservative MP Sir Patrick Cormack, said this:

> There are two enduring images of this country above all others: Constable's painting of Salisbury [...] and, from a more recent period, the picture of St Paul's in the Blitz, rising above the smoke. No nation can call itself civilised if it puts the spire of Salisbury or the dome of St Paul's at risk.[3]

The wartime image of St Paul's may still be traced in fresh reactions to the Cathedral which emerged particularly after financial deregulation of the City in 1986. This was the 'Big Bang' and is regarded as the most important economic event in the City since the War. In 1996 the Guildhall Art Gallery, the collection of the City of London Corporation, acquired *Blackfriars Bridge and St Paul's* by the British artist Anthony Lowe. It is considered to be among the most significant of the Guildhall's contemporary paintings and is a large (1.4 by 1.2 metres (4 feet 7 inches by 3 feet 11 inches)), bold and powerful view of the Cathedral, set amid the City as it was rebuilt after 1945. Vivien Knight, head of the Guildhall Gallery when the picture was acquired, commented: 'Lowe presents us with a crazily animated city, empty of human life, the dome of St Paul's gilded by light and surrounded by apocalyptic clouds.' She added: 'The clouds above the cathedral's metallic dome look like those of an apotheosis.'[4] This sense of apocalypse, of the light on the great dome of the Cathedral and

Anthony Lowe, *Blackfriars Bridge and St Paul's*, 1995, oil on canvas.

a moment of transformation, provides an unexpected link to Herbert Mason's wartime photograph, which contains precisely those characteristics. But where Mason photographed a savage air raid, Lowe possibly is painting the Big Bang's firestorm of money. In this reading, St Paul's is recast by an aggressive financial industry which is destroying the previous identity of the City.

A further fresh reaction to St Paul's can be found in the events of October 2011 to February 2012 when the Cathedral precinct was the site of a highly controversial protest by the anti-capitalist group Occupy London. The demonstrators had attempted to enter the London Stock Exchange, close to St Paul's, and their failure inspired a serendipitous move to the Cathedral, which became a platform from which to challenge the perceived moral failings of British business. The Cathedral was briefly closed, a senior member of the

Chapter resigned, and savage attacks were mounted in many sections of the media. The *Daily Mail* decided Occupy was a 'Rabble Without a Cause'[5] and, in an alliterative series of eulogies, branded them 'a shambolic crew of pot-smoking, part-time protesters who put partying before politics' (the only surprise is that none were also alleged to be predatory paedophiles). A more measured response came from Rowan Williams, the then Archbishop of Canterbury, who supported the protesters' call for a tax on British bankers.[6] Occupy, it would seem, had succeeded in a moral occupation of St Paul's.

One strand of a second political event – the Margaret Thatcher funeral – may be interpreted as the Right's reappropriation of the Cathedral. Her death, on 8 April 2013, produced a frenzy, which a range of observers described as an 'attempted canonisation' of the former Prime Minister.[7] In the nine days before the funeral, on 17 April, the *Daily Mail*, among others, campaigned to have her political record endorsed by a state funeral, though the details of the ceremony, complete with military honours, had been agreed some years earlier by the then Labour government and amounted to a state occasion in all but name. Central to the grandeur of the ceremony was its venue: St Paul's. Baroness Thatcher, proclaimed by the *Daily Mail* to be 'The Woman Who Saved Britain',[8] was the first former Prime Minister to be granted a funeral in the Cathedral since Sir Winston Churchill, and the association with the wartime leader was accordingly manipulated by the Right.

On the Left, Thatcher's death was marked by a number of celebratory bonfires in cities and former mining communities. The *Mail* condemned these 'Flames of Hatred', insisting that 'Thirty years of Left-wing loathing exploded in sick celebrations. Will her funeral now be targeted?'[9] Security fears, whether real or invented, resulted in a 4,000-strong police operation centred on St Paul's. Perhaps the decisive moment in the ceremony was the arrival of the coffin, draped in the Union flag, at the west front of the Cathedral, the scene just 18 months earlier of the Occupy protest.

Do these episodes represent a new meaning for the building? Will it continue to be contested by rival ideologies which sense that this unchanging building has a pliability to sustain wildly opposing views? However this possibility develops, it is already clear that the Cathedral can no longer be regarded solely, in Andrew Saint's words, as 'a symbol of togetherness'. That might, curiously, be regarded as the final achievement of the most divisive politician of the postwar era. And architectural historians await the funeral of Tony Blair with particular interest.

Notes

1   Marcus Binney, 'Wren's Baroque Vision is a Dazzling Showcase for Grand National Occasions', *The Times*, 17 April 2013.

2   Derek Keene, Arthur Burns and Andrew Saint (eds), *St Paul's: The Cathedral Church of London 604–2004*, Yale University Press (New Haven, Connecticut), 2004, Chapter 42.

3   *Lords Hansard*, 28 June 2012, column 330.

4   Vivien Knight, *Modern Pictures*, Guildhall Art Gallery (London), undated.

5   *Daily Mail*, 17 October 2011.

6   *Daily Telegraph*, 2 November 2011.

7   Those expressing this view ranged across the political spectrum from Sally Bercow, wife of the Speaker of the House of Commons, to Alastair Campbell, former Director of Communications under Tony Blair, to George Galloway, Respect MP.

8   *Daily Mail*, 9 April 2013.

9   *Daily Mail*, 10 April 2013.

CHAPTER 7

Photographs and Buildings (mainly)

BRIONY FER

The photographs that Adrian Forty (AF) has taken fill his books and fuelled his teaching. He followed Reyner Banham's watchword: that you should never talk about a building you have not seen. In practice, this also meant, have not photographed.

FILING CABINET

To describe the contents of AF's filing cabinets is to describe his collection of 35-millimetre slides. As an architectural historian, taking pictures of buildings was always his stock-in-trade. Now the storage system for images is on a computer; back then it was a repository of slides, all of which were taken by AF. A small proportion of his collection has been transferred, but the vast majority remains, now obsolete, in two grey filing cabinets heavy with images – laden, that is, with the physical weight of plastic mounts but also of a vast visual atlas.

Photographs record buildings (though not exclusively) but they also record AF's changing interests. Describing the contents of the filing cabinet is one way of describing how these have changed since 1970, which is around about the time when he began to build up his image-bank. In it, there are the things he wrote or lectured about as well as all the things he didn't – or else didn't get around to thinking about many years later. Often, the images are there just waiting to become useful.

Rather than see himself as a photographer, AF took photographs to do a job. It was always a matter-of-fact collection of images, whose principal use was to serve as the bedrock of his lectures and teaching, and which now continues in digital form. On the other hand he often spent many hours photographing a building, so clearly his relationship to photography was also – as it must be for all those architectural historians and critics who take photographs in this way – never quite contained within its classificatory system or the rationale imposed upon it.

TATTOO

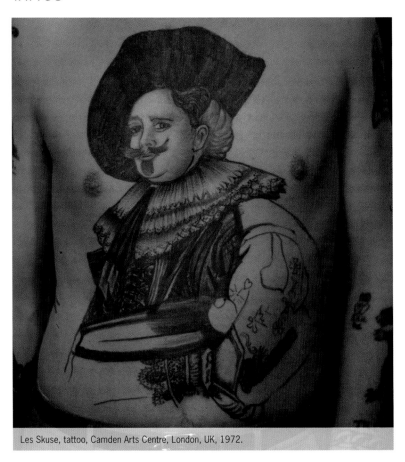

Les Skuse, tattoo, Camden Arts Centre, London, UK, 1972.

Between the sections on 'shoes' and 'textiles' there is a sheet marked 'tattoos'. Right at the very beginning of AF's professional life, around 1971 or 1972, in his first job after the Courtauld Institute, at the Bristol School of Art, he asked a leading local tattooist, Les Skuse, to come and give a talk to his students. AF was already interested in ideas about ornament. An exhibition of Les Skuse's work would later be held at the Camden Arts Centre, and the photographs he took at the opening of Skuse's show would later be used in lectures to Bartlett students on the origins of architecture. Both skin and walls could be seen as bearers of decoration freighted in culture and not nature. They were part of AF's already panoramic curiosity about everyday things that are taken for granted. Roland Barthes might not have discussed tattoos in his *Mythologies* (1957) but the images relate to AF's powerful response to that book's brilliant insights into 'what-goes-without-saying'.

HOME

Wells Coates, AD 65
EKCO wireless, 1934.

Barthes and trade magazines proved a powerful cocktail. The first article AF ever published was on wireless sets, in *AA Quarterly* in 1972,[1] and its first footnote was to Reyner Banham. It would be much transformed when it became part of his book on design, *Objects of Desire: Design and Society since 1750* (1986), which started life as a PhD under the supervision of Banham

RIZZI SCALE
PREFABBRICATA
SENZA PIANTONE
QUI'

Concrete factory, Vicenza, Italy.

after AF took a job at the Bartlett School of Architecture in 1973. But the gist – that objects are unable *not* to signify, and that technology is only part of the explanation as to why objects change their appearance – was already in place.

Trade magazines provided AF with images (he photographed them avidly), especially as he developed a way of thinking about how social processes were encrypted in the spaces we inhabit – in a domestic interior as much as the office. Of course, filing cabinets themselves would play a bit-part in these arguments: an example would be the way painting a filing cabinet red – one of Terence Conran's commercial successes at Habitat – effectively mixed up the symbolism and blurred the distinctions between home and office.[2]

From the early 1970s, AF was living in a collective household in West London. He lived with friends who were feminists, most importantly with Rozsika Parker, then a feminist art historian, later a psychotherapist. At the time she was writing the ground-breaking book, *Old Mistresses: Women, Art and Ideology*, with Griselda Pollock (published 1981). She and many others who talked around the kitchen table were associated with the Spare Rib Collective. AF would later call it 'the university' – meaning, I think, that for him, feminism was formative and as such influenced, if not always directly, his understanding of the role of gender in thinking about the spaces we live in, both public and private, as well as the objects within them.

CONCRETE

It is hard to remember a time before concrete, or before AF was interested in concrete. When he used to sail his wooden sloop on the Suffolk coast he would see the Atomic Weapons Research Establishment at Orford Ness from afar, with its pagoda-like structures on the skyline. Later, once it had been decommissioned, he would get to visit it, and photograph its concrete pavilions. Even when he was looking at buildings by Andrea Palladio (1508–1580) in Vicenza, a concrete staircase caught his attention, filed then under a section on 'prefabrication'. He would always be interested in the reasons why Greek houses were never finished, leaving their bare concrete structure revealed on the top storey (because tax was only payable on completion).

It is hard to be precise about the moment it stopped being simply about what the majority of modern buildings were made of, and became a pretext for travel and an attempt to chart its global drift across different contexts and cultures. AF quickly came to think of concrete not just as a building material but as a cultural medium. As a medium, it both consolidated and expanded his interests in what materials mean. Its very ubiquity allowed him to bring together an astonishing and eclectic range of buildings and building types, from bunkers to houses like Carlo Scarpa's Casa Ottolenghi (1974–9) on Lake Como, and films like Peter Collinson's *The Italian Job* (1969). The idea that concrete is always mediated through culture as a medium as well as a material re-describes a set of concerns with the ways in which architecture – like objects – has been mediated though social and symbolic processes that had preoccupied AF from the outset.

PHOTOGENIA

AF described *photogénie* as 'the process by which photography turns ordinary things beautiful',[3] adding that it does so by 'decontaminating' the scene. If 'photography's main service to concrete was to enhance its properties', then AF's own relation to photography was to resist that movement and to make images that did not enhance or exaggerate the aesthetic value of architecture over our social and lived relation to it. This often meant incorporating people

Carlo Scarpa, Brion Cemetery, Treviso, Italy, 1968.

(for scale) while keeping the image plain and clear. This does not mean that photography is neutral or objective but that it has to cut against the grain of itself. Because concrete has come to stand as abject in the culture in general, its seduction by and through photography becomes all the more startling. Any detail of a concrete surface is a case in point and inevitably ambivalent in some way. Perhaps there is always something of this ambivalence in photography's relationship to architecture in general.

But in the end it is not just about what things look like or how they are represented. Maybe photographs play a role that drawing might once have done in learning to look hard at something, honing and prolonging attention. In this sense a slide collection represents not just a record or memory bank, but images to think with. At the very least, it shows how architecture, for AF, could contain everything worth thinking about.

Notes

1 Adrian Forty, 'Wireless Style: Design of the English Radio Cabinet 1928–33', *Architectural Association Quarterly*, Vol 4, No 2, Spring 1972, pp 23–31.

2 Adrian Forty, 'Tycoon by Design', *Marxism Today*, Vol 27, No 7, July 1983, pp 36–7.

3 Adrian Forty, *Concrete and Culture: A Material History*, Reaktion (London), 2012, p 269.

CHAPTER 8

Stirling's Voice: A Detailed Suggestion

DAVID DUNSTER

In the methods of identification first published by Giovanni Morelli in 1876 and 1880, his argument was that artworks could be identified not by composition or theme or colour palette alone but by the ways the painter depicted the minor aspects of the painting: lace, hands, hair et cetera.[1] Further, the relationship between these incidentals was noted by Sigmund Freud,[2] an adjunct to his thoughts on parapraxes, though in earlier times Morelli did not view details as slips of the tongue. If we might reasonably take these observations one step sideways, then it can be argued that the repetitions of details themselves are neither slips nor parapraxes but identifying marks. These identifying details, by analogy with paintings, show a maturity that we could also refer to as a 'voice'.

I want to try to attend to the role of details in the work of one architect, James Stirling, not normally associated with that issue.[3] My argument concerns columns, handrails and windows in his work and proposes that the coherence of the handling of these details demonstrates the emergence of James Stirling as a voice.

Stirling spoke of his disinterest in structure as a mode of architectural expression; yet in his work we can trace the evolution of a load-bearing column support from the simple propositions of the University of Leicester Department of Engineering (1963),[4] to the focal role of a mushroom-headed column in the Library for the History Faculty at the University of Cambridge (1968), to its use in an oversized and possibly therefore expressive form in the sadly demolished housing scheme at Runcorn (1970s), to the column forms at the Neue Staatsgalerie art-gallery extension in Stuttgart (1983). There, the mushroom-head reappears at the theatre entrance, then inside the lecture room where it appears to hold up only a suspended glazed ceiling, and in the entrance hall where a ramp is supported by a column which tapers to attach to a horizontal slab, and unavoidably looks like a pencil stuck into a rubber. These columnar games suggest that there was no disinterest in the manipulation of structure. On the contrary, the columns mentioned play a distinctive role in the articulation of the public spaces. They also strongly evoke a visceral sensation of weight and support. Neither accidental nor programmatic, the columns are unique in the architectural production of that time. Moreover they were continually used by the office, and in the drawings approved by JS, as he signed himself.

By contrast to these advertisements of structure, the actual structure itself is suppressed, and rarely expressed except where there is some architectural benefit, as for example in the raking columns of the Florey Building in Oxford (1971), or the unbuilt project for Columbia University Chemistry Department (1980) where a huge truss carries the labs over an existing gymnasium and then appears to sit upon an almost dangerously small pin.

What kind of voice does this detailing reveal? Detailing and detailing routines are the almanac of any architectural office, tried, tested and catalogued as the 'way we do things'. Columns, in the case of the work discussed above, become more of a metaphor for structure than structure themselves. Perhaps this may be the quality of Stirling's details: they are both substance and metaphor. Most architectural offices will have a fairly standard way of handling glazing; in Stirling's case there is only one regularly occurring window – a circular hole nearly too large for the internal doors that it is housed in, or, in the rear elevation of the extension to the School of Architecture at Rice University in Texas (1981), a round off-centre window, capable of multiple readings and metaphors but clearly threatening the calm symmetry of that facade.

I suggest that these idiosyncrasies establish a signature: which is not to say that these are not the crucial themes of an artist's work, but to say that there are typical conditions, like hands and lace for Morelli's analysis, like columns and glazing, continually explored by that artist but secondary to any more major explorations. After the flats at Ham Common in Richmond-upon-Thames, Surrey (1958), there are no more real window details – light either enters through continuous glazing or through circular windows. The porthole appears first in the Andrew Melville Hall student residence at the University of St Andrews (1968) and dominates at Runcorn, then goes through to the Olivetti Training Centre at Haslemere, Surrey (1972) and beyond to the off-centre end elevation at Rice. Fat column heads first appear at the Cambridge History Faculty, become a forest at the unbuilt Olivetti Headquarters (designed 1971), and signal the entrance at Stuttgart. As well as these signature devices, there have to be ideas that connect. Movement around a building – 'circulation', in the medical parlance architects have adopted – is celebrated through planes, volumes and primary shapes. My purpose here is not to set up a series of 'looks-like' cues and clues, nor to suggest that these are in any way 'linguistic'. I am interested in understanding buildings not as a consumer, but to understand them as process and production, rather than the sensation of the viewer, the criticism which Nietzsche made of Kant's disinterested observer.[5]

English architecture in the 1960s, certainly as it was taught at The Bartlett and the Architectural Association, was obsessed with consistency. This was the last ditch of functionalism, the expression of structure, correct use of materials, and a literal attention to the expression of function. Form was the result, not the end. A concern with form led to that worst of all ends, arbitrariness. Robert Venturi was an American aberration; Max Bill and his buildings for the Hochschule für Gestaltung (School of Design) at Ulm in Germany (1955) were the ideal. Consistency became an end in itself and justified per se ugliness, just as sustainability does now. As with Le Corbusier, the engineer stayed a god.

Is that going too far? Perhaps. Stirling may have had problems of many sorts but he knew the problems of modern architecture and recognised the impossibility of necrophilia: from his student days he had criticised even those he idolised. One of his tutors, Colin Rowe, later taught that:

> I presume architectural education to be a very simple matter; and the task of the educator I am convinced can be quite simply specified as follows:
>
> 1. to encourage the student to believe in architecture and Modern architecture;

2. to encourage the student to be skeptical about architecture and Modern architecture;

3. and then to cause the student to manipulate, with passion and intelligence, the subjects or objects of his conviction and doubt.[6]

In the notes and ideas in Mark Crinson's excellent book *Stirling and Gowan*, the ferocity of Stirling's treatment of others – and even of his idol Le Corbusier – comes through. It is also clear from these notes for lectures that Stirling had a very clear idea of what he was about because he repeated so much of it and obviously had it off pat. This suggests that there was an inner logic, not quite a consistency, which developed from and was more careful of the detail – which is what I want to believe. Alternatively, Stirling was a fine actor with a limited memory.

So I might begin to suggest that the details were the safety net for the formal working, a sort of safety net for the wit, and for the contradictory desires. Colin Rowe, whose definition of architectural education I used above, also used Samuel Johnson's following definition:

> Wit, you know, is the unexpected copulation of ideas, the discovery of some occult relation between images in appearance remote from each other; an effusion of wit, therefore, presupposes an accumulation of knowledge; a memory stored with notions, which the imagination may cull out to compose new assemblages. Whatever may be the native vigour of the mind, she can never form any combinations from few ideas, as many changes can never be rung upon a few bells.[7]

Stirling had many bells, a veritable belfry some might say. Increasingly, it seems to me that his buildings became a collection and a collision of incidents, events strung out like jewels in a necklace, where the string is conventionally that walk through, the stroll that enlightens, the *promenade architecturale*.

In the 1960s there were three gods of architecture for me: Denys Lasdun, who had said that the job of an architect was to give the client what he never thought he could have; Robert Venturi, who opened up a new way of looking at buildings; and James Stirling, whose iconoclastic buildings designed with James Gowan were incomprehensibly exciting and to be copied – and that's the only way, I learnt later, to come close to how they might have been designed. Of these architects only Venturi turned out to be lovable as a person. I have no conclusion: we still need a critical appreciation of the work.

© David Dunster

Notes

1 See Carlo Ginzburg, 'Morelli, Freud and Sherlock Holmes: Clues and Scientific Method', *History Workshop Journal*, No 9, Spring 1980, pp 5–36.

2 To some of Morelli's critics it has seemed odd 'that personality should be found where personal effort is weakest'. But on this point modern psychology would certainly support Morelli: our inadvertent little gestures reveal our character far more authentically than any formal posture that we may carefully prepare.

3 In 2011 I gave a brief presentation at the Royal Academy in a symposium on the work of James Stirling which forms the basis of this paper.

4 The work of the partnership of James Stirling and James Gowan. It is hard not to assume that the workshops were primarily the work of Gowan and the tower block that of Stirling, though the creative and destructive interplay between them is hinted at by Mark Crinson in *Stirling and Gowan: Architecture from Austerity to Affluence*, Yale University Press (New Haven, Connecticut), 2012, pp 69–70.

5 Friedrich Nietzsche, 'On the Genealogy of Morals', in *Basic Writings of Nietzsche*, translated by Walter Kaufmann, The Modern Library (New York), 1968, Third Essay, Section 6, p 539: '[A]ll I wish to underline is that Kant, like all philosophers, instead of envisaging the aesthetic problem from the point of view of the artist (the creator), considered art and the beautiful purely from that of the "spectator" and unconsciously introduced the spectator into the concept "beautiful".'

6 See Colin Rowe, *As I Was Saying*, Vol 2, The MIT Press (Cambridge, Massachusetts), 1996, p 34.

7 Samuel Johnson, 'A Young Nobleman's Progress in Politeness', *The Rambler*, No 194, 25 January 1752, p 310, as quoted by Colin Rowe in *As I Was Saying*.

CHAPTER 9
Carte Blanche?

DAVIDE DERIU

'This is how space begins, with words only, signs traced
on the blank page.'

— GEORGES PEREC, *ESPÈCES D'ESPACES [SPECIES OF SPACES]* (1974)[1]

Staring at the blank screen in front of me, I began to wonder about the
space of architectural writing, the space of writing in general. What does
it mean to approach the surface of a white page, whether it be paper
or screen, as a 'space'? How will I respond to the solicitation of the empty
rectangle in front of me, which so insistently stares back? Will I hover over it,
tread across it, delve into it? By now I am already suspended over that void, in
thrall to the anxiety and pleasure it must cause, in varying measures, to anyone
who is drawn to it. Once a line has been thrown across this space, it feels a bit
like walking a tightrope: every sign marks a step across the abyss of the page,
and the web of words that forms before our eyes gives us the impression of
inhabiting that world, gradually, until we have reached an end. Is the writer's
act, then, somehow akin to that of the funambulist, ever intent on finding a
balance between an exhilarating sense of omnipotence and the awareness of
one's own limits in a grounded and finite world? Meanwhile, the hesitant walk
of words has become steadier and, along the way, this short piece has found
its title …

One way of thinking about architecture, then, might be to question the
notion of 'carte blanche' as a seemingly endless field of potentialities. Through
its material evolution from parchment paper to computer screen, this homelike
space has provided an immaculate cradle for various forms of representation:
a sort of primal scene that is silently shared by art, design and writing practices

alike.[2] As Kenya Hara reminds us, the invention of white paper brought about a new mode of perception with far-reaching consequences, not only in terms of practical applications but also of imaginative impact.[3] Hence, in our digital age, the enduring power of the blank sheet still evokes a zero degree of the creative imagination. Its symbolic force has received a further boost by the recent revival of utopian thinking over the past decade; for instance, a few years ago, Anthony Vidler opened a lecture at the Architectural Association speaking to the blank screen: 'As you may see, my first slide is a slide of utopia ... .'[4]

But what does it mean to recognise the white canvas as a space of potentialities? Historically, its cultural import has been related to the formation of a worldview based on subject–object relations. For Michel de Certeau, the blank page marked the advent of the 'scriptural economy' in modern societies. This shift occurred when writing became established as a concrete practice, challenging the primacy of orality in the production and reproduction of knowledge. As a result of this 'Cartesian move', the modern subject was empowered to master any field of human activity by taking a strategic distance from it and confronting it as a separate object. The blank page therefore became a 'place of production' open to different uses and, crucially, 'a place where the ambiguities of the world have been exorcised'.[5] By evoking *la page blanche* in distinctly spatial terms, de Certeau hinted at a terrain of operations with its own imaginative depth that could be managed and manipulated at will. A breeding ground of modern subjectivity:

> In front of his blank page, every child is already put in the position of the industrialist, the urban planner, or the Cartesian philosopher – the position of having to manage a space that is his own and distinct from all others and in which he can exercise his own will.[6]

This process of abstraction reached its apogee in the early 20th century, when the modernist avant-garde gave fresh impetus to the idea of tabula rasa in architecture and urbanism. In the work of Le Corbusier, for instance, the blank page was transformed from symbolic locus of production into a virgin land to be colonised by the *esprit nouveau*. An eloquent example is provided by the empty figure published in his seminal 1924 book, *Urbanisme*, bearing only the following line in its midst: 'Left blank for a work expressing modern feeling.'[7] For all its utopian thrust, however, the blankness was not meant to invite the whims of an unbridled imagination. Averse to romantic individualism, Le Corbusier invoked instead a gesture inspired by 'the most rational inquiry'; a work that would meet the demands of modern life. For the new zeitgeist favoured the rule over the exception: 'This modern sentiment is a spirit of geometry, a spirit of construction and synthesis. Exactitude and order are its essential condition.'[8] The provocative invitation to fill in the blank suggested a liberatory act yet, at the same time, a highly structured one. Adapting a famous surrealist epigram, we may add a retrospective subtext to Le Corbusier's caption: *Ceci n'est pas une carte blanche*.[9]

Fifty years later, a blank illustration opened an altogether different French book: *Espèces d'espaces*, Georges Perec's series of musings on space that zoomed out from the author's bed on to the wider world. As the author explained in the Foreword:

> The subject of this book is not the void exactly, but rather what
> there is round about or inside it […]. To start with, then, there isn't
> very much: nothingness, the impalpable, the virtually immaterial;
> extension, the external, what is external to us, what we move about in
> the midst of, our ambient milieu, the space around us.[10]

The enigmatically blank figure was in fact a citation of a previous literary work, Lewis Carroll's nonsensical poem *The Hunting of the Snark* (1876).[11] Perec sought to (dis)orient his reader with reference to the 'Map of the Ocean' used in Carroll's fictional quest for an imaginary creature. As related in the section of the poem titled 'The Bellman's Speech', the travelling crew mistrusted the conventional signs of cartography and praised Captain Bellman for finding a map they could all understand: '"A perfect and absolute blank!"'[12] Perec's mischievous reference to Carroll's map offers a vivid counterpoint to Le Corbusier's empty illustration. Carte blanche here is not a place of production to be harnessed towards modern progress, but rather a space of poetic imagination that revives, through parody, a faded historical precedent.

These different attitudes to the creative imagination of space intersect, unexpectedly, in the biography of the Turkish writer Orhan Pamuk, a one-time architecture student at Istanbul Technical University. Reflecting on why he did *not* become an architect, Pamuk recounts his long-standing fascination with Istanbul's old houses, whose everyday uses so often subvert their original design. To the architect's projective thinking, he preferred the 'accommodating imagination' whereby existing buildings are adapted to the ever-changing needs and tastes of their occupants: 'So the imagination in question is not in service to a person who is creating new worlds on a blank sheet of paper, it is in service to someone who is trying to fit in with a world already made.'[13] After ditching architecture to become a writer, however, Pamuk's creative activity was still confronted with an empty space – no less vertiginous than the one he had left behind:

> I abandoned the great empty architectural drawing sheets that thrilled and frightened me, making my head spin, and instead sat down to stare at the blank writing paper that thrilled and frightened me just as much.[14]

Pamuk has since been designing his novels in painstaking detail as though they were literary constructions, a further testimony to the porous boundary between the realms of words and buildings that is often traversed by architects and writers alike (think for instance of John Hejduk's poetry, of Jorge Luis Borges's architectures, etc). In hindsight, his change of path made him reconsider the raison d'être of architecture itself:

> Why didn't I become an architect? Answer: Because I thought the sheets of paper on which I was to pour my dreams were blank. But after twenty-five years of writing, I have come to understand that those pages are never blank.[15]

In a reversal of Bellman's speech, this anecdote prompts us to rethink the white page as an imperfect and relative space, a blank in which the ambiguities of the world are recognised rather than exorcised. Carte blanche, then, may also unfold into a critical space: one that symbolises not only a field of creative possibilities but also the inherent limitations that are inscribed in it. To cite Giorgio Agamben, we are confronted with the philosophical issue of 'potentiality', originally defined by Aristotle as the human faculty that manifests itself in the ability to do, or *not* to do something – that is, in the latter case, a voluntary privation of one's own power. Interestingly, Agamben uses poetry and architecture as examples of this faculty: '[W]e say of the architect that he or she has the *potential* to build, of the poet that he or she has the *potential* to write poems.' And, conversely, 'the architect is potential insofar as he has the potential to not-build, the poet the potential to not-write poems.'[16]

In some sense, the blank spaces framed by Le Corbusier and Perec can be regarded as partial acknowledgements of this potentiality: negative moments in which their architectural and poetic expressions were provisionally suspended. Far from being a nihilistic gesture, the acceptance of non-being might constitute the starting point towards a praxis that mobilises the critical and creative imaginations as mutually nourishing forces. Can we therefore imagine a blank space born out of the interplay between the architect's spirit of geometry and the writer's spirit of finesse? And what kind of space would that be?

Notes

1   Georges Perec, *Species of Spaces* (1974), translated by John Sturrock, Penguin (London), 1999, p 13.

2   Slavoj Žižek, for instance, refers to the whiteness of the film screen as a place onto which our inner drives are projected; that is, the place where the fragile relationship between reality and fantasy is played out. See *The Pervert's Guide to Cinema*, scripted and presented by Žižek, directed by Sophie Fiennes, 2006.

3   Kenya Hara, *White*, Lars Müller (Baden), 2010, p 14.

4   Anthony Vidler, 'The Necessity of Utopia', lecture, Architectural Association (London), 19 February 2007.

5   Michel de Certeau (1980), *The Practice of Everyday Life*, translated by Steven Rendall, University of California Press (Berkeley, California), 1984, p 134.

6   Ibid.

7   Le Corbusier, *The City of To-morrow* (*Urbanisme*, 1924), translated by Frederick Etchells, Dover Publications (Mineola, New York), 1987, p 40.

8   Ibid, p 38.

9   The reference is to René Magritte's 1929 painting *La Trahison des images* [The Treachery of Images]. In Le Corbusier's blank figure, the message was placed right in the middle of the rectangular frame: the text was elevated from caption to slogan, temporarily occupying the place of a future work.

10 Perec, *Species of Spaces*, p 5.

11 Lewis Carroll, *The Hunting of the Snark*, Macmillan (London), 1876.

12 Ibid. Henry Holiday's original illustration of Bellman's 'Ocean-Chart' included a series of illogical orientations written all around the edges of the empty frame.

13 Orhan Pamuk, 'Why Didn't I Become an Architect?', in *Other Colours: Essays and a Story*, translated by Maureen Freely, Faber & Faber (London), 2007, p 306.

14 Ibid, p 307.

15 Ibid.

16 Giorgio Agamben, 'On Potentiality', in *Potentialities: Collected Essays in Philosophy*, Stanford University Press (Stanford, California), 1999, p 179.

CHAPTER 10

Buildings: A Reader's Guide

ELEANOR YOUNG

I first visited the British Library (completed in 1997) fifteen years ago. The sensations are still imprinted on my skin: cascades of volumes, a dogleg dash down to drop bags, brilliant brass atop smooth bright Portland stone, rich King's Library, cool, calm and light humanities at one with the scholarly promise of oak and leather under your elbows and pen. I tingle as I think of it.

But I haven't been back for years. The British Library is possibly the building I treasure the most in my home city of London, I pass by it regularly and yet it is not the abiding presence it should be. I have never had the excuse to write about the British Library over a decade of architectural journalism. I missed the long drawn-out run-up, the many crises looming then overcome. I missed its opening in 1997, the journalists' typical moment to reflect on and critique a building. Few people now seem to celebrate this masterpiece – despite the fact the desks are congested with writers, documentary researchers, students and academics. It seems to come down to two things: its face to the city and its turbulent, lengthy gestation. After all, to get into it you have to apply for a reader's ticket, and who goes through that palaver to see inside a rather lumpen brickscape? Who could guess that inside it could be so transformative, so fulfilling yet full of promise?

On the day the host city for the 2012 Olympics was announced, I was at the Pompidou Centre in Paris. Paris was frontrunner for winning the Games. I would have been happy to avoid the endless over-time, over-budget stories that I was convinced would define a London Olympic win. They were not

Colin St John Wilson, British Library, London, 1997.
The lofty ascension from the foyer entrance to the knowledge of the reading rooms.

worth the short-lived 'honour'. At the same time, reminding myself of Paris's modern architectural legacy was sobering; London had nothing to compare to IM Pei's pyramid at the Louvre (1989) or Jean Nouvel's Institut du Monde Arabe (1987). There appeared to be no room amid London's Victoriana for a *Grand Projet*[1] or a public, urban flowering of the architects of our time, Zaha Hadid and David Chipperfield; even Richard Rogers's best City work felt tucked away. (Of course, London won and gave Hadid and Hopkins a chance to build public icons; I have a pack of Top Trumps London 2012 Venues to prove it.)

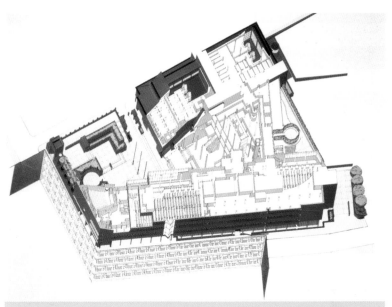

Colin St John Wilson, British Library, London, 1997.
The stacks and secret spaces of the British Library in the architect's axonometric.

But reel back and consider London's buried beauty. The British Library *is* up there with Paris's *Grands Projets*. And directly comparable to one: I had peered with awe at Paris's Bibliothèque Nationale de France (1996, designed by Dominique Perrault) and its sunken tree canopy alongside glass towers. But I had not filed the British Library under the category of London's great modern architecture. It lacks the urban presence or a singular form to burn its greatness on the eye of the beholder. Its series of roofs and walls are visible but not memorable. Its apparent gift to the city, the enclosed courtyard, presided over by Eduardo Paolozzi's statue *Newton* (1995), confuses rather than calms. And for streetscape: matching the brick doesn't help when it has as its next-door neighbour the gloriously gothic St Pancras Hotel (1876, designed by George Gilbert Scott), rising up from the Euston Road, competing for attention.

Prince Charles described the British Library as looking like 'the assembly hall of an academy for secret police' in his 1988 attack on contemporary architecture.[2] But by then, still years off the opening, the building had already

Colin St John Wilson, British Library, London, 1997.
Enclosure and release from the stacked volumes of this reading room.

been redesigned several times for an initial location in the Bloomsbury area of London, and its site had been moved north – at which point one of the two lead architects, Sir Leslie Martin, retired. Professor Sir Colin St John Wilson (Sandy Wilson), who remained on the project, later referred to the library as his '30-year war'[3] – though it ended up taking 35 years from the original commission in 1962. Both critiques of the library and the obituaries for Wilson referred extensively to the saga. But few delved into the qualities of the building itself.

For the British Library to become more than a beautiful research den for the literary and academic, its story has to be turned around. The creative process and the experience of the building have to be brought to the fore. It is impossible to do that in such a short piece as this, but there are perhaps a few pointers in the British Library's design influences and antecedents.

The British Library and Wilson do not fit into the still-fluid postwar canon of Brutalism, Postmodernism and High-Tech. Helpfully, Wilson himself defined another route through in his book *The Other Tradition of Modern Architecture: The Uncompleted Project* (1995). Alvar Aalto, Hans Scharoun, Hugo Häring and Frank Lloyd Wright were the architects he set against the stark Le Corbusian tenets of Modernism which Wilson felt had won CIAM's battle for ascendancy and dominance. The Other Tradition is more textured and complex with light, space and materials. It calls for a greater agility and imagination with internal volumes. All these things the British Library has in abundance.

It is interesting to look at the influences not just of those Wilson studied and wrote on, such as Swedish architect Sigurd Lewerentz, but also those he worked closely with. He started work with a gifted, stylistically fractured young generation at London County Council (LCC). They included Alison and Peter Smithson, James Stirling and Bill Howell (later of Howell Killick Partridge & Amis). Tracing the way they spun out their architectural ideas – words and buildings – into the world is fascinating. The British Library can be read and reread in the light of the vocabularies of each of those architects, and parallels can be drawn – Stirling's processional routes, Howell's use of light and so on.

Perhaps the most obvious influence is Martin, who led the LCC Architects' Department and worked closely with Wilson teaching at Cambridge and ultimately on the earlier plans for the British Library. Martin was a leading light in the design of the Royal Festival Hall (1951), which shares with the Library a tumbling sense of public space upon public space – masterfully interrogated by Adrian Forty.[4]

The rather more compact form of the St Cross Building (1965) at Oxford – worked on by both Martin and Wilson – originally housed three faculty libraries and shares a lot with the British Library. The enclosing and ascending diagram, with a staircase feeding a cluster of top-lit reading rooms, marks out both buildings. The main reading rooms are uncannily similar in plan and sensation. The scale of the British Library means that the distinctive planar massing of St Cross is lost and the buff brick and anodised aluminium give way to the brasher red brick, considered to be critical to a London project in this position.

Buildings are treasure houses of stories – even if they are not built on books as the British Library is. I studied with Forty as I was trying to apply journalism to architecture. And though my favourite days were visits where we would arrive imbued with the *Architectural Review* view from the 1930s to listen with fresh ears to Adrian deconstructing both the writing and the building, the theory side of the teaching made what we were doing explicit.

Michel Foucault, Walter Benjamin, Henri Lefebvre and more each yielded their own obsessions, making a *Grand Projet* (or not) of every human construction.

Different approaches to one object still intrigue me. After a press visit for a major opening it is fascinating to compare and contrast accounts (the voice and 'spin' of the main protagonists is often very clear). My colleagues and I at the *RIBA Journal* have experimented with applying the filter of a theme (collaboration, cosiness, money) to a whole series of buildings when editing an issue. Though this thematic approach is often used in academia, it is an unacknowledged trope in architectural criticism. In recent architectural journalism Ellis Woodman (*Building Design*) or Peter Davey (*Architectural Review*) are particularly notable for picking up and developing a small number of themes, certain architectural genealogies, materiality and aesthetics.

I find my writing tending towards the people behind the building, in them and around them, the traces of ideas and the words made flesh. It seems the only way to capture the wider idea of the architectural project. At 126,970 square metres (1,366,693 square feet), the British Library is a large chunk of land; but as a text, it is one that readers – users, critics, librarians, tourists – still have to define for themselves.

Notes

1   '*Grands Projets*' (Grand Projects) is the collective name given to a programme of eight major buildings initiated by French President François Mitterrand to provide Paris with modern architectural monuments. The Louvre Pyramid, the Institut du Monde Arabe and the Bibliothèque Nationale de France were among them.

2   First stated by Prince Charles in the BBC television documentary programme *A Vision of Britain*, 1988. Published in HRH The Prince of Wales, *A Vision of Britain: A Personal View of Architecture*, Doubleday (London), 1989.

3   Fiona MacCarthy, 'A House for the Mind', *The Guardian*, 23 February 2008, http://www.theguardian.com/books/2008/feb/23/architecture.art (accessed 11 December 2013).

4   Adrian Forty, 'The Royal Festival Hall – A "Democratic" Space?', in I Borden, J Kerr, J Rendell with A Pivaro (eds), *The Unknown City*, The MIT Press (Cambridge, Massachusetts), 2001, pp 201–12.

CHAPTER 11

The City and the Event: Disturbing, Forgetting and Escaping Memory

GRISELDA POLLOCK

The *Geometry of Conscience* (2010), created by Chilean artist Alfredo Jaar (born 1956), is sited underground in the city-centre plaza beside the Museum of Memory and Human Rights in Santiago, Chile. Thirty-three steps lead down from the sunlit plaza to a door in front of which a guard is positioned. Only 10 people at a time are allowed to enter into a space that is kept completely dark for one full minute. Silence is also requested. At the end of the dark minute, gradually over 90 seconds illumination increases from 0 to 100 per cent, allowing the viewers' eyes to adjust. The light reveals a back wall composed of rows and columns of silhouettes, light shapes of heads set against the dark background. The side walls are mirrored so that the 10 or fewer people present in the space and the hundreds of silhouettes replicate to infinity on either side. Darkness returns to engulf the viewers, but retinal after-images remain, impressing the flashing presence, through dots of a million lights. The silhouettes represent victims of the Pinochet dictatorship (1973–90) established violently on the first 9/11 with the deposition and death of Salvador Allende, the democratically elected President of Chile. The silhouettes are also taken

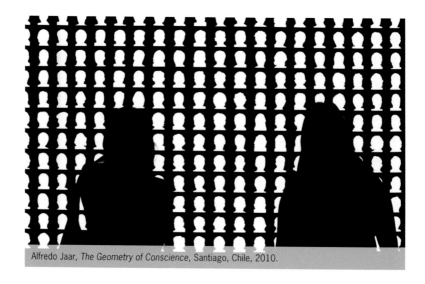
Alfredo Jaar, *The Geometry of Conscience*, Santiago, Chile, 2010.

from anonymous Chileans living at the time of the making of the memorial in 2010. Thus the past is mirroring the 17 million Chileans living now, seeking to rediscover a common history rather than to bury a traumatic past.

Alfredo Jaar's work falls into the difficult space between architecture and contemporary art. There is architectural thinking. There is also what Mieke Bal, writing of sculptor Louise Bourgeois, named 'architecturality' – a dimension of architectural thinking or effect that may be mobilised non-architecturally.[1] There is also aesthetic thinking, which may well, as in installation art, use space and constructed elements in pursuit of certain affects, sometimes provoking associational thought. The architectural already both performs and represents its thinking through structure, foundation, elevation, enclosure, seclusion, monument, sacredness, functionality and so forth. The body-mind's experience of space and place is shaped by that which it enters, inhabits or is impressed by when confronting the architectural. In the aesthetic operations of an artwork that makes space and spacing part of its grammar, the body-mind is the activated site of a contemplative, participatory subjectivity taken out of the lived spaces of designed and constructed spaces and places to encounter that which has been set apart, and which has been calculated to produce affect and response distinct from everyday habitations and environments.

Alfredo Jaar, *The Geometry of Conscience*, Santiago, Chile, 2010.

Alfredo Jaar cannot be said to be making installation art. Nor is he constructing built environments. The logic by which his extraordinary work operates defies both ends of the admittedly simplified opposition I have set up. The aesthetic dominates, I would argue because Jaar subjects every element of the spectator's experience to the choreography – the movement – of his piece. The departure from the level of the everyday happens as the visitor descends the steps, reversing, however, the usual architectural trope of mounting steps to an elevated space such as a temple or church, a format often borrowed for the museum. Descending into a crypt or tomb (with its deathly aspect), the visitor encounters the guard, the gatekeeper at the entrance to an underworld. This Cerberus, guardian of the portal to Hades, is recast as a kindly museum guide. Advised of the rule of silence, another association – with sacred space – colours the visitor's anticipated experience. But then the power of the artist asserts itself over the visitor, who has given him- or herself over to his protocol. Darkness engulfs and persists for a disorienting minute. Complete darkness is dramatic, dispossessing our senses of all the information they need to be able to orient the body in space, to operate at all. Then, gently and with care, the light returns. Light and darkness are mythic and magical in their absolute opposition. Phenomenologically powerful forces are thus played over the bodies and minds of the viewers to prompt a series of symbolic oppositions: blindness and vision, death and life, being and image. Flanked by mirror glass, the viewers lose their sense of spatial frontiers and substance as they reflect each other *en abyme*. I am reminded of the minimalist work of American sculptor John McCracken (1934–2011) who created such an effect in an untitled work at the Documenta 12 exhibition in Kassel (2007) by mirroring the entrance hall of the Fridericianum museum where it was held. The reversal of the silhouette makes faces shaped by the darkness from which they are cut out become points of light. Actively resisting the iconic use of the photograph in the memorial practices of many survivors of Latin American dictatorships in which people were 'disappeared', the silhouettes capture the singularity of each head without capturing or fixing the gaze. The viewers, shadowed dark against the screen of lighted heads, become counter-silhouettes, participating with their living presence in the perpetual rewriting of collective memory and current responsibility for knowledge of the human dimension within the political.

I want to make a conversation between this work and *Rue Santa Fe*, a film named after a street, Calle Santa Fe in Santiago, completed in 2007 by fellow Chilean, Carmen Castillo (born 1945), former teacher of Latin American history, now writer and documentarist. Castillo was earlier a political militant in the Movimiento de Izquierda Revolucionaria (MIR – Revolutionary Left Movement) and partner of Miguel Enriquez, a brilliant neurologist who became the movement's leader and supporter of the elected President Allende. With the Pinochet coup that led to the suicide of Allende, Enriquez and Castillo and their four-year-old daughters went into hiding rather than exile to engineer the Resistance. In October 1974, their hiding place was betrayed and the house was assaulted. After a gun battle, Enriquez was killed. Castillo, pregnant, was shot and left bleeding on the street. She was taken to hospital, and deported into exile rather than being killed. How she came to be taken to hospital, and the reason for the leniency in her sentencing, were a mystery. Living in Paris, Castillo became a writer and made films. In 2002, she risked returning and began a campaign to find and buy the house on Calle Santa Fe in which she had lived in that last year between the first 9/11 (11 September 1973) and 5 October 1974. This marked the beginning of the preparation of her French-titled film, as a cinematic journey back from long exile in Paris to Santiago. The project brought her into contact with the young men and women of the Chilean Left today.

Two events are significant for me in this context from this long film (2 hours 43 minutes). Firstly, Castillo realises that her poignant investment in the house on Calle Santa Fe and her need to make this place as a memorial does not touch the younger generation. They and their activism now are themselves Enriquez's living monument. Castillo merely lays a plaque in the pavement where he died. Secondly, during one of her returns to the Calle, she is introduced to a former neighbour, a man unknown to her at the time they both lived on the street. He tells her that it was he who called an ambulance and forced its nervous driver to take the almost unconscious woman to hospital, waiting with her until a doctor treated her. His simple act of immense courage prevented the police from killing Castillo or disappearing her. Just an ordinary man, not a political person, this neighbour kept her in public view and it was that publicity that ensured that she was taken to a hospital and saved and merely expelled. His gesture of compassion and the students' energy transform Castillo's fixated relation to the site and moment of the trauma of 5 October 1974. But on that day an ordinary man did something simple and humane that allowed the deadliness and estrangement from Chile, frozen in the dark history of her suffering and exile, to be warmed and illuminated by an act beneath and beyond the organisation we call 'politics'.

I offer this excursus on the *Geometry of Conscience*, and *Rue Santa Fe*, as brief but related reflections on the materiality of memorialisation but also

These scattered fragments of memory have opened a door for me.

Carmen Castillo, film still from *Rue Santa Fe*, 2007, produced by Les Films d'Ici.

The ambulance driver and I
took you to the hospital,

Carmen Castillo, film still from *Rue Santa Fe*, 2007, produced by Les Films d'Ici.

on the subtle play between structuration – the architectural, be that formal or constructed – and the affecting encounter – the aesthetic, be that durational or choreographed. The documentary film-maker journeying back to a country in search of a house that she wanted to reclaim in order to appease the problem of unfinished memory allows the architectural but also symbolic and affective site, the house, to become the catalyst for the kind of enlivening of memory that Jaar also seeks: uncontained by the monuments that enable forgetting, memory reshaped as life becomes a living force that must also acknowledge the moment that is the present in which the call to responsibility is made, one to one. Both instances attest to the necessity for movement as the opposite of monumentalisation. The creation of something precarious and contingent on the human encounter transcends the pairing of remembering and forgetting and their partner forms, anamnesis and repression, in order to figure, continuously in Jaar's work and in the flash of recognition in Castillo's film, the vitality of active memory as movement.

Note

1   Mieke Bal, *Louise Bourgeois' Spider: The Architecture of Art-Writing*, University of Chicago Press (Chicago, Illinois), 2001.

CHAPTER 12

The Most Modern Material Of Them All ...

HILDE HEYNEN

t is a somewhat casual remark, in Adrian Forty's *Concrete and Culture: A Material Story*, but it set me thinking:

> All around the Mediterranean, across Latin America and in shanty towns throughout the world, there are simple, framed structures built out of reinforced concrete, whose relationship to modernity [...] is decidedly questionable.[1]

Forty specifies that he takes modernity to be 'a distinctive form of industrial organisation and of labour relations', which makes the statement consistent. I nevertheless want to challenge it. Is modernity really only about industrial organisation and labour relations? What if we understand modernity in a broader sense? What if we understand it to be – as Marshall Berman would have it[2] – about the experience of the new and the hope for emancipation? What if we were not to see modernity as something that emanates from the West and slowly radiates to the other parts of the world, but rather as a set of hopes and dreams that can be appropriated in many ways and that gives rise to multiple variants? What would concrete's relationship be to these multiple modernities?

Forty casts concrete as a material that is at the same time modern

Noël Naert, Collage: house and road, village and town, Kabylia, 1992.

and unmodern: modern because of its rather recent emergence as a material intimately related to the industrial production of Portland cement and because of its allegiance to technology; unmodern because of its embedded crudeness, its primitivism and its popularity among multitudes of unskilled, uncultured and unruly people inhabiting especially the poorer parts of this planet. For me, on the other hand, this ambivalence is exactly the reason why concrete is *not* unmodern, but rather the most modern material of them all.

Let us have a look at the magnificent drawing shown here, which was made by Noël Naert after extensive fieldwork, with André Loeckx, in the early 1980s in Kabylia, Algeria.[3] The drawing shows, in one view, the triple reality of the built environment in that particular region in the mountains. On the upper left-hand side, there is a village high in the hills, overlooking mountain passes and arid highlands. It is the traditional Kabylian village whose houses have been immortalised by Pierre Bourdieu's description in 'La maison kabyle ou le monde renversé' [The Berber House or the World Reversed] (1960).[4] At the right-hand side, in the more fertile valley, is the colonial town of Tizi Ouzou, originally built in grid form by the French and extended by the mass housing blocks realised by the socialist government in the first decades after decolonisation. The drawing is dominated however by the image of a few buildings in the foreground, which do not belong to the village nor to the town. They are situated along a road, which interconnects several of the mountain villages and eventually leads to the town. Along this road we find the new constructions initiated by returning migrants, who go abroad to earn the money to support their families, and who return each summer to frantically work on their buildings, which are often left unfinished when they depart once again to Paris or Lyon.

Modernity, I have argued earlier, can be conceived of in different ways.[5] For those who hold a *programmatic* outlook, modernity is seen as a project: a project to change the world for the better, to improve conditions of life, economically, socially, politically, culturally and to enhance equal opportunities for everyone. For them the basic experience of modernity – that 'all that is solid melts into air' – is but the consequence of that ongoing experiment in generating progress. For others, who are less confident maybe in the progressive pace of history, the *transitory* aspect of modernity is paramount: for them the fleetingness of the moment, the impermanence of everything once thought to be immutable and the very versatility of objects and people constitute one giant machinery of endlessly fascinating effects of change. Even without concentrating on its supposedly beneficial outcomes, they appreciate modernity for its very ephemerality and for its continuous production of ever new and unexpected situations. This image, it seems to me, captures both of these aspects of modernity. It refers, on the one hand, to the contrast between an age-old tradition (the mountain villages) and the programmatic intentions of first a colonial and afterwards a revolutionary government (the town in the valley) – programmatic intentions that did not meet with unqualified success (to say the least). On the other hand, however, the image superposes upon this contrast a more transitory moment: the permanently unfinished building that seems to stand for a modernity-in-the-making, not yet achieved, maybe never to be achieved, but still eagerly sought and passionately shaped.

This skeleton that is gradually filled in – every year one room or one floor, and maybe some years nothing at all – speaks of hopes and dreams, of solidarity and confidence. It might embody the life savings of an extended family, and – who knows? – it might remain unfinished and uninhabited, if troubles between family members result in a conflict that stalls further construction, or if the political situation grows so unstable that one doesn't dare to invest any longer. This is an everyday kind of modernity, to which architects barely contribute (although the builders certainly picked up bits and pieces of the architectural typologies and the construction methods customary in the places they migrated to). It is also a hybrid kind of architecture, combining local aspects (references to tradition, local materials, local labour) with global elements (the concrete skeleton, the workshop-below-apartments-above configuration). This kind of architecture is, indeed, vernacular: it is anonymous, popular, widespread and local. Being vernacular, however, doesn't make it traditional. On the contrary: in contrast with the traditional Berber houses of the mountain villages, these frame constructions belong to an idiom that I would call a *modern vernacular*.

For me – and here I differ from Forty – shanty towns, squatter settlements and slums are definitely modern: they do not belong to a time frame that is somehow 'behind' or that would belong to the past; they cannot be seen as 'not-yet-modern', because they are in many respects the contemporary – and hence modern – spatial correlate of a globalising economy. The endless belts of self-built settlements that make up such a large section of so many megacities are part and parcel of a globalising economy.[6] Almost all the megacities of the South have come about as spin-offs of colonialism and imperialism – many of them barely existed before the beginning of the 19th century. Their explosive growth is the result of restructuring processes that are clearly bound up with this globalising economy. Migration patterns, agricultural reforms, shifts in industrialisation, growth of services, ever-increasing tourism – these and similar processes are the driving forces that transform the planet into a world of cities. In as far as we understand modernity to be about these major changes, it is not the province of some technology-minded architects in the North, but it is really a word that describes the hopes and dreams of individuals most everywhere, and it is a condition that takes on multiple forms.

In that sense, reinforced concrete is the material that quintessentially catches the dialectics of these modernities. As an accessible, and by now almost everywhere readily available material, it lends itself to many different uses and interpretations. In the hands of the best architects and engineers, it becomes a sophisticated material that allows for highly layered and complicated technological and cultural achievements. In its very accessibility, however, it also lends itself to humble uses that translate everyday dreams of modest people into built reality. Because of its plasticity it can be used as an improved version of much older building materials like earth or mud, thus allowing for some continuity of forms and building methods while at the same time performing better in a technical sense (stability, maintenance, cleanliness). Its ubiquitousness as a building material is offset by its suitability to be moulded into diverse shapes and typologies, which is compatible with the multiple modernities coexisting across the world. Even its most questionable characteristic, I would argue, renders it unmistakably modern: the fact that the massive production of Portland cement produces such high amounts of carbon emissions, and is thus threatening the very sustainability of the ecological balance that supports our economies, might be seen as indicative of the unsustainability of modernity itself. For is it not the very success of our endeavours to change the world that has resulted in effects that we didn't foresee but nevertheless caused? And is that not the most prominent, the most dramatic, even the most tragic aspect of all our multiple modernities?

Notes

1   Adrian Forty, *Concrete and Culture: A Material History*, Reaktion (London), 2012, p 29.

2   Marshall Berman, *All That Is Solid Melts Into Air: The Experience of Modernity*, Verso (London), 1985.

3   André Loeckx, 'Kabylia, the House, and the Road: Games of Reversal and Displacement', *Journal of Architectural Education*, Vol 52, No 2, 1998, pp 87–99.

4   Pierre Bourdieu, 'La maison kabyle ou le monde renversé', in *Deux Essais sur la société kabyle*, Université de Lausanne (Lausanne), 1960; published in English as 'The Berber House or the World Reversed', *Social Science Information*, Vol 9, No 3, April 1970, pp 151–70; abridged version, 'The Berber House', in Mary Douglas (ed), *Rules and Meaning: The Anthropology of Everyday Knowledge*, Penguin (Harmondsworth and New York), 1973, pp 98–110.

5   Hilde Heynen, *Architecture and Modernity: A Critique*, The MIT Press (Cambridge, Massachusetts), 1999, pp 8–14.

6   Mike Davis, *Planet of Slums*, Verso (London), 2007.

CHAPTER 13

'Things that People Cannot Anticipate': Skateboarding at the Southbank Centre

IAIN BORDEN

When the complex of the Hayward Gallery, Queen Elizabeth Hall and Purcell Room in London – what is now sometimes called the Festival Wing at the north end of the arts-focused Southbank Centre – was first dreamt up in the early 1960s, the architects were a team at the London County Council (later Greater London Council) led by Sir Hubert Bennett and Norman Engleback, but also including Ron Herron, Warren Chalk and Dennis Crompton.

Significantly, the last three belonged to the radical architecture group Archigram, who had many innovative ideas about architecture and cities. Above all, Archigram believed in modern architecture as an exciting part of how people live their lives. For Archigram, this was not architecture as sterile glass-and-steel office buildings, as dreary Welfare State hospitals and schools designed by faceless committees, but as something full of the mobile, changing,

Skateboarder Matt Fowler in the Undercroft area of the Festival Wing.

popular and dynamic culture of groovy 1960s life. This architecture was to be exhilarating and multicoloured, made of buildings which walked on stilts, which transformed into different shapes and functions, which you could wear on your body, which plugged into you and you into them. It was architecture as part of living, breathing, happening urban life, and it was meant to be open to everyone.

It was Archigram's ideas therefore which led to the meandering high-level walkways and open-sided ground-level spaces ('Undercroft') of the Festival Wing. In particular, and importantly for skateboarding, there was a strong suggestion that some spaces of the Festival Wing should not be overtly prescribed for particular people or activities, but rather be left open for unpredictable and unknown uses. As Adrian Forty comments in a video about the complex, this was a 'great idea' – thinking of architecture as being 'populated with all sorts of activities' and that 'things that people cannot anticipate' will 'happen around the building'.[1] And so when the Festival Wing opened in 1968, the architects quite deliberately had no precise idea about who would use the Undercroft and in what ways.

Consequently, when skateboarding came along in the mid-1970s, it fulfilled this architectural promise, providing exactly the sort of unexpected eruption of creativity for which the architects had hoped. Where the designers had produced flat spaces interrupted by a series of surprisingly and apparently uselessly angled banks, the skateboarders saw these very same slopes as providing a freely accessible version of the commercial skate parks which were then being constructed in London and across the world. The roof of the Undercroft was another great attraction, allowing skateboarders to enjoy their movements relatively sheltered from Britain's inclement weather. Here, under the protective ceiling, up and down the angled banks, and in between the curious Doric-mushroom columns, the skateboarders freely emulated the surf-style skateboarding then being favoured in magazines like *Skateboard!* and *Skateboarder*.

As this suggests, this is much more than the history of a building as concrete structure, and is also the history of what people have done there. As philosopher Henri Lefebvre has argued, architectural and urban space is made up of the physical places we use (in this case the Festival Wing's Brutalist concrete and spaces), the conscious ideas we have of buildings (such as the architects' designs), and also people's actual experiences of buildings.[2] In addition, as Lefebvre also argues, people's everyday lives are the most important part of our cities and histories – what we do with our bodies, who we talk to, how we love, think and feel, what we truly enjoy and value.[3]

And so skateboarding is also absolutely part of the Southbank Centre, not as a history of architecture as a static monument, or as a great architectural invention, or as a symbol of the national Festival of Britain (which took place earlier on this extensive site), but as a place where people – skateboarders – have done something with their bodies and have created something quite extraordinary as a dynamic expression of youthful energy and joy.

Nor has skateboarding been a short-lived moment in the Southbank Centre. Rather, skateboarding has now been in the Undercroft and other spaces there for nigh on forty years, making it very probably the oldest place in the world which has been subjected to skateboarding continuously and intensively throughout this period.

Just how focused skateboarding usage has been was particularly evident during the 1980s and 1990s. In these years, after many skate parks closed at the end of the 1970s, skateboarding became more street-based with skateboarders using the 'ollie' move to ride up on to the ledges, benches, handrails and other paraphernalia of everyday city streets. The Undercroft changed too, becoming less like a free skate park and more like an urban street, somewhere appropriated by skateboarders for their own pleasure. It changed again in 2004, when the first skate-able concrete blocks were added by the skateboard-arts group The Side Effects of Urethane, quickly followed by niceties such as lighting, CCTV and a benign police presence to reduce petty crime. Railings and yellow lines helped demarcate a skateboardable space for which the Southbank Centre could take out liability insurance, and so could legally allow skateboarding to occur. Murals and graffiti also started to arrive, marking the Undercroft as a centre for various urban arts, and not just for skateboarding.

As a result of all this, the Undercroft has achieved near mythic status as the epicentre of UK skateboarding, where tens of thousands have learned their craft, from novices to professionals, and from hardcore locals to occasional visitors. The Undercroft is then UK skateboarding's most precious home, its original Garden of Eden, its mother ship and its oldest sparring partner – all rolled into one. It is also a place of pilgrimage for skateboarders globally, coming long distances to roll across one of skateboarding's most hallowed grounds. If there were to be just one heritage blue plaque put up to skateboarding, it would surely go here.

But this is never a matter purely of heritage, in which case a simple museum, book or documentary could stand in for skateboarding at the Festival Wing. Instead, the real value of skateboarding lies not in visual records or words (like these), but in the act of skateboarding itself, when someone does that simple thing and stands on a skateboard to express themselves in motion. This movement also takes its meaning from its architectural context – and in the Undercroft, for example, we find an extraordinary collision of Brutalist architecture and youthful bodies, where dark concrete, rough textures and echoing acoustics meet

Skateboarder Mike Manzoori at the Festival Wing.

splashes of colour, sudden adrenaline and the rasping, grinding, sliding sound of skateboards. These contrasts suggest all kinds of things, not least that the arts are far more than painting and sculpture, that noises as well as music are parts of urban soundscapes, that everyone has a right to public space and to be creative within it, that we should not have to pay for a coffee or buy something for every moment we exist outside our homes, that great architecture can encourage unusual and surprising activities, and that people can become urban citizens in a myriad of different ways. Under the belly of the beast, these juxtapositions create amazing lived-in architecture, produce dynamic city spaces, and so meet the theories of Lefebvre and Archigram all at once.

All of this means that the 2013 proposals to move the main focus of skateboarding from its Undercroft location to a different one on the Southbank Centre site – 125 metres (410 feet) south along the River Thames to a similarly sized 1,200-square-metre (13,000-square-foot) area underneath the Hungerford Bridge – have a great deal to live up to.[4] This new skate spot will need to be at once everyday and purposeful, subtle and enticing, dark and colourful, moody and seductive, noisily resonant and punctuated with moments of silence; it will need to be a great place to skateboard with ledges, banks, rails and steps – just like the existing Undercroft – but above all, it must avoid the character of an overtly designed skate park or skate plaza. It cannot be offered up as a fully sanctioned skateboarding-only facility complete with fees, fences and rules, but must be a freely open space, shared by all, yet one which skateboarders can appropriate and localise, and so help to create a vibrant public space in the full sense of that term.

Above all, it is worth remembering why so many non-skateboarders – and not just skateboarders themselves – also come to the Festival Wing and Undercroft. People from all over London, the UK and the wider world enjoy seeing the Undercroft's unique combination of skateboarding-against-concrete, of unruly disorder amid increasing sanitisation, of darkness and danger as well as of light and surety, and so witnessing a truly public space in action. This is important stuff, and in many ways transcends the immediate needs of skateboarding to speak to a larger question as to the kinds of public spaces we desire in cities today. Above all, skateboarding at the Southbank Centre – whether at the Festival Wing, Undercroft, Hungerford Bridge or any other of its spaces – suggests that public spaces can be so much richer than typical shopping malls or high streets. It suggests that different people doing different things perceive, use and enjoy architecture and city spaces in different ways. It suggests that, in turn, we would like our city spaces to be similarly different and varied, at once loud and quiet, rough and smooth, colourful and monochrome, flat and angled. And, above all, it suggests that we most enjoy cities and buildings when they both comfort and challenge us, when we feel we can be relaxed and excited, when they indeed provide us with things which we cannot anticipate. Skateboarding at the Southbank Centre is but one small part of this process, but it is a very important one.

Notes

1 'The Festival Wing', video on http://www.thefestivalwing.com (directed by Clare Hughes for the Southbank Centre, 2013).

2 Henri Lefebvre, *The Production of Space*, Blackwell (Oxford), 1991.

3 See, for example, Henri Lefebvre, *Everyday Life in the Modern World*, Continuum (London), 2002; and Henri Lefebvre, *Introduction to Modernity: Twelve Preludes September 1959 – May 1961*, Verso (London), 1995.

4 See, for example, 'The Hungerford Bridge Skate Space', video on http://www.youtube.com/watch?v=NcAymfoOh5Q (uploaded by the Southbank Centre, 9 September 2013).

CHAPTER 14

'Truth, Love, Life': Building with Language in Prague Castle under Masaryk

IRENA ŽANTOVSKÁ MURRAY

Adrian Forty's description of the critical categories of the modernist understanding of 'truth' has been indispensable: 'expressive' in 'the sense of a work being true to its inner essence or the spirit of its makers', as Goethe put it; 'structural', that is, one that discloses a direct correspondence between internal structure or material content and the external appearance of the work; and lastly, 'historical', a work is representative of its time.[1] In what follows, I shall briefly illustrate the role of language in the collaboration between Thomas Garrigue Masaryk (1850–1937) and the architect, Jože Plečnik (1872–1957). Masaryk's daughter, Alice Garrigue Masaryk (1879–1966) served as an intermediary. Both Masaryk's writings and Alice's extensive correspondence with Plečnik form important sources of evidence.[2]

Recent architectural scholarship (Damjan Prelovšek, Akos Moravánszky, Eve Blau, Friedrich Achleitner Anthony Alofsin) has shown how questions of language have always been deeply embedded in Central European political, social and intellectual discourse. And no wonder, for on the eve of its disappearance, the Austro-Hungarian Empire consisted of a dozen distinct linguistic nationalities. The linguist, Roman Jakobson, once vividly evoked Masaryk's description of his student days in Vienna in the 1870s: 'Vienna isn't German, she isn't Czech, in fact she has no national characteristics when it comes to language; Vienna is Austria, that is, polyglot.'[3]

Masaryk understood language as a dual process of expression (*Ausdrucksmittel*) and communication (*Mittel zur wechselseitigen Mitteilung*).[4] Language as it is used in society shaped a chapter in the history of Prague Castle; it made possible its transformation from a neglected regional seat of the Habsburg Monarchy into the symbol of a new, *democratic*, state. Masaryk

JA Comenius, Joh. Amos Commenii Orbis Sensualium Pictus: hoc est, Omnium principalium in Mundo Rerum, & in vita Actionum, Pictura & Nomenclatura = Joh. Amos Commenius's visible world: or, a nomenclature, and pictures of all the chief things that are in the world, ... in above an 150 copper cuts written by the author in Latin and High-Dutch. ... Translated into English by Charles Hoole, ... for the use of young Latin scholars, 1705.

had expressed his thoughts on this point repeatedly both before and after Czechoslovakia was established as an independent state in 1918. As its first President, Masaryk, the one-time student of the philosopher and psychologist Franz Brentano and later a professor of philosophy himself, embraced language in its social context as the driving force of his agenda, starting with the so-called 'Washington Declaration', the founding document of the new Czechoslovak state.[5]

The post-World War I collaboration between Masaryk and Plečnik, as mediated by Alice Masaryk, generated a significant new linguistic layer: that of *epistolary* language. Alice conveyed – and sometimes interpreted – her father's wishes and the overall brief itself; their shared sense of public responsibility, indeed of moral duty, was as powerfully expressed in her letters as in Masaryk's own writings.

Thus, in *The Making of a State*, Masaryk wrote that: 'To transform the Prague Castle, a purely monarchic building, into a *democratic* building, to think through [the concept] of *democratic* garden ... these are serious problems that should concern our best artistic minds.'[6]

Accordingly, Masaryk's ideas of governance and of collective memory were the informing principles that aimed to create a layered and referential landscape. He wanted the castle to constitute a reconceived *typus* in the hierarchy of public spaces, not for Prague alone but for the entire nation. Memory, as recollection, imagination and *ingegno*, informed the symbolic action. To introduce change into the dense, charged, circumscribed spaces of Prague Castle can be understood as a language analogy in the terms of creating *new relationships*. Polysemy was a characteristic, even dominant, feature of this process: a kind of Semperian analogy between linguistic and artistic transformation in which a common *Urform* is implicitly carried forward.

When Masaryk wrote in 1929 that 'progress is achieved by the true relationship to tradition',[7] he was unknowingly echoing Jože Plečnik, who already in 1902, while still a student of Otto Wagner in Vienna, had set out his own course as an architect along similar lines. 'Like a spider,' he had written, 'I aspire to attach my strand to tradition and from there I want to weave my own web.'[8]

Akos Moravánszky has recently drawn attention to the work of the French linguist, Henri Gobard, and his categories of vehicular, referential and mythical language that can be meaningfully deployed to describe the process of actualising the past.[9] These means include foundation legends, proverbs, and, in a higher form, a broadly shared literary canon which depends on value recognition, rather than profound knowledge. Frequent references to Plato, Saint Augustine, Dante and Goethe in the exchanges between the Masaryks and Plečnik helped to create a shared transnational language rather than drawing on a specific national context.[10]

Referential language in particular is bound up with traditions in their multiple forms, as defined by actualisation of the past tense, a 'dialogue with distance', and by efforts to revivify not the past, but the *values* of the past (the *'passé pérénnisé, ktema eis aei* of Thucydides').[11] The letters of the Masaryks and Plečnik abound with frequent references to antiquity, the Mediterranean, and Greek mythology and its figures, most notably Prometheus and Sisyphus. 'The Slavic Acropolis' of Alice's letters shows also how she attempted to create a hybrid vision of the Prague Castle precinct.

The language of their correspondence is often enigmatic enough to invite speculation in interpretation of key passages. A striking example is the repeated reference to 'Labadie' or 'Labadea', which first appears in two separate letters of early February 1924 and continues to crop up occasionally through to 1927. At first glance this seems to suggest ideas related to the Presidential apartment or the Column Hall, but could equally stand for the Bull Staircase which connects the Third Castle courtyard with the southern gardens.

Lebadeia (modern-day Livadia) was a sacred city on the east–west route to Delphi, renowned for its oracle and cult of Trophonios, as well as for the sanctuary of Zeus Basileus replete with inscriptions relating to its process of construction. The cult itself was rooted in the architecture with which it maintained a special bond. The Masaryks were well aware of the extensive description of the cult as it appears in Pausanias, whose magisterial *Description of Greece* (present in several editions in Masaryk's own library) contains perhaps the most extensive account of Lebadeia handed down to us. The 'sacred precinct' invoked by Alice in her 'Labadea letters' to Plečnik, as well as the descent into the 'oracular chasm' in the discussion of the Bull Staircase and the passageway and staircase in the Column Hall in Prague Castle, may have struck both correspondents as a powerful analogy.[12]

There is another, perhaps even more compelling reason why the oracle at Lebadeia appealed to both correspondents. The importance of memory and forgetfulness in the cult of the shrine, coupled with the power of predicting the future, were aspects which could not but have attracted them. In the Prague Castle project they were working to enshrine a recovered past in symbol and metonymic form while also creating for an as yet indiscernible future.

As Masaryk's writings and epistolary exchanges among the three protagonists indicate, the notion of 'truth', in its many nuances, was a key concept in the project. As both philosopher and statesman, Masaryk was able to perceive the visionary and the pragmatic to an unusual degree. Accordingly, his conception of truth, as conveyed in the language of his writings, did not merely encompass expressive, structural and historical understandings of the term, but represented the utmost moral and spiritual category for him.

In his introduction to Alain Soubigou's biography of Masaryk (2002), the late Václav Havel invokes the essence of Masaryk's thinking by emphasising his 'profound conviction that the real source of political action lies, and must lie, within the moral sphere and that truth itself is first and foremost a moral category'.[13] Havel thus puts specific emphasis on the secondary position of such apparently sacrosanct terms as national identity. And he quotes Masaryk himself: 'Let us stop appealing to Czechness, to Slavness, to patriotism, but [rather], let us demand the truth, let us bear witness in support of truth.'[14]

In her final letter to Plečnik in November 1956, Alice Masaryk expressed the same sentiment with regard to the monumental obelisk which Plečnik had designed for the Third Castle courtyard but which they both considered unfinished. She wrote: 'I hope that the sign on the obelisk will read Truth, Love, Life.'

Notes

1   Adrian Forty, *Words and Buildings: A Vocabulary of Modern Architecture*, Thames & Hudson (London), 2000.
2   Alice Masaryk's letters to Plečnik are preserved in the Architectural Museum in Ljubljana, Slovenia. They were translated into English by the author as part of her PhD thesis.
3   Roman Jakobson, 'Jazykové problémy v Masarykův díle', in *Masaryk a řeč* [Masaryk and Speech], Kroužek (Prague), 1931, pp 29–47.
4   TG Masaryk, *Versuch einer concreten Logik*, C Konegen (Vienna), 1887.
5   *Declaration of Independence of the Czechoslovak Nation*, Masarykův ústav (Prague), 1998.
6   TG Masaryk, *The Making of a State: Memories and Observations, 1914–1918*, Allen & Unwin (London), 1927.

7 TG Masaryk, *The Ideals of Humanity and How to Work*. Arno Press, (New York), 1971.

8 Plecnik, J. Unpublished letter to his brother, Andrej, in Vienna, 1902. Archives of the Architectural Museum, Ljubljana.

9 Akos Moravánzsky, *Competing Visions: Aesthetic Invention and Social Imagination in Central European Architecture, 1867–1918*, The MIT Press (Cambridge, Massachusetts), 1998.

10 Irena Žantovská Murray, *'Our Slav Acropolis': Language and Architecture in the Prague Castle under Masaryk*, PhD dissertation, McGill University, 2002, pp 13–15, 169. Viewable at http://digitool.library.mcgill.ca/webclient/ StreamGate?folder_id=0&dvs=1381360930482~425, McGill University Library website (accessed 9 October 2013).

11 Henri Gobard, *L'aliénation linguistique: analyse tétraglossique*, Flammarion (Paris), 1976. 'Actualisation' (or 'foregrounding') was a term coined by the Prague Linguistic Circle.

12 It is possible to imagine that President Masaryk himself was tacitly seen as the immured oracular figure of Trophonios in these speculations.

13 Alain Soubigou, *Thomas Masaryk*, Fayard (Paris), 2002.

14 Vaclav Havel, 'Preface', in ibid, p 11.

CHAPTER 15

Le Corbusier: Lies, Damned Lies and Statistics

JAN BIRKSTED

When reflecting on research theories in architectural history and their methodological implications, a sentence by Adrian Forty springs to mind:

> There seems no reason to suppose that [...] language will not continue to be as productive a source of ideas to architecture as it ever was.[1]

In research over the years, language, and by extension sign systems, have been two interdisciplinary models that have encouraged me to observe and to analyse in greater depth than would otherwise have been possible. But it was GM Trevelyan who wrote:

> Let the science and research of the historian find the fact, and let [...] imagination and art make clear its significance.[2]

It sounds so simple: find the facts and then interpret their significance. But what to do when the facts are deliberately hidden, falsified or otherwise manipulated? This is often the case with the most mythical figures and events in history. For example, Cézanne, an archetypal modernist striving for originality and celebrity, operated specific strategies to craft his own legend.[3] So did Picasso, for whom the problem was doubly complex because he had to reinvent himself as working within *la tradition française*. And so too was the case for one Charles-Édouard Jeanneret (1887–1965), who, from the small Swiss town of La Chaux-de-Fonds, had to engage in epic battles to metamorphose into the great French architect Le Corbusier, climaxing in his state funeral in the symbolic Cour Carrée of the Louvre, televised and presided over by André Malraux.[4]

Of this meteoric and irresistible rise, the historian can detect clues here and there. In 1937, in *Le concert sans orchestre* [The Concert with no Orchestra], his historical novel about life and friends in La Chaux-de-Fonds, Jean-Paul Zimmermann used the character of a musician called Courvoisier to represent the architect Le Corbusier, and hints at how he began his pre-1917 ascent:

> The musician was very preoccupied, frequently absent from town, and, on his returns, he immersed himself in his work without giving sign of life. [...] One day, in the street, Vitus complained that Courvoisier [Le Corbusier] was dropping his friends. [...] 'He is unloading ballast. That is how you rise.'[5]

Indeed, in his rewriting of his own life as legend, Le Corbusier virtually erased the details of these first thirty formative years of his life in La Chaux-de-Fonds to present his creations as a series of immaculate conceptions. He described in his *Œuvre Complète* how:

> Intuition produces flashes of unexpected insight. Thus in 1914 the perfect and complete conception of an entire system of construction, anticipating all future problems.[6]

In his 1975 interview with H Allen Brooks, Marcel Montandon, draftsman on Le Corbusier's Villa Schwob (1916) in La Chaux-de-Fonds, retorted with suppressed irritation: 'You have no idea of the extent to which he copied!'[7] And in 1926, Le Corbusier himself described confidentially to Josef Cerv the existence of his double-faced strategy:

Le Corbusier is a pseudonym. Le Corbusier creates architecture, recklessly [...] It is an entity free of the burdens of carnality. He must (but will he succeed?) never disappoint. Charles-Édouard Jeanneret is the embodied person who has endured the innumerably radiant or wretched episodes of an adventurous life [...] Ch É Jeanneret and Le Corbusier both sign this note together, Warmest regards, Paris 18 January 1926.[8]

Now, faced with such complex facts, the 'science and research of the historian' need to establish special procedures to observe and interpret such facts beyond what is available to the naked eye. This is where the interdisciplinary models of language and of sign systems come in. Rosalind Krauss has explored the notion of 'clue' as 'what was never considered, what

Les Francs-maçons [The Freemasons] by Serge Hutin (Tardy imprint, Éditions du Seuil (Bourges), 1960): a book much read and heavily annotated by Le Corbusier towards the end of his life, now in the Fondation Le Corbusier.

was inadvertent, unconscious, left by mistake'.[9] Similarly, Carlo Ginzburg has sought to examine the detective methods described by Arthur Conan Doyle and Edgar Allan Poe, who, in *The Purloined Letter* (1844), describes the case of a document that, paradoxically, is nearly invisible because of its extreme visibility 'full in view of every visitor […] to delude the beholder into an idea of its worthlessness'.[10] But, what then is the nature of such clues? To be able to clarify and categorise them would help historians to spot them, to analyse the myths that they sustain, and to reveal the historical structures behind them.

It is here that Charles S Peirce's theory of signs becomes relevant. For Peirce, relations between signs and their objects were either 'icons', 'indexes', 'symbols' or 'traces'. Peirce defined the 'icon' (such as painted portraits) as representations 'so completely substituted for their objects as hardly to be distinguished from them';[11] the 'index' (such as smoke from a fire) as relating existentially, causally or factually to the object since it 'asserts nothing; it only says "There!" It takes hold of our eyes, as it were, and forcibly directs them to a particular object, and there it stops';[12] the 'trace' as an index indicating a past presence (such as footsteps in the sand); and, finally, the 'symbol' (such as flags) as recalling the object on grounds of habit, custom or convention. In recent research about Le Corbusier, a recurring series of iconic resemblances between Corbusian architectural *partis* (plans, elevations, sections, architectural character) and the *partis* of an 18th-century architect, François-Joseph Belanger, were noticed. To corroborate these, the full range of additional Peircean signs (indexes, traces, symbols) would be needed. Several indexical inscriptions were found: a hitherto-unnoticed reference to a book about Belanger in Le Corbusier's *Carnet Paris Automne 1913*, in which he describes it as 'amazing – to be bought'; and, in Le Corbusier's *New World of Space* (1948), an actual sketch by Le Corbusier of Belanger's Temple Grotto.[13] Peircean 'traces' of Charles-Édouard Jeanneret were still needed for further corroboration, which were found in the memoirs of scholars who read books about Belanger in the Bibliothèque Nationale when the young Jeanneret was doing so too. Finally, Peirce's symbolic consistency was needed: extensive evidence of the cultural interest in, and publications about, Belanger in Paris at that time were documented. Thus, following Peirce's rule that 'in a perfect system of logical notation, signs of these several kinds must all be employed',[14] icons, indexes, traces and symbols all supported each other and accorded with their cultural context.

A postcard of a favourite watering hole in La Chaux-de-Fonds, sent to Le Corbusier by his friends after his 1917 departure to Paris, now in the Fondation Le Corbusier.

This brief analysis of the use of sign theory to organise historical clues suggests some implications. By extending the concepts of icon, index, trace and symbol to previous research publications to detect hidden facts in their interstices and between their lines, such previous research is itself transformed into primary source material, thereby enlarging the range of empirical data that we can use to progress our knowledge.

The concepts of icon, index, trace and symbol can also be extended to visual materials. There is a tendency to use architectural photographs to discuss architecture, but photographs are *not* architecture; they are representations of architecture (which, to complicate matters, is itself a form of representation).[15] And so by extending these concepts of icon, index, trace and symbol to photographs, they too can be used as primary sources to disclose additional information in architectural history.[16]

I would therefore propose the extension of Adrian Forty's statement – 'there seems no reason to suppose that [...] language will not continue to be as productive a source of ideas to architecture as it ever was'[17] – as an interdisciplinary model to the field of architectural history, with two provisos: that it be dynamic and rhetorical, rather than following the static model of language proposed by Ferdinand de Saussure.[18] Peirce's theory therefore has to be amended, as its categories are too cut-and-dried. Icons, indexes, traces and symbols in fact crisscross and overlap. A footstep in the sand is both a trace of a passage and an icon of a foot sole. A flag is simultaneously a symbol of a nation, a trace of the wind and an index of the wind's direction. Such dynamics generate new meanings through their interactive transformations.[19]

Using linguistic and sign systems as models has been critiqued because of their inability to deal with time and change. In reply, I would quote Fredric Jameson for whom, when mapping sociocultural configurations, the very opposite is the case: 'where everything is historical, the idea of history itself has seemed to empty of content. Perhaps that is, indeed, the ultimate propaedeutic value of the linguistic model: to renew our fascination with the seeds of time.'[20]

With this expression, 'the seeds of time', a second and recent sentence by Adrian Forty about the inherently unstable relations between concrete and culture springs to mind. It raises issues and questions about the concept of 'culture'.[21] What is 'culture'? When applying dynamic linguistic and sign models to research methods in architectural history, culture is seen to be a panoply of social latencies that individuals operate, selectively and strategically, in trying to achieve their aims, objects, intentions and beliefs. Thus, cultures, societies and history are inherently changing and unstable formations – which raises the two fundamental questions of history: of the relations between present and past, and of agency, that is of the relations between individual strategy and sociocultural formation. In this respect, the lies, and even more so the damned lies, of history are the true and proper materials of historical research, whose statistical-like patterns the historian needs to unravel.

Notes

1 Adrian Forty, *Words and Buildings: A Vocabulary of Modern Architecture*, Thames & Hudson (London), 2000, p 85.

2 GM Trevelyan, 'The Present Position of History' (inaugural lecture as Regius Professor, delivered at Cambridge, 27 October 1927), in GM Trevelyan, *Clio, A Muse*, Longmans, Green & Co (London), 1913, pp 177–96 (p 196).

3 See Richard Shiff, *Cézanne and the End of Impressionism: A Study of the Theory, Technique, and Critical Evaluation of Modern Art*, University of Chicago Press (Chicago, Illinois), 1984.

4 See JK Birksted, *Le Corbusier and the Occult*, The MIT Press (Cambridge, Massachusetts), 2009.

5 Jean-Paul Zimmermann, *Le concert sans orchestre*, Éditions Victor Attinger (Neuchâtel), c 1937, p 96.

6   Le Corbusier and Pierre Jeanneret, *Œuvre Complète 1910–1929*, Les Éditions d'Architecture (Erlenbach-Zurich), 1930, 1946 reprinting, p 23.

7   'Vous ne savez pas à quel point il a copié!' (Marcel Montandon interview with H Allen Brooks, November 1975, H Allen Brooks Archives, Yale University Library, MS 1784, Box 104).

8   Le Corbusier letter to Josef Cerv in William Ritter's guest book, 18 January 1926 (Fonds William Ritter, Bibliothèque Publique et Universitaire de Neuchâtel).

9   Rosalind Krauss, *The Optical Unconscious*, The MIT Press (Cambridge, Massachusetts), 1993, p 253.

10 Edgar Allan Poe, 'The Purloined Letter' in Edgar Allan Poe, *The Purloined Letter and Other Tales*, The Holerth Press (London), 1924, pp 5–29 (pp 26–7).

11 Charles S Peirce, *The Essential Peirce: Selected Philosophical Writings, Volume 1 1867–1893*, Indiana University Press (Bloomington and Indianapolis), 1992, p 226.

12 Ibid.

13 Le Corbusier, *New World of Space*, The Institute of Contemporary Art (Boston, Massachusetts), 1948.

14 Peirce, *The Essential Peirce*, p 227.

15 Roland Barthes's distinction between photographs and snapshots must here be borne in mind.

16 For an example of this, see JK Birksted, *Modernism and the Mediterranean: The Maeght Foundation*, Ashgate (London), 2004.

17 Forty, *Words and Buildings*, p 85.

18 For the history of such dynamic theories, see Tzvetan Todorov, *Théories du symbole*, Éditions du Seuil (Paris), 1977, and Gérard Genette, *Figures III*, Éditions du Seuil (Paris), 1972. One such dynamic model of language is Mikhail Bakhtin's.

19 Such crisscrossing and overlapping can have powerful effects: in Roland Barthes's *Camera Lucida* in the classic example of the photograph of his deceased mother, the photograph is simultaneously icon (of her appearance), trace (of her existence) and symbol (of his own loss) (Roland Barthes, *Camera Lucida: Reflections on Photography*, Hill & Wang (New York), 1981). Such dynamic transformations are well documented by Julia Kristeva in *Proust and the Sense of Time*, Faber & Faber (London), 1993, and by Paul de Mann in *Blindness and Insight: Essays in the Rhetoric of Contemporary Criticism*, Routledge (London and New York), 1983.

20 Fredric Jameson, *The Prison House of Language: A Critical Account of Structuralism and Russian Formalism*, Princeton University Press (Princeton, New Jersey), 1972, p xi.

21 Adrian Forty, *Concrete and Culture: A Material History*, Reaktion (London), 2012 p 296.

CHAPTER 16

During Breakfast

JANE RENDELL

This visual essay is part of a larger project, conducted through my practice of site-writing, which explores transitional spaces in architecture and psychoanalysis: how architecture situates, and is situated by, objects (and subjects) of desire. This particular iteration focuses on a building – with Art Nouveau motifs inspired by naturalistic forms – commissioned by a member of the bourgeois class, and occupied during the Russian Revolution by a psychoanalytic nursery, closely linked to larger debates concerning the relation between Marxism and psychoanalysis. Sigmund Freud was widely read in Russia, and his essay of 1920, 'Beyond the Pleasure Principle', which introduces the notion of the death drive, was in part influenced by a 1912 essay written by Sabina Spielrein, a psychoanalyst who worked in the nursery. Translated into Russian the year the nursery was closed, Freud's essay deals with the tension in the psyche between life and death, and in psychoanalysis between biology and history.

My own essay is composed of four strands of material evidence, which intertwine words and images, present and past, to suggest how one building has been experienced over time. This building is a villa, designed by the architect Fyodor Schechtel for Stepan Pavlovich Ryabushinsky, a member of a wealthy banking family, and constructed in Moscow between 1902 and 1906. From 1921 the building was occupied by a psychoanalytic nursery, headed by Vera Schmidt, first named the 'Children's Home Laboratory' and then, from 1922, 'International Solidarity'. From its founding in 1923, by psychoanalysts Otto Schmidt, Ivan Ermakov and Alexander Luria, until it was closed by Stalin in August 1925, the villa also housed the State Psychoanalytic Institute, which offered an outpatients department, lectures, workshops and publications.

During breakfast Genja (2 years, 10 months) was very stubborn. Eventually the following scene took place: Genja asked for a small plate to put his piece of bread on it. I gave it to him. He angrily pushed it away: 'Don't want this, want another one.' Before I could give him another one, Wolik (3 years, 3 months) pointed at the plate that Genja had rejected, and said: 'But I want just that one. It's mine, the one with the small black spot.'[1]

One of them, Vladimir Ottovich Schmidt, whose mother, Vera Fedorovna, worked there as a tutor, shared his memories: he did not remember the inner decoration and building plan well, but clearly remembered a huge half-round window that seemed unreachably high for the child.[2]

Freud made his debut as a revolutionary. The degree of opposition which psycho-analysis elicited in official academic circles, bears incontestable witness to the fact that it was guilty of having severely infringed age old traditions of bourgeois morality and scholarship and had overstepped the limits of what is acceptable.[3]

The first floor housed a dining room with a long table and benches; the room near the balcony housed the medical aid point.[4]

Instantly Genja grabbed the very same plate, seemingly in order to tease Wolik, and did not want to give it back at any price. Wolik tried to snatch away the plate, but Genja did not let go of it. This is when I had to intervene, in order to put an end to the quarrel at the table. As Genja was already upset and I did not want to provoke him even more, I persuaded Wolik to let him keep the small plate. Wolik agreed, but sat there with a scowling look on his face. Even the other children seemed to be dissatisfied with this decision. Hedy (3 years, 5 months) said: 'No, this is Wolik's plate. Genja did not want to take it and Wolik did; Genja wanted it later; Wolik wanted it earlier.' At this point Wera, who was lying in bed, called for me. From a distance I observed what happened.[5]

In front of our eyes, a new and original trend in psychoanalysis is beginning to form in Russia, which, with the help of the theory of the conditional reflexes, attempts to synthesize Freudian psychology and Marxism and to develop a system of 'reflexological Freudian psychology' in the spirit of dialectical materialism.[6]

At the age of 21 I became a secretary of the Russian Psychoanalytic Society, whose chairman was professor Ermakov [...] We were given a beautiful house – Ryabushunskiy's mansion, a place where Gorky later lived, I had a wonderful room, decorated with silk wallpaper, where I arranged regular meetings of psychoanalysts every two weeks. Our psychoanalytic society was on the mansion's ground floor and its first floor housed the 'psychoanalytic nursery school'.[7]

Where are we to look for the root of the stormy progression of the historical process? Freud provides us with a highly interesting and deeply materialistic answer, i.e. if in the deep recesses of the human psyche there still remain conservative tendencies of primordial biology and if, in the final analysis, even Eros is consigned to it, then the only forces which make it possible for us to escape from this state of biological conservatism and which may propel us toward progress and activity, are external forces, in our terms, the external conditions of the material environment in which the individual exists.[8]

Artyom Fyodorovich remembers Annushka Albuhina – a cook – treating children with milk in a big kitchen at the basement.[9]

I had barely turned away, when Wolodja (2 years, 10 months) got up from his seat, took the plate from Genja and gave it to Wolik: 'Take it, Wolik, it is yours.' Genja started crying. Wolik was drinking coffee, the plate lying next to him. He picked it up a couple of times, turned it around in his hands and put it down again. Finally he resolutely handed it to Genja. 'Take it, Genja. I already played with it, now you play.' Genja calmed down instantly and took the plate, gently stroking Wolik's hand: 'I love you, Wolik,' Wolik: 'I love you too.' The children were laughing happily. Genja: 'Am I your friend, Wolik?' Wolik: 'Yes, you are.' Hedy: 'And mine too!' Ira and Wolodja: 'And mine! And mine!' Genja is happy, all faces are smiling.[10]

At the beginning, the nursery was a day-and-night residency, but in the autumn of 1926 a plywood partition was installed across the stairway, and children started to come just during the day and only to the first floor. In the spring the nursery-school was closed.[11]

Bourgeois science is giving birth to materialism; such labour is often difficult and prolonged, but we only have to find where in its bowels materialistic buds are showing, to find them, to rescue them and to make good use of them.[12]

The first strand of this composition comprises photographs I took in July 2012 of the Gorky House-Museum – the building as it is today. The other three strands are made of words taken from text-based sources associated with the building's history and its connections to psychoanalysis. The italicised text is taken from diary extracts concerning events that took place in the Children's Home Laboratory on 16 June 1923, and which were later published in *Psychoanalytical Education in Soviet Russia: Report about the Children's Home Laboratory in Moscow*, a report written by Vera Schmidt and published in 1924. The plain text is taken from a publication concerning the building's history, incorporating memories of those who occupied it, including the psychoanalyst Luria, and children who lived there when it was a nursery, such as Stalin's adopted son, Artyom Sergeyev. The bold text is taken from the 1925 introduction, co-authored by Luria, to the Russian translation of Freud's 'Beyond the Pleasure Principle'.

Notes

1 V Schmidt, 'Annex: Extract from the Younger Group's Diary: On the Development of a Social Sense, 16 June 1923', in V Schmidt, *Psychoanalytical Education in Soviet Russia: Report about the Children's Home Laboratory in Moscow*, translated from the German by Anna Guelzow, Internationaler Psychoanalytischer Verlag (Leipzig, Vienna and Zurich), 1924, p 30.

2 NL Penezhko, VN Chernuchina and AM Marchenkov, *Schechtel, Ryabushinskiy, Gorky* (*The House at Malaya Nikitskaya, 6*), translated from the Russian by Yuriy Milevskiy, 'Nasledie' (Moscow), 2000, p 74.

3 L Vygotsky and A Luria, 'Introduction' to the Russian translation of Freud's 'Beyond the Pleasure Principle', translated from the Russian by Theresa Prout, in R van der Veer and J Valsiner (eds), *The Vygotsky Reader*, Basil Blackwell (Oxford), 1925/1994, pp 11–18 (p 10). First published in Sigmund Freud, *Po tu storonu principa uduvol'stvija*, Sovermennye Problemy (Moscow), 1925, pp 3–16.

4 Penezhko, Chernuchina and Marchenkov, *Schechtel, Ryabushinskiy, Gorky*, p 77.

5 Schmidt, *Psychoanalytical Education in Soviet Russia*, p 30.

6 Vygotsky and Luria, 'Introduction' to the Russian translation of Freud's 'Beyond the Pleasure Principle', p 10.

7 Penezhko, Chernuchina and Marchenkov, *Schechtel, Ryabushinskiy, Gorky*, p 75.

8 Vygotsky and Luria, 'Introduction' to the Russian translation of Freud's 'Beyond the Pleasure Principle', p 10.

9 Penezhko, Chernuchina and Marchenkov, *Schechtel, Ryabushinskiy, Gorky*, p 77.

10 Schmidt, *Psychoanalytical Education in Soviet Russia*, p 30.

11 Penezhko, Chernuchina and Marchenkov, *Schechtel, Ryabushinskiy, Gorky*, p 78.

12 Vygotsky and Luria, 'Introduction' to the Russian translation of Freud's 'Beyond the Pleasure Principle', p 10.

CHAPTER 17
[American] Objects of [Soviet] Desire

JEAN-LOUIS COHEN

Between the Allied victory over Nazism, symbolised by the encounter of the Red Army and the US Army on the Elbe in April 1945, and the famous 1959 'kitchen debate', held in Moscow by Nikita Khrushchev and Richard Nixon, as well as in years to follow, when academic modernism was endorsed in Soviet architecture and design, the observation of American design never ceased in the USSR and was practised in all the professions and industries, but maybe most prominently in architecture.

Throughout the 1920s and the early 1930s, American themes abounded in avant-garde designs. In a collage published in 1926, Kazimir Malevich inscribed one of his 'Architectons' against the skyline of downtown Manhattan. Ivan Leonidov designed in 1934 his Narkomtiazhprom skyscraper on Moscow's Red Square, representing the silhouette according to the worm-eye patterns used in Erich Mendelsohn's photographs of American cities.[1] Amerikanizm pervaded mass culture, as jazz bands became popular, and shaped particularly Soviet cinema. After unauthorised borrowings, such as the production of a copy of the Fordson tractor by the former Putilov factories in Leningrad, the import of American technology became one of the key factors in the success of the first of the Soviet regime's Five-Year Plans (1928–33). The material skeleton of Soviet industrialisation was forged in American factories, such as the one Albert Kahn Associates built in Chelyabinsk for the production of tractors (1932).[2]

During the Second World War, a new wave of American technology reached the Soviet Union. Thanks to the Lend-Lease agreements, thousands of vehicles and aeroplanes were ferried by sea and land to the Eastern front. The offensive movements of the Red Army were largely facilitated by the massive delivery of Studebaker trucks. Direct relationships were established in the field of architecture, thanks to the works of the National Council of American–Soviet Friendship and its ad hoc committee, chaired by Harvey Wiley Corbett, which organised an American–Soviet Building Conference in New York. The most engaged project of the Committee was an exhibition prepared by Douglas Haskell, editor of *The Architectural Record*, and architect Simon Breines. Frederick Kiesler made a design for the show, which was shipped to Moscow but apparently never shown in the USSR.[3]

After the start of the Cold War, the new condition was reflected, if not even preceded, in the field of technological 'transfer'. The history of the Soviet atomic bombs and of espionage in the US has been told, but the production of the very vector of the bomb also deserves some attention. One of the most extraordinary cases of reverse engineering took place between 1945 and 1947, when four B-29 Superfortress bombers, which had made an emergency landing in Siberia after having raided Tokyo, were dismantled and copied, piece by piece, from the airframe to the electronic equipment, in order to produce Tupolev's Tu-4.[4] The redesign and re-engineering of the bomber became a massive effort of industrial coordination, as shown by the displays Tupolev's team had to organise in order to plan the subcontractors' work.

On the architectural 'front', an experience of American technology had been brought back by Viacheslav Oltarzhevsky, an architect who had emigrated in 1924 and had worked in New York with Harvey Wiley Corbett. Sent to the Gulag in 1938 after his return, Oltarzhevsky was freed thanks to American ambassador Averell Harriman and resumed work on a sort of Russian equivalent to the US's definitive style guide the *Architectural Graphic Standards*, in which he reproduced patterns and measurements based on American examples. This was the case with rather exotic programmes such as batteries of escalators derived from American department stores, or luncheonette counters.[5]

With the rapid development of the Cold War, the 'accursed' double of Americanism, ie anti-Americanism, re-emerged. Critic David Arkin, who in 1936 had translated Lewis Mumford's 1924 volume *Sticks and Stones*, was accused in 1949 of being an 'ideologue of cosmopolitanism in architecture'.[6]

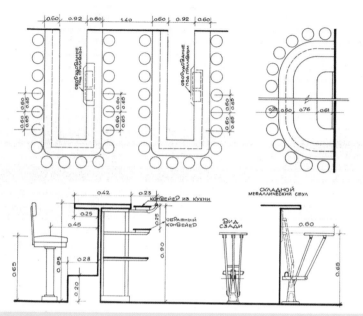

The organisation of American luncheonette counters.
Plate from Viacheslav Oltarzhevsky, *Gabaritny spravochnik arkhitektora*, Moscow, 1947.

The new skyline of Moscow, a programme coordinated by Dmitri Chechulin, following a decision taken in January 1947 by the Council of Ministers of the USSR, would be shaped by the experience acquired by Oltarzhevsky.[7] In fact, the general principle of the distribution of the 'seven sisters' in Moscow's urban space derives from a polygonal, multi-centric scheme proposed in 1929 by architectural renderer Hugh Ferriss in his *Metropolis of Tomorrow* and commented upon in 1934 in Moscow by Alexei Shchusev.[8]

In the realm of automobile production, American design was also unequivocally recycled.[9] The design of Soviet cars had been since the earliest period derived from American or sometimes German models. In Gorky, the GAZ factory had been built with Ford and the Austin Company between 1929 and 1932. Its designer Andrei Liphart conceived the M20 Pobeda, which would be produced between 1946 and 1958, with more built under licence in Poland. The car was a hybrid of a Ford 1942 sedan and a 1942 Nash. Its meaning for

The automobile GAZ M20 Pobeda in front of a condensed Moscow skyline.

postwar Soviet citizens is made clear by an illustration featuring the car on the background of the 'seven sisters' pressed together, so as to suggest the idea of a dense skyline. The mise-en-scène suggested that, with the joint production of the Pobeda and the high-rise buildings, Russia was catching up with America.

In 1953, Liphart started working on the GAZ M21 Volga, similar to the 1952 Ford, and which entered production in 1956. The next step in an apparently endless process was the launch of the Chaika, a new *apparatchikmobile*, put in production in 1959, this time a synthesis of many late 1950s American cars.

In the last months of Stalin's life, 'the sharpening crisis of architecture and town planning in post-war America' had been discussed. The attack was focused on modernist slab buildings, considered as 'functionalism for the rich'.[10] The discipline itself was redefined, being brought down from the Parnassus of the arts to the more prosaic condition of a domain of technology. But the relationship to the US would rapidly be restored. The visit of Khrushchev to America in 1959 led Russian audiences to discover cities and landscapes until then invariably shown as decaying urban ruins or paradise for the privileged. American city planning ceased to be the cynical expression of capitalism to become a field of observation.

АРХИТЕКТУРА США

Arthur Drexler,
Arkhitektura SShA,
1965.
Cover designed
by Chermayeff &
Geismar.

Inscribed in a new pattern of cultural exchange, after nearly 14 years of interruption, the 1959 American National Exhibition in Moscow, with its 2.7 million visitors, marked a threshold in the Soviet citizen's understanding of American technology and civilisation.[11] Besides the four kitchens exhibited, which prompted a memorable discussion between Khrushchev and Vice-President Nixon, an architectural section presented most of the buildings that had been criticised in the past years. The slogan of 'catching up with America' was replaced by 'passing America'.[12]

Translations of Western architectural books resumed in the 1960s. Interestingly, at a time in which a new emphasis was being put on consumption, one of the first would be Gruen and Smith's *Shopping Towns USA*. Study trips led to solid reports, such as the one published after a visit of New York, Washington and Los Angeles by Mikhail Posokhin, who had in the meantime become the head architect of Moscow.[13] Meant 'for service use' only, and printed in numbered copies, the book included the compulsory views of American slums. But the architectural objects shown and discussed in detail were unquestionable modernist icons: Lever House (by Gordon Bunshaft of Skidmore, Owings & Merrill, 1952), the Seagram Building (Mies van der Rohe,

View of Los Angeles from the air, page from Mikhail Posokhin, *Gradostroitelstvo v SShA*, Moscow, 1965.

1958) and the World Trade Center (Minoru Yamasaki, 1972) in New York, and the type of the shopping centre, which was being discovered and used to design the new Russian *Univermagi*, or universal stores. Also, the geography of architectural Americanism was extended to new territories, beginning with Los Angeles.

The effects of the observations made since the mid-1950s led to new urban schemes in the Soviet cities, which could be interpreted in their relationships with American cases. Posokhin's own Kalinin Prospekt, built in Moscow to commemorate the 50th anniversary of the 1917 Revolution, was no less brutal in razing historical blocks of the Arbat quarter than the plans for 6th Avenue in New York, developed since the early 1940s. The very bourgeois slabs criticised in the early 1950s were now considered essential features of a modern city centre, and the most banal Manhattan skyscrapers were more likely precedents for the Intourist Hotel – built on Gorky Street between 1965 and 1969 to designs by an unknown architect – than Mies van der Rohe's rigorous Seagram Building. In sum, despite rapid changes in the political discourse, from the wartime alliance to the dark late Stalinist age, and to the times of Khrushchev and his followers, the reference to America remained so powerful in defining technical and aesthetic ideals that it resisted the most violent diatribes, and imposed on Russian soil a peculiarly hybrid culture. Having escaped direct Americanisation by refusing the Marshall Plan, the USSR had been shaped in its material and visual culture by a pervading Americanism.

Notes

1   Jean-Louis Cohen, 'L'Oncle Sam au pays des Soviets: le temps des avant-gardes', in Jean-Louis Cohen and Hubert Damisch (eds), *Américanisme et modernité, l'idéal américain dans l'architecture*, Flammarion (Paris), 1993, pp 403–35.

2   Sonia Melnikova-Raich, 'The Soviet Problem with Two "Unknowns": How an American Architect and a Soviet Negotiator Jump-Started the Industrialization of Russia, Part I: Albert Kahn', *Journal of the Society for Industrial Archeology*, Vol 36, No 2, 2010, pp 57–80.

3   Richard Anderson, 'USA/USSR: Architecture and War', *Grey Room*, No 34, Winter 2009, pp 80–103.

4   Yefim Gordon and Vladimir Rigmant, *Tupolev Tu-4: Soviet Superfortress*, Midland Publishing (Hinckley), 2002.

5   Viacheslav Oltarzhevsky, *Gabaritny spravochnik arkhitektora*, Izdatelstvo Akademii Arkhitektury SSSR (Moscow), 1947.

6   Arkh. A Peremyslov, '"Ideolog" kozpolitizma v arkhitekture D. Arkin', *Arkhitektura i Stroitelstvo*, March 1949, p 8.

7   Viacheslav K Oltarzevsky, *Stroitelstvo vysotnykh zdanii v Moskve*, Gos. izd. Lit. po Stroitelstvu i Arkhitekture (Moscow), 1953.

8   AV Shchusev and LE Zagorsky, *Arkhitekturnaia organizatsia goroda*, Gosstroiizdat (Moscow), 1934, pp 17–20.

9   Lewis H Siegelbaum, *Cars for Comrades: The Life of the Soviet Automobile*, Cornell University Press (Ithaca, New York and London), 2008.

10   Nikita Khrushchev, quoted in Catherine Cooke (with Susan E Reid), 'Modernity and Realism: Architectural Relations in the Cold War', *Russian Art and the West: A Century of Dialogue in Painting, Architecture, and the Decorative Arts*, in Rosalind P Blakesley and Susan E Reid (eds), Northern Illinois University Press (DeKalb, Illinois), 2007, pp 172–94.

11   Jack Masey and Conway Lloyd Morgan, *Cold War Confrontations: US Exhibitions and their Role in the Cultural Cold War*, Lars Müller (Baden), 2008.

12   Susan E Reid, 'Who Will Beat Whom? Soviet Popular Reception of the American National Exhibition in Moscow, 1959', *Kritika: Explorations in Russian and Eurasian History*, Vol 9, No 4, 2008, pp 855–904.

13   Mikhail Posokhin, *Gradostroitelstvo v SShA*, Otdelenie nauchno-teknicheskoi informatsii pri NII teorii, istorii i perspektivnykh problem sovetskoi arkhitektury (Moscow), 1968.

CHAPTER 18
Words and Buildings
JEREMY MELVIN

'Sir John will be here shortly,' intoned a green-jacketed attendant with the air of an undertaker at a funeral where the quick only just outnumber the dead. Footsteps, a few muttered imprecations, and then as if animated from some alchemical fusion or, as I was later to speculate, awakened from slumber in a 4,000-year-old sarcophagus, a tall, stooping man appeared. Once he started speaking though, the cobwebs disappeared, and his words became shafts of light which seemed to order the fragments into their correct and meaningful places. It was as if the Ruinart champagne flowed again and Sir John Summerson dissolved into his predecessor, namesake and posthumous patron, Sir John Soane.[1]

It was not quite like that, of course, one Saturday afternoon in November 1983 when half a dozen first-year students from The Bartlett were trying to make sense of a newly set assignment, to describe Sir John Soane's Museum. Coming from an academic schooling which valued anything literary over anything numerate, where the visual and musical scarcely registered, and brought up on the pithy verbless sentences in Nikolaus Pevsner's *Buildings of England* – I thought I could acquit myself well. But I had greatly underestimated that difficulty of matching words to buildings and could not possibly match Summerson's fluency. In the second part of the task we each had to take a different building – mine was Denys Lasdun's library building for the School of Oriental and African Studies in nearby Bloomsbury (1973) – and I think by the end of it we were all far less naive but also rather more intrigued by the possible relationships of words to buildings.

Nearly 20 years later, in 2000, the same tutor who had set that task published *Words and Buildings*.[2] It is a crucial book, not because it was the first publication to look at the territory – Ben Jonson and Inigo Jones had a fair old spat about the relationship between words and architecture when they devised court masques in the 17th century – but because it was systematic as well as being even-handed in its sensitivity to the peculiarities of language and those of architecture.[3] On top of that, it gave an unusually powerful insight into that much noted but rarely analysed characteristic of the architectural world in the post-World War II period: its curious resistance to outside interference, commentary or criticism.

Reyner Banham hinted at this characteristic in his essay in Pevsner's festschrift, 'Revenge of the Picturesque'.[4] Recalling in 1967 the conditions of the early 1950s, he wrote 'the younger generation found an apparent solidarity between their intellectual mentors in Queen Anne's Gate, their instructors at the Architectural Association, and their superiors when they qualified and went to work for largely Socialist-dominated local government bodies like the London County Council'.[5] Right at the end of his life Banham would identify the tissue that held this belief system together – the drawing: 'Even before architectural drawings achieved the kind of commercial value they can claim nowadays, they had such crucial value for architects that being unable to think without drawing became the true mark of one fully socialised into the profession of architecture.'[6]

The contrast with the passage from John Evelyn that Forty cites in the introduction to *Words and Buildings* is striking.[7] Evelyn defined four types of architect: the *architectus ingenio* who met the Vitruvian prescriptions for architectural knowledge; the *architectus sumptuarius*, the client or patron; the *architectus manuarius* or artisan; and the *architectus verborum*, the architect of words. Each type was vital to the project of architecture. After World War II the Welfare State did create a need to redefine Evelyn's four parts: the *architectus sumptuarius* could no longer be characterised as a wealthy individual patron but needed some concept of the public body as a client, and of members of the public as 'users', while new methods of production were leaving the idea of the *architectus manuarius* as purely an artisan some way behind. But was the architectural establishment's redefinition of 'architecture' purely around the updated *architectus ingenio* appropriate or helpful? Especially when, as Banham perceptively noted, its key argument for this sleight of hand was implicitly to invoke the concept of *disegno*, the Renaissance theory of drawing – precisely the same concept that Inigo Jones used to great effect in his argument with Ben Jonson regarding the superiority of the architect's contribution over the poet's to court masques.[8]

And what of the *architectus verborum*? At a conference on 'Rethinking the 1950s' held at the Architectural Association (AA) in October 1992, during the early stages of the serious work on *Words and Buildings*, Forty gave a paper which hinted at his insights to come.[9] He outlined several of the key words he had already identified, including 'simple', 'simplicity' or even better 'sober simplicity' as terms of high approbation. An intervention from Alison Smithson – 'We didn't think our work was simple, but we did think most other architects were simple-minded' – magisterially cued up Forty's concluding point: that the failure of the architectural world to find a way of using language to convey what it was trying to do, how it was trying to contribute to society, meant that these ideals and their potential simply could not be expressed in ways anyone outside the closed circle – Banham's 'black box' – could understand. The way was left for reactionaries and other nihilists to devise a language of ridicule and exaggeration that played up all the symptoms of failure without giving any space to the underlying achievements. It is perhaps no coincidence that postmodern architects – Charles Moore and Robert Stern, to name two – tend to be better writers than their modernist counterparts.

Forty probably ruffled more feathers than Alison Smithson's. Her generation included several members who might be considered *architecti verborum* like Colin Rowe, Alan Colquhoun, Robert Maxwell and Kenneth Frampton.[10] Each of these made a contribution to how architects understand architecture and often in a positive way. Rowe in particular opened up an approach to looking at the past even if his motives and methods were not strictly historical.[11] The problem was that none of them found an effective way of relating their insights to any external discourse – from the expanding field of art history, to the increasing interest of national newspapers in covering architecture. Banham specifically notes difficulties the *Observer* experienced in trying to find competent architecture critics who could explain the discipline to their readership.[12] For all its erudition, the work of the writers mentioned above tends towards the glorified technical manual, telling architects what they need to know about other architects and the history of their discipline in order to design 'better' buildings.

This is certainly one important aspect of what an *architectus verborum* should do. But especially the heady Welfare State experiment of making architecture something other than a plaything for wealthy patrons, and produced by means other than traditional craft, did require a different level of explanation. At the time of the AA conference, five years after completing the MSc in the history of modern architecture with Forty and Mark Swenarton, I was in the early stages of a peculiar and variegated career that has spanned academic architectural history, journalism and curating.[13] Academic architectural history is of course for academics, though not all of them architects; my journalism was largely for professional publications, but the forays I made into more mainstream circles were eye-openers to the amount of knowledge – and jargon – that even well-edited architectural publications took for granted.

My experience made Forty's line of thought from the undergraduate task of 1983 to his AA conference contribution seem very relevant. Without a way of relating specifically architectural thinking to other modes of intellectual activity – popular and academic – the chances of creating any level of understanding with the public, opinion-formers or politicians would be remote.

Armed with this slightly pessimistic realisation, my career slowly turned towards curating. It is its own practice which is at least and possibly rather more complex than either academic work or journalism, precisely because it has to span the worlds of scholarship and popular perception. Curators have to be aware of new research and creative activity – sometimes to undertake it – but they also have to devise ways of presenting those ideas, themes and works so they appeal to a broad audience. Fortunately curators have a wide range of tools to achieve this, including selection of material, placement of objects in relation to each other and the exhibition space, the creation of atmosphere, and even, in some institutions, their own tradition and expectations that visitors may have from previous visits.

This may move some way beyond any meaningful definition of the *architectus verborum*, but it is reasonable to suggest that exhibitions may be able to fill part of the gap left by the excision of the *architectus verborum* in the postwar period. They have the potential to create popular but meaningful encounters with architectural ideas, which might be taken for granted when met in a building in everyday use, but can come to life in the space defined by an exhibition.

On top of that, it could be argued that the exhibition is the cultural forum of our time. Most arts institutions, even those with fabulous permanent collections, devote large resources and take massive risks to organise temporary exhibitions that will bring in visitors who might otherwise postpone their visit. This is a parallel to the significant increase in cultural tourism, 'weekend-breaks', and generally greater mobility which has come with greater affluence and, in general, higher levels of education. But in various guises the exhibition is the medium through which ideas are presented and developed in all the other visual arts.

Architectural exhibitions have some distinct features: very few institutions have sufficiently large and distinguished collections to mount permanent displays;[14] and the apparent impediment of being unable to exhibit 'real buildings' invites and demands innovation and imagination in the type, mode, medium and display. They may even need something of the performative about them. The result is that architectural exhibitions inevitably have more similarity to temporary exhibitions than to permanent displays.

It was through Inigo Jones – himself as *architectus ingenio*, his *architecti sumptuarii*, and his *architecti manuarii* – that the course of English architecture irrevocably absorbed the classical tradition. Arguably it was through his collaboration on the court masques with Ben Jonson – his notably unpliant *architectus verborum* – that these concepts of classical thought became embedded in a wider level of social and cultural understanding. Their argument opened up the possibility of discussing different cultural practices in relation to each other, both their internal dynamic and their external perception. It is just possible that the architectural exhibition might be able to do something analogous to that. Here, perhaps, is the challenge for *architectura verborum de nos jours*.[15]

© 2014 Jeremy Melvin

Notes

1   Sir John Summerson (1904–1992), legendary and largely autodidactic architectural historian who pioneered (in the UK at least) systematic study of the development of cities (in *Georgian London*, Pleiades Books (London), 1945 [and many subsequent editions by various publishers]), and the construction industry (see, for example, 'Charting the Victorian Building World', in *The Unromantic Castle and Other Essays*, Thames & Hudson (London), 1990), pp 175–92. Curator of Sir John Soane's Museum, 1945–84.

2   For anyone who has not yet twigged it, the tutor in question was Adrian Forty.

3   See 'Poet and Architect: The Intellectual Setting of the Quarrel between Ben Jonson and Inigo Jones', in *The Renaissance Imagination: Essays and Lectures by DJ Gordon*, collected and edited by Stephen Orgel, University of California Press (Los Angeles, California and London), 1975, pp 77–101.

4   Reyner Banham, 'Revenge of the Picturesque: English Architectural Polemics, 1945–1965', in John Summerson (ed), *Concerning Architecture*, Allen Lane (London), 1968, pp 265–73.

5   Ibid, p 266. The Architectural Press, publisher of the *Architectural Review* and the *Architects' Journal*, was based at Queen Anne's Gate.

6   From 'A Black Box: The Secret Profession of Architecture', in *A Critic Writes: Essays by Reyner Banham*, edited by Mary Banham, Paul Barker, Sutherland Lyall and Cedric Price, University of California Press (Berkeley, California and London), 1997, pp 292–99 (p 298).

7   Adrian Forty, *Words and Buildings: A Vocabulary of Modern Architecture*, Thames & Hudson (London), 2000, p 11.

8   'A Black Box: The Secret Profession of Architecture', p 298; 'Poet and Architect: The Intellectual Setting of the Quarrel between Ben Jonson and Inigo Jones', pp 94–5.

9   The present author attended this conference and reviewed it for *Building Design*. See Jeremy Melvin, 'Reviewing the Fifties', in *Building Design*, 9 October 1992, p 14. Alison Smithson went on to express regret that the terms she and Peter had devised did not enter common critical vocabulary.

10 Colin Rowe (1920–1999), Alan Colquhoun (1921–2012), Robert Maxwell (1923–), Kenneth Frampton (1930–). All were British-educated architects – some of them legendary – who rose to academic prominence in Ivy League universities in the United States.

11 In his Acceptance Address for the Royal Gold Medal for Architecture in 1995, Rowe explained the impetus behind his essay 'The Mathematics of the Ideal Villa', which compares buildings by Le Corbusier and Palladio: 'Reyner Banham thought it was an attempt to make Corbu respectable, while, really, it was the other way round: *Hey you guys, here's Palladio and let's take a look*' [author's italics]. *The Journal of Architecture*, Vol 1, No 1, p 6.

12 Banham, 'Revenge of the Picturesque: English Architectural Polemics, 1945–1965', p 266 footnote.

13 In which both Forty and Swenarton, also a legendary architectural historian and teacher and now James Stirling Professor of Architecture at Liverpool University, have been significant influences and mentors.

14 And those that do, such as the RIBA, lack the resources to show more than a fraction of their holdings for a fraction of the time.

15 I offer this thought not just as an *apologia pro vita sua*.

CHAPTER 19
Slow Hard Look

JEREMY TILL

My first encounter with Adrian Forty was at the Bartlett School of Architecture in the early 1990s. He had asked me to give a lecture on Italian gardens. The invitation was surprising enough because there was a divide between the Peter Cook side of The Bartlett (to which I had been recruited) and the rest of it. Adrian was one of the few people who made the effort to traverse the boundary, and this in itself is indicative of his take on the efficacy of architectural history: it is not there as a dry set of internalised narratives, but as an active force that engages with, and informs, architectural culture and design. Unless he believed this, why else would he have run a lecture course for first-year architects, planners and builders at The Bartlett? Get them young, get them to see the importance of ideas and the way that these are played out in history, and so in design. I suspect that it did not all make complete sense to those first-years, but I also know that those lectures stuck in the memory banks of generations of Bartlett graduates, and in this it might be argued that they were more influential than the seminal master's course, whose graduates make up so many of this book's contributors.

Adrian ran this first-year course for over 30 years, a commitment way beyond the call of duty for one of the world's most important architectural historians. That he did it for so long is a mark of his intellectual persistence and generosity, and also a suggestion of the importance that he attaches to the role of architectural history as a productive force for change. Given the reputation of the first-year course, I was both honoured and worried when he invited me, a noisy design tutor and nascent theorist, to lecture on it, especially since it was for the opening lecture. I was given the responsibility of participating in probably the first lecture that these students ever received at The Bartlett. The topic was 'walls', a clever engagement tactic by Adrian to introduce architecture not through the distant Greeks, but through the immediacy of something very tangible.

I had a 15-minute slot, and with the naivety of relative youth attempted the entire history of walls in 900 seconds, as a badly extended *pecha kucha*. This approach was, of course, hopeless, as was clear from watching Adrian's contribution to the subject, in which he took a single idea and gently dropped it on a range of subjects as a means of elucidating them. I learnt from this and came back next time with just bricks as symbol and material of wall. But even my run through from the Pantheon of classical Rome to Swedish architect Sigurd Lewerentz was too cursory, so by the third year the lecture was only about Lewerentz's Church of St Peter at Klippan (1966), the brickiest of bricks and the walliest of walls that I know. It was a slow hard look at the cavity detail and the way that the doors are planted on, rather than framed by, the wall (and so the massiveness of the wall is asserted) – and in this slow hard look I could say more about walls than in any superficial skip through history. Three slides did more than a complete carousel.

It is the persistence of Adrian's slow hard look that is, for me, the most remarkable quality of his work, and marks him out from so many contemporary traits. There is much debate about how the financial strictures of higher education are determining a new intellectual landscape. In particular, critics see the various UK research assessment exercises (RAE 2008 and REF 2014) as mere accountancy tools framed by neoliberal ideologies. Thus the production of research as 'outputs' becomes little more than the production of any commodity. Books are salami-sliced into bite-sized chunks for consumption by the research assessment teams. Academics update their CVs on a weekly basis. Conference papers are smashed together into hodgepodge collections, which are then called 'books'. A hierarchy of peer reviewing perpetuates, and commodifies, a certain set of established values and methods. I could go on, but the point is that academic life has become no different from any other area of life in being exposed to the machinations of the market, and so to accompanying acceleration and proliferation.

Flying in the face of this contemporary urge to speed, Adrian is a procrastinator. Now, that might appear very rude of me, but only if one follows the received usage and implications of the term. However, I take the lead of my intellectual mentor, Zygmunt Bauman, in seeing procrastination in a much more positive light. To quote Bauman at some length:

Cras, in Latin, means 'tomorrow' [...] *Crastinus* is what belongs to tomorrow. To *pro*-crastinate, is to place something among the things that belong to tomorrow. To *place* something there, which implies right away that tomorrow is not that thing's natural place, that the thing in question does not belong there of right [...] 'To procrastinate' means *not* to take things as they come, *not* to act according to a natural succession of things. Contrary to an impression made common in the modern era, procrastination is not a matter of sloth, indolence, quiescence or lassitude; it is an *active* stance, an attempt to assume control over the sequence of events and make that sequence different from what it would be were one to stay docile and unresisting.[1]

Bauman's last sentence is, for me, a good description of a type of critical history that releases meaning from the past.

Such procrastination does not come easily; it is the result of the slow hard look. Again, suggesting someone is slow might appear derogatory given the espousal of acceleration in contemporary life. However, generally things that are produced and consumed quickly also pass quickly. In Adrian's case the obverse is true: those books produced once every ten or so years have an incredible resilience that transcends fleeting trends. Just as slow food can be savoured and returned to, so slow history bears, almost demands, revisiting. *Words and Buildings: A Vocabulary of Modern Architecture* (2000) is not exactly bedside reading in our house, but it certainly could sit on our shelf of well-thumbed recipe books as something to return to time and again.

Then there is the hardness of the slow hard look. Not in the sense of difficult (Adrian's writing is enviously readable and accessible, making the density of his scholarship buoyant), but in terms of the intensity of the critique. To some extent this is a sleight of hand. There is in all the work an underlying theoretical and political thrust, but somehow the depth of the analysis makes the argument appear self-evident and so avoid any ideological impulse. The hardness of the look brings all of us along with it.

Finally there is the look. To look at things might seem to be an essential trait of a historian, but Adrian is especially fastidious in using objects as the source of evidence. Where others attach buildings to genealogies of events and people, or else subsume them to theoretical constructs, Adrian starts with stuff as the source of interpretation. The genealogical or theoretical approach can result in the displacement of architecture into other territories, and with this it is dematerialised. This tends to reduce the potential of history to be accessed by designers, whereas Adrian's looking at stuff reveals lessons that architects can relate to, because that is what the best of them also do. But Adrian's slow hard look is much more than a formally or aesthetically determined act (which is where some architects concentrate, and then leave, their looking). It places the material of architecture within the complex of human and non-human networks, and with it brings the inert to social life. In *Concrete and Culture: A Material History* (2012), concrete, the most apparently dumb and solid of materials, is made lively in all its cultural and political constitutions. He opens the book by saying 'cursory inspection of even the most debased lump of concrete rapidly takes us into a fugacious world of beliefs and counter-beliefs, hopes and fears, longings and loathings'. But his far-from-cursory exegesis then shows us concrete in all its slippery glory, defying classification and becoming the substance of stories.

So, when others or I rush headlong into another transitory project, we need to remember that slow hard look, breathe deeply, and procrastinate.

Note

1   Zygmunt Bauman, *Liquid Modernity*, Polity Press (Cambridge, Massachusetts), 2000, pp 155–6.

CHAPTER 20

Topography, Biography and Architecture

JOE KERR

It's patently obvious to any teacher, if not always to students, that the consequences of a good education are only fully realised after the event; it takes a slow process of synthesis and maturation before a difficult lesson is properly learnt. I knew immediately that the year I spent studying at The Bartlett nearly thirty years ago would prove to be profoundly transformative, but I could not know the extent to which its influence would continue to reverberate throughout my subsequent career. Perhaps the simplest way to illustrate this would be to describe the manner in which it shaped and modified my relationships with the two historians who have cast the longest shadow over my own thoughts and ideas.

I grew up in a house that was bursting with generations of old books, devoted to subjects in which I had little interest; but in among the dusty old tomes on art, music and literature, I was guided by a prescient parent to a handful of architectural texts that became my constant companions in adolescence. I'm certain that two of these books in particular were responsible for stimulating a youthful curiosity to the extent that it grew into my governing passion. There's no surprise in the texts that I was weaned on, for they would have been staples in many postwar British households: in my case a tattered Pelican copy of Nikolaus Pevsner's *Outline of European Architecture* (first

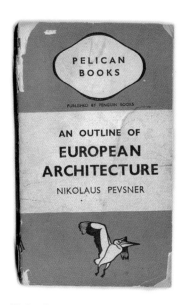

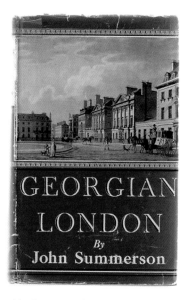

Nikolaus Pevsner, *An Outline of European Architecture*, Penguin (Harmondsworth), 1942.

John Summerson, *Georgian London*, Pleiades Books (London), 1945.

published in 1942) and a pristine hardback edition of Sir John Summerson's *Georgian London* (first published in 1945).[1]

Of the two, it was undoubtedly Pevsner who exerted the most powerful early influence; for whilst I poured over the thick wad of images sandwiched in the middle of Summerson, the text seemed as dense and unleavened as its subject matter, and its restrained and equivocal tone offered little guidance to an unformed mind eager for authoritative opinions. Pevsner, on the other hand, fired a youthful imagination with all the fervour and righteousness of the modernist manifestos of his German youth. The finality of his pronouncements made it a simple matter to adopt them, and I became a wholehearted disciple, embracing uncritically the (in)famous first line that 'A bicycle shed is a building; Lincoln Cathedral is a piece of architecture'[2] and absorbing without question that the Victorians had achieved extraordinary things, but that hereafter things had gone rather badly. Today it's merely amusing to quote the assertion that 'For the next forty years, the first forty of our century, no English name need here be mentioned', but I shudder to think what damage such a proposition had on my intellectual development.³ However, while the *Outline* may have laid the foundation for my personal Pevsnerian cult, it was the well-thumbed volumes of his *Buildings of England* that sealed my love affair. Browsing over the browning pages of *London Volume 2: Except the Cities of London and Westminster* (1952) offered to the imagination an exotic world of great soot-stained railway termini from the age of mechanical engineering and of visionary housing schemes in a new era of social engineering.

The marvel of these guides is that they offered judgements rather than opinions. My favourite instance of his scathing criticism comes in the very first volume, an extremely slim guide to Middlesex, a suburban realm that must have confounded this émigré apologist for the Modern Movement:

> Wood Green. The Inventory of the Royal Commission says: 'No Monuments Known', and there is indeed nothing in the borough worth more than a cursory glance.⁴

Thus it was that I entered the MSc in the History of Modern Architecture, complete with an autodidact's prejudices and misconceptions; however, that was all about to change. The principal effect of Adrian Forty's teaching on me was to force my prior accumulation of partial and haphazard knowledge and opinion through the filter of a rigorous methodological approach, and to compel me to subject all that I thought I knew to a painful critical evaluation. The first victim of this intellectual culling was my dearly loved mentor Nikolaus Pevsner, whose Hegelian failings were cruelly exposed to my acute embarrassment. His great survey of Western architecture,⁵ which had previously held the status of scripture, was now reduced to an obsolete artefact of purely historical interest.

The greater shock however was to learn that my other adolescent companion was held in the highest esteem at The Bartlett. It was revelatory to discover how this grand old man of the establishment had pioneered – at least in a British context – a heavily Marxist-inflected reading of architectural history, albeit with no reference to its ideological underpinning, written as it was at the height of the Second World War. While in retrospect Summerson's own application of his highly constructionist historical method seems crude and dated, nonetheless as I now re-read his oft-quoted line on the first page of Chapter 1, that 'The story is made up of topography, biography, and architecture, and I shall try and weave these three together', I am instantly transported back to the seminar in which this revelatory statement was discussed and interpreted.[6]

Shortly afterwards my small class of perhaps half a dozen students were taken on a visit to Sir John Soane's Museum, also a favourite haunt since childhood, and were given a class by the great man himself. I confess to being so overawed that I only briefly conversed with Summerson, but I vividly remember him pulling Robert Adam (1728–1792) drawings from drawers, and displaying for us presentation drawings of Soane's (1753–1837) major buildings by Joseph Michael Gandy (1771–1843) and other pupils.

But the lesson that cemented itself into my imagination was the delightful conceit employed by Summerson to frame the whole narrative of *Georgian London*, a device described in the opening chapter 'Air-View', in which he invites the reader 'to imagine yourself suspended a mile above London; and to imagine yourself staying up there for a period of time proportional to two centuries, with the years speeding past at one a second ... The life of a city, condensed so, would be dramatic. It would give the same startling impression of automatic movement, of mindless growth. For a town, like a plant or an ant-hill, is a product of a collective, unconscious will, and only to a very small extent of formulated intention.'[7] This brilliant passage draws on the established technique of time-lapse photography, but synthesises it with the then emerging technology of aerial reconnaissance (and also of course with a materialist imperative), hence ironically presenting to the reader much the same viewpoint of London as the Luftwaffe pilots whose destructive raids had in part impelled him to write the book.

But most significantly, with this device Summerson created a robust enough frame to encompass both the general development of a city and simultaneously a consideration of its major monuments, and to develop his thesis that 'Taste and wealth – these are the two basic things in Georgian London.'[8] While we may take issue with this simple binary, the simplicity and elegance of the method continues to impress. Hence when nearly two decades later I had my own chance to contribute to the vast corpus of literature on London,[9] I was happy not only to acknowledge a long-standing debt, but also to add a contemporary dimension to this historically specific method. I once again invited the reader to suspend themselves above London, albeit merely for a 25-year span.[10] However I then addressed a major limitation in Summerson's method when applied to the contemporary city; 'because London's significant growth is no longer significantly outwards, but upwards and even downwards as well, making it difficult to read from the air alone. Instead, we might usefully update his visual device by thinking in terms of a cross-section across the city, cutting above and below ground level to reveal the true scale of development that has taken place across the metropolis.'[11]

Further, and in light of the profound theoretical transformations that have shaped our contemporary urban understanding, I argued that 'in truth our privileged vantage point has merely indicated the general contours of change, and has placed us at too great a distance to focus on the individual lives of any of London's multitude of citizens. Yet, ultimately, it is the minuscule shifts and adjustments in daily experience that should matter most to us. In reality it is the view from the pavement rather than from far above it that is most revealing about the ways in which the city is actually changing.'[12] By adding these extra triangulations, I hope that I breathed new life into an old but still-seductive narrative device.

Thus it was that lessons learnt at The Bartlett have continued to reverberate throughout my subsequent career, not in this case by imposing new knowledge, but instead by intervening in my pre-existing relationship with two great architectural historians, and by equipping me with the necessary critical tools to learn from their work anew. Having paid homage to Summerson, I have a suspicion that I will attempt something similar with Pevsner in the future. But right now, I'm grateful for this opportunity to record the debt I owe to the tutor who set me on the path that I have followed ever since.

Notes

1   First published as: Nikolaus Pevsner, *An Outline of European Architecture*, Penguin (Harmondsworth), 1942; John Summerson, *Georgian London*, Pleiades Books (London), 1945. I can't say exactly which editions I originally encountered, as rather carelessly I can no longer lay my hands on them.

2   Nikolaus Pevsner, *An Outline of European Architecture*, Penguin (London), sixth jubilee edition, 1960, p 15.

3   Ibid, p 394. It is not surprising, but in retrospect perhaps a little depressing, that the *Outline* was still on my

required reading list as an Art History undergraduate nearly 40 years after it first appeared.

4   Nikolaus Pevsner, *The Buildings of England: Middlesex*, Penguin (Harmondsworth), 1951, p 174. The individual buildings in the area fare little better, for instance Alexandra Palace is described on the following page as 'one of the most extensive and most prominently placed of London buildings; there is not much else to be said about it'.

5   The title *An Outline of European Architecture* is misleading, given the attention paid to America, particularly in the later revised editions.

6   John Summerson, *Georgian London,* Penguin (Harmondsworth), Peregrine Edition, 1978, p 17. I have specifically referenced this revised edition as it has my name inscribed in the front, with the date of my first month at The Bartlett; not only that, but the words 'topography, biography, and architecture' have been faintly underlined, no doubt in preparation for that very seminar.

7   Ibid, pp 17–18.

8   Ibid, p 26.

9   Joe Kerr and Andrew Gibson (eds), *London From Punk to Blair*, Reaktion (London), 2003.

10 Joe Kerr and Andrew Gibson (eds), *London From Punk to Blair*, Reaktion (London), 2nd edition, 2012, p 23.

11 Ibid, p 25.

12 Ibid, p 27.

CHAPTER 21

Of Character and Concrete: The Historian's Material

JOHN MACARTHUR

'Are sullen lumps of concrete, steel and glass animated by the words we shower on them?' asks Adrian Forty in the first lines of *Words and Buildings: A Vocabulary of Modern Architecture* (2000). It is a question comprehensively answered in that book and substantiated in Forty's recent *Concrete and Culture: A Material History* (2012). Few would now agree with the alternative Forty posits: 'Or does every word spoken or written about it diminish a work of architecture and deprive it of a part of its being?'[1] *Words and Buildings* overcomes the fallacy of this too-easy opposition. The equivocations of architectural concepts are not some simple inadequacy of language, but are historical phenomena that are often longer lived than structures of masonry or metal. Forty would probably not choose to say that the pages of *Concrete and Culture* 'animate' concrete, but how can we describe the action of a historian on their 'material', particularly when that material includes not only beliefs about the stuff of building, but also abstract concepts such as 'character'?

Architects work not only with construction materials but also types, concepts and codified values of the kind described in *Words and Buildings* – an architect without brief or site can still be working on 'flexibility' or 'structure'. *Concrete and Culture* explains that to work in concrete is to work with ideas – that concrete has a history and identification with national building traditions, or, indeed, the contrary belief that concrete is the first truly modern material, free of history and locale. This sense of the word 'material' when arranged with 'technique' and 'content' is a way to understand the mediums that distinguish the different art disciplines.[2] The material of an artist is not only 'stuff', but also a proper understanding of how it defines the artist and the art discipline. What sculptors formed, their proper 'content' or substance, was, for a long time past, the human figure made by carving stone, or moulding and then casting in bronze. Gianlorenzo Bernini's (1598–1680) skill in carving and finishing marble to appear as flesh or cloth, would be mere unthinking technique (indeed something less than technique) if at the moment of cutting the stone he were not also making present the millennial task of sculpture as a whole in producing its privileged subject or content, the human form. Architectural theory in the last century was dominated by attempts to make 'space' the privileged content formed by architecture, and to argue this in part from the affinity of framed structures in reinforced concrete with modern ideas of space. An architect's use of sequential spatial planning techniques such as the architectural promenade, or to take a more ubiquitous case, putting windows in the corners of rooms, shows a grasp of the potentiality of the concrete frame, and hence, a contribution to the mastery of architecture's proper content – 'space'.

History complicates this schema. One definition of art lies in its attributes as a certain kind of transcendence. What does it mean to appreciate the art of the past; to make it live alongside our art at the same time as we understand that we are cut off from it by the differing beliefs and aspirations of past societies? 'Character' is such a historical concept.[3] It once named a significant part of the content of architecture but now we can only understand it as what was once thought. Forty's 'vocabulary of modern architecture' follows an etymological method, spending a great many pages in the periods preceding modern architecture, and thus risks becoming a kind of antiquarianism. While Forty shows that 'character' continues through the 20th century as a debating point, particularly around the relative values of understanding architecture as rhetoric or sensory experience, 'character' does this as a historical remnant, as a term, the origins of which are forgotten while still demanding to be accounted for.

Bound up in 18th-century theory, 'character' – and a linked word, 'decorum' – described something like the mood or grace with which a building's purpose was expressed, and the appropriateness of such an expression to a place and a time.[4] If we seek to understand as well as to appreciate the buildings of an architect such as John Soane (1753–1837), then we need scholars such as Forty to rebuild 'character' for us.[5] Only then can we understand what Soane was striving to form as he worked the given material of his day, the classical orders and their implied relation of geometry and the body. Our sensory experience of the house and museum at Lincoln's Inn Fields might be the same as that of people of Soane's day, but it would be anachronistic to name the contents of Soane's architecture, the stuff on which he worked, as 'space' rather than 'character'. This is not to say that such anachronism is not productive, and even a principal task of architectural history. Wölfflin thought of style in something like this way, the possibility of having feelings in common with the people of the past despite no real knowledge of their beliefs and aspirations.[6] Knowing the concept of 'character' is, at a mundane level, no different from knowing of Soane's thwarted aspirations for his sons' architectural education. For us, these matters are historical context to a presently available experience, while for Soane, they were intrinsic. Put the other way around, we can only have a history of architecture, separated from a history of everything, by this ability to see an ongoing project of forms and affects riding over a succession of 'contents'.

One can read this historicity of contents through *Words and Buildings*. 'Character' and 'history' are the words most obviously past; these are keywords of the 18th and 19th centuries mortified in modernist discourse. 'Function' and 'truth' belong with modernism but are 'historical' by the end of the 20th century. 'Type' and 'context' had a big run in the later 20th century (and carried the corpse of 'character' along with them), but are looking quite sick today with the failure of another big word, 'urbanism'. 'Space' and 'form' are still going strong. Despite the historical research into the invention of the concept of space in the late 19th century, and the delirium about autogenic form coming out of parametric design, it is quite difficult to think of such terms from the outside, to see how they function in the way that we can understand how 'history' did in 19th-century discourse. The role of the historian then is a complex one. Telling us what we do not know about the old architecture we value can help us imagine a similar distance from the architecture in which we are entangled by our present interests and beliefs.

Now, materials also have a history. As Forty shows, this is a matter not only of breakthroughs in chemistry and engineering calculation, but of national pride, economic necessity and aesthetic matters: explorations of aggregate colour and the patterns of shuttering, of feeling for lumpenness or precision. Forty writes that it is more useful to think of concrete as a medium than as a material, and I agree, but I am interested in the relation between concrete as Forty presents it and the 'words' of the earlier book. Concrete is at one level just like 'character'. It is what the discipline of architecture conceptualises as a proper substance to be formed in a certain historical period, it is a content in the sense that we say that the content of a letter is its significance or import. But at the same time, concrete is a 'material' in the sense that it is the stuff that architects form, each of them recognising and exploiting its varied properties, and it is recognising this twin-level relationship that seems to me important. What concrete is for architecture is both the fine finishes, sharp arrises, and structural redundancy of Tadao Ando's (1941–) concrete, and the high engineering but crude finishing of Vilanova Artigas (1915–1985).[7] At the same time, the work of these and other architects of import assumes a pre-existing ideational status of concrete. A priori, concrete is more than a means to achieve form as it guarantees that what is formed by an architect of merit will have significance beyond the completed building. This aesthetic theory of the relation of making buildings to architecture as a discipline also has a historical dimension. We could argue that what is wrong with putting classical columns and entablatures on buildings today is not only that the concepts of character and decorum are not cognate with present architectural discourse, but that to do so would deny that architecture had a history in any meaningful sense. If the phases of architecture build one on another in such a way that they can be described historically, then this history lies in the intersection of social and technological history with a succession of contents and materials that are proper to architecture. We still love Soane, just as we listen to the music of Beethoven, and if, as I have argued, it is a mis-statement of our own historical position to repeat these old forms, then is it mere nostalgia to still be affected by them?

Forty shows us that this is not the case; his materials are architectural as much as historical. Modern architecture is made of character as much as of concrete. Old concepts and old forms are the sedimented material from which modern forms are made. When we experience the light airy classicism of Soane, the way in which columns and entablature seem to become surfaces and frames to volumes, what we experience at a sensory level is also a historical matter. It is not that historical distance has allowed us to see through the confused terms of Soane's day, but rather that Soane's grappling to form the classical elements around concepts of character, makes a kind of substance that will go on to be available to and valued by later architects. What makes architectural history of more than antiquarian interest is the way in which old concepts become the given materials of a subsequent moment. Forty shows us that the past is not a mine of forms and materials available for our exploitation. Rather, history presents us with materials, and an architecture of substance is one that understands this obligation.

Notes

1   Adrian Forty, *Concrete and Culture: A Material History*, Reaktion (London), 2012.

2   I hope that I can assume a degree of common sense and familiarity in my usage of these terms, although I am drawing rather freely and loosely on the aesthetic theory of Theodor Adorno. At one level this is an odd thing to do, as Forty's generous character as an author and clarity of expression contrast sharply with Adorno's magisterial persona and rebarbative prose. While Forty does refer to Adorno on issues of nature and memory (see Adrian Forty, *Words and Buildings: A Vocabulary of Modern Architecture*, Thames & Hudson (London), 2000, p 238, and *Concrete and Culture*, p 200), this essay does not argue some general relation between their thought. It is rather my attempt to open questions of how the aesthetic experience of architecture and the making of architecture relate historically. See: Theodor W Adorno, *Aesthetic Theory*, University of Minnesota Press (Minneapolis, Minnesota), 1997. I have also referred to: Lambert Zuidervaart, *Adorno's Aesthetic Theory: The Redemption of Illusion*, The MIT Press (Cambridge, Massachusetts), 1991; Shierry Weber Nicholsen, *Exact Imagination, Late Work: On Adorno's Aesthetics*, The MIT Press (Cambridge, Massachusetts), 1997.

3   Forty, *Words and Buildings*, pp 120–30.

4   Ibid, pp 120-30; and Peter Kohane and Michael Hill, 'The Eclipse of a Commonplace Idea: Decorum in Architectural Theory', *Architectural Research Quarterly*, Vol 5, No 1, 2001, pp 63–77.

5   Forty, *Words and Buildings*, pp 126–7.

6   Heinrich Wölfflin, *Principles of Art History: The Problem of the Development of Style in Later Art*, translated by MD Hottinger, Dover (New York), 1950. Frederic J Schwartz, 'Cathedrals and Shoes: Concepts of Style in Wölfflin and Adorno', *New German Critique*, No 76, 1999, pp 3–48.

7   Forty, *Concrete and Culture*, pp 126–31.

CHAPTER 22
Spectres of Marx in City X

JONATHAN CHARLEY

Apart from his investigations into fixed capital, rent theory and the urban transformation of 19th-century Paris, Karl Marx (1818–1883) wrote very little directly about architecture and the built environment. His collaborator Friedrich Engels (1820–1895) wrote considerably more. But even

"*Believe it or not Comrades, it was here in a bar on La Grand-Place that I wrote a draft of the Communist Manifesto. Capital wanted a city built in its own image, and I can think of no better example than here, resplendent as it is with Town Hall, Law Court and the Guild Houses of merchants and Master craftsmen, an ebullient display of gilted confectionary, a mere stone's throw away from utter penury and misery.*"

Marx in Brussels.

"I sometimes like to sit in the graveyards of the bourgeoisie amongst the pretentious monuments dedicated to bandit merchants, plantation owners and capitalists. It reminds that their vanity and lust for glory does not end with their death. It is also from up here that I can contemplate the immense landscape of commodity forms that make up this city, and how easily the social relations between human beings assume, in our minds, the fantastic form of a relation between things."

Marx in Glasgow.

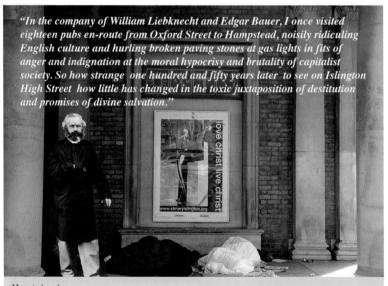

"In the company of William Liebknecht and Edgar Bauer, I once visited eighteen pubs en-route from Oxford Street to Hampstead, noisily ridiculing English culture and hurling broken paving stones at gas lights in fits of anger and indignation at the moral hypocrisy and brutality of capitalist society. So how strange one hundred and fifty years later to see on Islington High Street how little has changed in the toxic juxtaposition of destitution and promises of divine salvation."

Marx in London.

156

"*The capitalist city boasts architectural and urban wonders that can match the achievements of the Egyptians, Romans and medieval Kings. Its mirror reflection however displays a history of violent destruction and deeply engrained patterns of social and spatial inequality. It is why I laugh at the absurd contemporary fondness for the word sustainability, for the real history of capitalist society and its cities, is that of the constant revolutionising of production, the uninterrupted disturbance of all social conditions, and everlasting uncertainty and agitation.*"

Marx in Marseilles.

when taken together they didn't write a lot. So it is ironic and telling that their writings have proved to be such an inspiration to some of the 20th century's most profound thinkers on urban matters who have collectively changed the way we think about the city.[1] What follows are five short journeys in the company of Marx into a fictitious city – City X.

COMMODITY

> The wealth of societies in which the capitalist mode of production prevails appears as 'an immense collection of commodities' [...] Initially the commodity appeared to us as an object with a dual character, possessing both use-value and exchange value.[2]

When stripped of its poetic narratives and spectacular urban gestures, City X emerges as an extensive landscape for capital accumulation, in which the political history of the built environment can be read through the scars of a three-hundred-year battle to seize control of the shifting dialectic of its commodity

157

forms. On one side of the conflict stand militant brigades. They build barricades, turn palaces into libraries, and churches into workers' clubs. They passionately defend collective rights to the city, the principles of democratic planning, and prioritise the *social use value* of buildings. At particular historical moments they have challenged the whole basis of capitalist building production and even mounted full-scale urban social revolutions. Assembled opposite are heavily armed disciples of laissez faire. They are ready to fight to the death to defend an ideology of economic self-interest, private property and free markets. Their priority is to maximise the *exchange value* of built commodities, even if the pursuit of profit requires the subordination of a building's social worth and environmental performance. It is the latter economic regime flying under the banner of neoliberalism that currently governs City X. As a consequence, large swathes of the population have denounced the enlightenment and returned to a belief in magic. It is understandable, for how else are citizens able to explain the insane commercial logic that measures quality in quantitative terms, and stamps a price tag on every fragment of the city, from pediment to pavement, window to wall, and home to hovel? No longer a literary or philosophical dystopia, in City X the total commodification of everyday life verges on becoming a reality.

LABOUR

> The labour process [...] is the universal condition for the metabolic interaction between man and nature, the everlasting nature-imposed condition of human existence.[3]

In response to the collapse of reason, a clandestine manifesto is hastily printed. It tells the citizenry that buildings are not the result of a sorcerer's spells, but of the common expenditure of human labour in both its particular purposeful and abstract physiological senses.[4] It is their own labour, then, that provides the fantastic forms of buildings and settlements with meaning, equivalence and distinctiveness. From classical antiquity onwards, the history of City X is thus revealed not only as a history of object forms, but as a history of changing methods of production. It is in fact a city that has been forged under the whip hand of the overseer, the priest and the capitalist by the collective labour of slaves, serfs and wage-workers. It is a history that tells of an epic struggle between the domination of workers within the construction labour process, their quest for freedom from exploitation, for control over the means of production, and for the opportunity to realise their full creative potential. But this is a story that is seldom recalled or understood. Instead, the ideological inversion of the city's real history persists in the minds of its citizens so that despite the fact that the multi-layered history of the labour process is embedded in every urban block, the city stands before them not as product of their labour and of the accumulated knowledge of thousands of years, but as a fetishised and alienated thing.[5]

TECHNOLOGY

> Here we have, in place of the isolated machine, a mechanical monster whose body fills whole factories, and whose demonic power, at first hidden by the slow and measured motions of its gigantic members, finally bursts forth in the fast and feverish whirl of its countless working organs.[6]

At the dawn of capitalism the building sites and workshops of City X still operated on the basis of measure and value, and echoed with the sound of chisel on stone, axe on wood and the voices of master craftsmen and journeymen. But it was an ancient world that was soon to be swept away by the advent of competitive tendering and the arrival of capitalist contractors and proletarian armies. Urban construction exploded, and City X began to pulsate with the clang of steam-driven machines that could dig, plane and manufacture components. Then came pile drivers, cranes and assembly lines that churned out brick and concrete, while thundering on the periphery were furnaces and rollers that turned the bowels of the earth into sheets of shining steel and glass. But still this was not productive enough, and the factories of City X were streamlined with the sleek automated systems of advanced machine production that threatened to expel living labour altogether. Meanwhile, on site, the slopping shimmer of trowels was all but drowned out by the wrenching of spanners and rivet guns. At long last the prefabrication of buildings clipped together with the same efficiency as cars and aircraft seemed a real possibility. Some even imagined a future in which energy would be free and heavy labour would become a distant memory. It was tragically naive. For technological innovation in capitalist economies is not so much driven by ideas of equitable social progress as it is by the economic competition between rival capitalists to maintain the rate of profit and dominate the market. If to this story of rapacious inventions that pump every last drop of surplus from workers we were to add a chapter on how military technology has merged with urban management systems to track and monitor the movements and behaviour of citizens, it is small wonder that the population of City X is haunted by images of intelligent machines which will one day extinguish life as we know it.[7]

CAPITAL

> The bourgeoisie has disclosed how it came to pass that the brutal display of vigour in the Middle Ages, which reactionists so much admire, found its fitting complement in the most slothful indolence. It has been the first to show what man's activity can bring about. It has accomplished wonders far surpassing Egyptian pyramids, Roman aqueducts, and Gothic cathedrals; it has conducted expeditions that put in the shade all former Exoduses of nations and crusades.[8]

Relentless acts of enclosure, clearances and privatisations have slowly transformed the concept of the common ownership of land into a fantasy, while talk of participation in the decision-making process provides sour comfort for a citizenry who have little say in what gets built and where. But this should come as no surprise; after all, the ruling ideas in any epoch tend to be those of the ruling class, and that goes for architecture as well.[9] There are traces of heterotopias, rival ideologies and other ways of making buildings, but they struggle to be remembered in a city that for centuries has tirelessly devoted itself to the worship of God, Dikē and Mammon. Capital demanded a city to be built in its own image, and so it was. The resources of the earth were mobilised and decimated, and whole continents were reassembled with imperial violence. Simultaneously an extraordinary civic construction project was put in motion to provide all the institutions necessary; to educate and discipline mind, body and soul; to produce and exchange commodities; to lubricate the circulation of money; and to provide everything with legal right. Little has changed in terms of the architectural dimensions of political power and capital accumulation except for the forms that are used to claim mastery over history. If once the citizenry knelt in front of the Stock Exchange, Law Court and City Hall, now they pay homage to the headquarters of finance capital and pay with their lives to enter gargantuan retail mausolea.

CRISIS

> From time to time the conflict of antagonistic agencies finds vent in crises. The crises are always but momentary and forcible solutions of the existing contradictions. They are violent eruptions which for a time restore the disturbed equilibrium.[10]

Amid the ruins and relics of speculative bubbles, the peddlers of the bourgeois utopia pound the pavements of City X, selling the idea that capitalism is the eternal and most natural form of economy, and that sustainability and managed equilibrium is achievable. It is a beguiling proposition, but one that bears no resemblance to the empirical evidence of economic history. This suggests another reality, that crises of whatever complexion – political, economic or social – are not aberrations or exceptions, but the rule. In parallel to the history of City X as a triumphant tale of uninterrupted progress is a history dominated by patterns of uneven development, ingrained socio-spatial inequality, cycles of boom and slump, overproduction, environmental degradation, designed obsolescence and the periodic destruction of technology. It is a history in which rents soar to giddy heights in towers and monuments of glass, steel and concrete which moments later lie abandoned. It is a history of ceaseless waves of creative destruction that lap the foundations of every street and building, threaten communities and annihilate bonds of solidarity. City X doesn't sing anymore, it groans and spasmodically expands and contracts like a sick panting beast that has gorged for too long on indigestible myths.

Notes

1   The list is extraordinary and includes authors such as Henri Lefebvre, Manuel Castells, Mike Davis, David Harvey,

Edward Soja and Fredric Jameson.

2   For Marx's analysis of the dual aspects of the commodity form see, Karl Marx, *Capital Volume I*, Penguin (London), 1976, pp 125–31.

3   Ibid, p 290.

4   For Marx's analysis of the dual aspects of *labour* that mimics that of the commodity, see ibid, pp 131–7.

5   In short, 'a definite social relation between men that assumes, in their eyes, the fantastic form of a relationship between things': ibid, p 165.

6   Ibid, p 503.

7   Marx suggested that it would be possible to write a history of the inventions since 1830, as a series of technological innovations whose sole purpose appeared to be to supply 'capital with weapons against the working class'! Ibid, p 563.

8   Karl Marx and Friedrich Engels, *The Communist Manifesto*, Penguin (London), 2002, p 222.

9   Karl Marx and Friedrich Engels, *The German Ideology*, Lawrence & Wishart (London), 1985, p 64: 'The ideas of the ruling class are in every epoch the ruling ideas, i.e. the class which is the ruling material force of society, is at the same time its ruling intellectual force. The class which has the means of material production at its disposal, has control at the same time over the means of mental production, so that thereby, generally speaking, the ideas of those who lack the means of mental production are subject to it.'

10 Karl Marx, *Capital Volume III*, Progress Publishers (Moscow), 1984, p 249.

CHAPTER 23
History by Design
JONATHAN HILL

The command of drawing – not building – established the architect's status. The term 'design' derives from *disegno*, meaning drawing, which associated the visual arts – architecture, painting and sculpture – with the realm of ideas. In the new division of labour, architects acquired complementary means to practise architecture that were as important as building, namely drawing and writing, creating an interdependent, multidirectional web of influences that stimulated architects' future development. To affirm their new status, architects began to theorise architecture both for themselves and for their patrons, ensuring that the authored book became more valuable to architects than to painters and sculptors, whose status was more secure and means to acquire commissions less demanding. In contrast to the architectural drawing, which is seen in relation to other drawings and a building, the painting is unique and need not refer to an external object, thus appearing further removed from the material world and closer to that of ideas.

Leon Battista Alberti's *De re aedificatoria* [Ten Books on Architecture], *c* 1450, was the first thorough investigation of the Renaissance architect. Francesco Colonna's *Hypnerotomachia Poliphili*, 1499, was the second architectural book by a living writer published in the Renaissance and the first to be printed with illustrations, establishing the multimedia interdependence of text and image that has been essential to architectural books ever since. One model for the architectural book, *Hypnerotomachia Poliphili* is a fictional narrative illustrated with pictorial images in which love is lost and won among monuments and ruins in a sylvan landscape. A second model is the analytical manifesto illustrated with orthogonal drawings, such as Andrea Palladio's *I quattro libri dell'archittetura* [The Four Books of Architecture], 1570. The relationship between history and design was central to Colonna and Palladio, but their historical references have different purposes. In one book they enrich a specific story, in the other they legitimise generic solutions. A further literary model, the manual conveys practical knowledge and is illustrated with diagrams. But these models are not hermetic and many architectural books refer to more than one, as is the case in Palladio's attention to practical matters.

FACTUAL HISTORIES

Describing actual events and others of his invention, Giorgio Vasari's *Le vite de' più eccellenti pittori, scultori e architettori* [The Lives of the Most Eminent Painters, Sculptors and Architects], 1550, was the first significant history of art and architecture. In the 16th century, history's purpose was to offer useful lessons; accuracy was not necessary. In subsequent centuries, empiricism gave greater emphasis to the distinction between fact and fiction, which came to transform history. Rather than Vasari's focus on individual achievements, historians employed a comparative method to characterise changing cultural, social and economic processes in which specific protagonists were contextualised. By the 19th century, the art and architectural historian was established as a distinct practitioner and history was assumed to be objective. Science is supported in its claim to objectivity by the presence of its objects of study before the scientist. No archive, however complete, can return the historian to the past and no history is more than an interpretation. Any history expresses a particular ideology, as does any scientific statement. Whether implicit or explicit, a critique of the present and prospect of the future are evident in both.

FACTUAL FICTIONS

In valuing direct experience, precise description and a sceptical approach to 'facts', empiricism also created a fruitful climate in which the everyday realism of a new literary genre – the novel – could prosper as 'factual fictions'.[1] In contrast to the earlier romance, the novel concentrated on contemporary society and the individualism it professed. The uncertainties of identity were ripe for narrative account. Notably, Daniel Defoe's *Robinson Crusoe*, 1719, which is often described as the first English novel, is a fictional autobiography.

The early novels – fictional autobiographies – developed in parallel with early diaries – autobiographical fictions. People have written about themselves for millennia but the formation of modern identity is associated with a type of writing that Michel Foucault describes as a 'technology of the self'.[2] As Paul de Man remarks: 'We assume that life *produces* the autobiography as an act produces its consequences, but can we not suggest, with equal justice, that the autobiographical project may itself produce and determine the life and that whatever the writer *does* is in fact governed by the technical demands of self-portraiture and thus determined, in all its aspects, by the resources of his medium?'[3] Equivalent to a visual and spatial diary, the process of design – from one drawing to the next and from one project to another – is itself a fictional autobiography, a 'technology of the self', even when a number of collaborators are involved, formulating a design ethos for an individual or an office.

DESIGN HISTORIES

From the Renaissance to the early 20th century the architect was a historian in the sense that a treatise combined design and history, and a building was expected to manifest the character of the time and knowingly refer to earlier eras. Modernism ruptured this system in principle if not always in practice, but it returned with vigour in the mid-20th century.

Architects have used history in different ways, whether to indicate their continuity with the past or departure from it. Even early modernists who denied the relevance of the past relied on histories to justify modernism's evolution. To some degree, mid-20th-century architects merely reaffirmed an appreciation of history that was latent in a work such as Le Corbusier's *Vers une architecture* (Towards an Architecture), 1923. But the Second World War was more technological than the First, and atomic devastation undermined confidence in technological progress, which early modernism had emphasised as a means of social transformation. Modernism's previously dismissive reaction to cultural memories was itself anachronistic. The consequence was not just to acknowledge modernism's classical heritage but also to place a concern for history at the heart of architecture once again.

To explain his conception of a building in dialogue with its surroundings and contributing to an evolving historical continuity, Ernesto N Rogers quoted from TS Eliot's 'Tradition and the Individual Talent', 1917, in which Eliot emphasises that the present alters our understanding of the past as much as the past influences the present.[4] Equally indebted to Eliot, Denys Lasdun noted the value that he placed on innovation as well as tradition: 'The existing monuments form an ideal order among themselves, which is modified by the introduction of the new (the really new) work of art among them.'[5] Confirming the prevalence of such ideas, Vincent Scully concluded that the architect will 'always be dealing with historical problems – with the past and, a function of the past, with the future. So the architect should be regarded as a kind of physical historian'.[6] A reinterpretation of the past in the present, transforming them both to some degree, each building is a new history. The architect is a historian twice over: as an author and as a designer.

CREATIVE MYTHS

Histories and novels both need to be convincing but in different ways. Although no history is completely objective, to have any validity it must appear truthful to the past. A novel may be believable but not true. But recognising the overlaps between two literary genres, Malcolm Bradbury notably describes his novel *The History Man*, 1975, as 'a total invention with delusory approximations to historical reality, just as is history itself'.[7]

Associating designs with histories and stories, Lasdun remarked that each architect must devise his or her 'own creative myth', which should be 'sufficiently objective' and also have 'an element of subjectivity; the myth must be partly an expression of the architect's personality and partly of his time, partly a distillation of permanent truths and partly of the ephemerae of the particular moment'.[8] The 'creative myth' may be a private inspiration or a public narrative that is disseminated widely, either to architects, or to users, or to societies. Lasdun concluded: 'My own myth [...] engages with history'.[9]

As a design is equivalent to a history, we may expect the designer as well as the historian 'to have a certain quality of *subjectivity*' that is 'suited to the objectivity proper to history', as Paul Ricoeur concludes.[10] But the designer does not usually construct a history with the rigour expected of a historian, and we expect the designer to display other qualities of subjectivity as well. A design is also equivalent to a novel, convincing the user to suspend disbelief. Part-novelist, part-historian, the architect is 'the history man'. We expect a history or a novel to be written in words, but they can also be cast in concrete. An architectural book can be a history and a novel, and so can a building.

While a prospect of the future is implicit in many histories and novels, it is explicit in a design, which is always set in the future and imagined before it is built. The most creative architects have always looked to the past to imagine a future, studying an earlier architecture not to replicate it but to understand and transform it, revealing its relevance to the present and future. Twenty-first-century architects should appreciate the shock of the old as well as the shock of the new.

Notes

1   Lennard J Davis, *Factual Fictions: The Origins of the English Novel*, University of Pennsylvania Press (Philadelphia), 1996, p 213.

2   Michel Foucault, 'On the Genealogy of Ethics: An Overview of Work in Progress', in Paul Rabinow (ed), *The Foucault Reader*, Random House (London), 1984, p 369.

3   Paul de Man, *The Rhetoric of Romanticism*, Columbia University Press (New York), 1984, p 69.

4   Ernesto N Rogers, 'Continuità', *Casabella Continuità*, December 1953–January 1954, p 2.

5   TS Eliot, 'Tradition and the Individual Talent', in *Points of View*, Faber & Faber (London), 1941, pp 26–7, filed in Lasdun archive, RIBA Library Drawings and Archives Collections, Victoria & Albert Museum, London.

6   Vincent Scully, *American Architecture and Urbanism*, Thames & Hudson (London), 1969, p 257.

7   Malcolm Bradbury, 'Author's Note', in *The History Man*, Secker & Warburg (London), 1975.

8   Denys Lasdun, 'The Architecture of Urban Landscape', in Denys Lasdun (ed), *Architecture in an Age of Scepticism: A Practitioner's Anthology*, Heinemann (London), 1984, p 137.

9   Ibid, p 139.

10 Paul Ricoeur, 'Objectivity and Subjectivity in History', in *History and Truth*, translated by Charles A Kelbley, Northwestern University Press (Evanston, Illinois), 1965, p 22.

CHAPTER 24

Angel Place: A Way In to Dickens's London

KESTER RATTENBURY

On the sixth day of May 1857, Charles Dickens went back to the Marshalsea, the debtors' prison where his improvident father had been locked up for three months in 1824. He was a few days away from finishing his latest novel, *Little Dorrit*, which is principally set in, and entirely structured around, this prison – indeed, all but the last episodes had already been published. But he had not revisited the prison while he was writing. In fact, he had not been back to the Marshalsea at all in those thirty-odd years. Given that he was one of the most famously wide-walking Londoners ever, and that one of the quickest ways to Rochester (where he was just buying his childhood dream home, Gads Hill) would have been straight past the front gate, this suggests that he – like his released prisoner, William Dorrit – had taken pains to avoid it.

This, however, was the time to confront his ghosts. In his Preface (originally an Afterword to the last instalment in 1857) Dickens describes his visit to 'the outer front courtyard, often mentioned in this story, metamorphosed into a butter-shop', and yet, further on, he notes that the visitor to Marshalsea Place 'will look upon the rooms in which the debtors lived; and will stand among the crowding ghosts of many miserable years'.[1]

To start with, I found *Little Dorrit* behaved rather like the butter shop.

There it stood, right where you might expect to find an entrance to the apogee of writer-place. Dickens's London is surely the most potent of all literary versions of a world city, surely the one where the novels and the real social history have fused fast into working, living, experience. And it is surely the one where different kinds of writing – fiction, journalism, social and speculative histories – lie most tightly packed together. Surely this book would open some fissure into this immensely real and successful world. And yet, like the butter shop, *Little Dorrit* seemed to be blocking my way in.

The power of Dickens's London can be disconcerting. Vladimir Nabokov, Peter Ackroyd and John Sutherland have all pounded through his tempestuous metaphors, his swirling polemic structures of fog and water, dust and mud: the great scenery which Dickens hammers into place around his famous stories. But that quality of over-the-top, bravura performance also seemed like a theatrical diversion from the quiet, pervasive realities which also form this astonishing phenomenon – that Dickens's London is, somehow, *still* London today.

Little Dorrit has two of these big, hammy metaphors. There is the collapsing house of Clennam – literally and metaphorically, the family, business and building are on their way down. But bigger by far is the shadow-of-the-Marshalsea-wall, the motif of sunlight and shade which patterns and structures and organises the book, a metaphor so strong it can make you groan aloud when reading – and maybe, fail to notice exactly what it is doing.

But then, on rereading the book and the footnotes (houses in the real London *did* simply collapse),[2] and the Preface and the appendix about the real Marshalsea, and after finally walking down to Borough myself one evening, *Little Dorrit* opened up and let me in.

Strangely, this was to do with the architect – or anti-architect – Cedric Price. Price is one of those people unbelievably famous in architectural circles, and very little known outside them. He was the 20th century's greatest designer of near-unthinkable alternatives. An architect who once told a client that they didn't need an architect, they needed a divorce. Who was delighted when his projects were demolished, and horrified when they were listed. Who said, when asked on radio what to do about York Minster (it had been struck by lightning and was leaning on its foundations): 'Flatten it.'

Not surprisingly, Price built little and takes some explaining. If I were writing for non-architects, I'd explain that his ideas lie behind epic, popular projects like the Pompidou Centre and the London Eye, and that he was the 'real' designer with the engineer Frank Newby of the aviary at London Zoo (usually credited to Lord Snowdon). And I'd certainly explain that Price made you see the world differently. He never produced normal seductive imagery, but had you puzzle through hundreds of maps, plans, diagrams, sketches, fragments of information – maybe about drains, or buses, or views – to try to force your brain to imagine the very different conditions he was proposing. And in doing so, you found the way you saw the world had changed, a little, forever.

Price loved Dickens, and especially *The Pickwick Papers*. He always carried a copy with him and he owned at least fifteen copies (at any rate, that's the total I came to by counting through *Cedric Price: Retriever* (2006), the catalogue of his library made by Eleanor Bron and Samantha Hardingham after his death). There was an important connection between Dickens and Price, but till that moment, in noisy, gritty, ugly, thundering South London, I hadn't really understood what.

But then, much as Price's projects might suddenly clarify in your mind, the great scenario of Dickens's London was suddenly revealed to me, because the Marshalsea wall was still there. And it is green with moss on its northern side, the side that never saw the sun. It was, simply, real.

Angel Court, leading to Bermondsey, the passage used by Dickens for his walk in 1857, is now built over. Instead, you go through Angel Place, an unpromising passage under a modern public library, squeezing through the vanished butter shop and gatehouse into the yard itself. A more recent building stands on the footprint of the building where William Dorrit (and John Dickens, and Tom Pythick) lived. And, cut right down to near-normal proportions, is the bottom part of the Marshalsea wall, whose shadow closes and warps the hopes and possibilities of those incarcerated there.

Dickens's Marshalsea building was a long, tight tenement; the 'yard' around it was only the width of an alley or very narrow street. The poor side (of course) faced northeast. The wealthier side, facing southwest, *should* have looked across St George's Churchyard towards the Surrey hills, but for that massive wall, cutting off air, and the view and the sunlight Dickens adored. When John Dickens had been shut up there, he said (with true, Micawberian flourish) that 'the sun set on him forever'.

Dickens explains that the wall was lowered 'when the building got free'. That's important, because neither maps, nor the current reality show you the conditions of the Marshalsea like the novel does. The old wall was more than three storeys high, with spikes on top. Little Dorrit, from her attic in the gatehouse, can only just glimpse over the top; her father, on the second floor, can only see its shadow.

All this is explored by Helen Small in Appendix II of my copy of *Little Dorrit*,[3] pointing to a wealth of further sources in a rich footnoted realm where fact and fiction are briefly allowed to lie together. And this, too, seems somehow to relate to Cedric Price. To really imagine architecture you have to put all sorts of information together in your head – and not just rely on pictures. The historical images are actually very confusing: there were two different Marshalsea sites, both off Borough High Street, and even when you get the right one (and some people don't) the prison is often shown across a wide yard which cuts away or predates the all-important wall, or shows it later on, 'when the place got free'.

The Marshalsea was *real*, super real; and the metaphors projected off its wall and through the book describe *real* conditions: psychological, physical, and fundamentally architectural in a sense that is so rarely noticed or described. The sense in which it shapes and conditions our lives; the way it can go on doing so, long after the world that produced it has moved on.

Dickens was a real bloodhound for urban history. The morphology of London drives a surprising amount of his plots (he gives us our best urban analysis of Chancery in *Bleak House*). His detailed, critical, analytic performance of London runs alongside, and ahead of, the urban mapping which retrospectively charted the chaotic, exponential growth of the world's first megacity. He was, of course, an insider – and someone whose skills ranged from semiprofessional acting and famous public performances to parliamentary reporting. He *combined* dramatisation and accuracy; perhaps it's this fusion of spectacular performance and forensic precision which gives his writing its analytical strength.

Dickens doesn't tell you what the Marshalsea looks like from outside because there was nothing to see. The 'hero', Arthur Clennam, comes across it by stalking his mother's silent dressmaker, Little Dorrit, who suddenly turns off Borough High Street into a small yard and through an open gate; indeed all kinds of characters, real and fictional, fail to find the prison. Because the Borough's ancient plot layout makes a very peculiar kind of prison in itself. Borough High Street was for centuries the main road leading south from the single bridge across the Thames. Long, narrow, weirdly deep plots squeezed together so that as many coaching inns and wayside businesses as possible could grab their tiny, precious scrap of lucrative street frontage onto the teeming traffic leaving or entering London (some of those inns are still there, and Price and Dickens both loved them).

The Marshalsea simply moved into the existing urban maze. Its gateway was built around what was there, and its presence in the public realm vanished. An unmarked entrance off a busy street, leading to one of the nameless back-lots of this teeming, booming, scarcely mapped part of London. It was a bizarre accident of non-planning which defines the institution where William Dorrit disappeared without comment for twenty years. The Marshalsea was society's *oubliette*.

Architecturally, Dickens is dead accurate. The Marshalsea even vanished from the *maps* that were being scrupulously produced in this period. It has a shadowy cartographic presence because the building *used* to be the King's Bench County Jail, marked as such in 1795 when the building was not quite so tightly built around, and again in the Wallis map of London of 1801. But as the Marshalsea prison itself, it keeps flickering out. In Darton's map of 1814 it is drawn, but unlabelled. By 1820, in Pigot's *Miniature Guide* to 'every street, court, alley and public building', it is blotted out by a number, and not even distinguished from the mass of urban development around it. It is shown on Smith's *New Map of London* of c 1830, but has vanished again on Mogg's *Strangers Guide to London* of 1834. It is marked as 'Gaol', but not named, on Cary's map of 1837. It then vanished again by 1850 – by which time it had in fact closed, even though the buildings were not demolished till the 1870s.[4]

Little Dorrit's great metaphor is thus a piece of proper architectural history and criticism. The Marshalsea really *was* a place that vanished from public life. The shadow of the Marshalsea wall *is* a real shadow. The sun and shade which frame the book, which structure and name its chapters and its sections with their poverty and wealth; their patches of love and gloom, their happiness and horrors, all derive from the Marshalsea's real shadow. And it was a *constructed*, deliberate, architectural shadow.

For someone built that wall high. A far lower wall, a railing would have been enough to keep people in. Other parts of the prison had a lower wall, and in the King's Bench debtors' prison, a short distance to the west (and described in Dickens's *Nicholas Nickleby*) long-term debtors could even pay to live in the 'rules', which were houses outside the prison. The physical purpose of the Marshalsea wall was, deliberately or subconsciously, a form of architectural, social *punishment*. As Dickens wrote of his fictitious prisoner, 'the sensation of being stifled, sometimes so overpowered him, that he would stand at a window holding his throat and gasping. At the same time, a longing for other air, and a yearning to be beyond the blind blank wall, made him feel as if he must go mad with the ardour of his desire.'[5]

This is fantastic architectural critique; way beyond what usually passes for informed architectural commentary. And, because it was *like* Cedric Price's own unusual view, I could see far more clearly how architectural and unusual his analysis is, in the many areas where their concerns now appeared so powerfully to overlap. Both shared an active drive for reform, and made keen observations of how property resists this. There was also in both Dickens and Price a bitter criticism of institutions. They saw importance in maps, journalism and social analysis. The strong connection with theatre, both personally and as a way of interpreting a shifting world. The deeply moving ideal of home and the perverse, perennial nostalgia. The heartfelt call for drains before churches.

And both used an essential mix of types of writing and other information which were used to cook up something quite distinct, with a life of its own. That new vision of Dickens's London as a great, dramatic performance of reality whisked away my architectural 'problem' with Dickens's London, replacing it with an aperture, or field of vision, which now began to grow. Because Dickens, like Price, shows you London in a different way; not to do with how it *looks*, but to do with how it *works* – theatrically, socially, structurally, politically, dramatically, humanly – all around us, every day.

Notes

1   Stephen Wall and Helen Small, 'Preface', in Charles Dickens, *Little Dorrit*, Penguin Classics (London), 1998, revised edition 2003, pp 5–6. Charles Dickens's *Little Dorrit* was first published in 1857.
2   Ibid, p 983. According to the book's footnotes, Dickens had to deny that he had taken the idea from a fall of houses in the Tottenham Court Road earlier that year.
3   See Appendix II by Helen Small in the above-cited edition of *Little Dorrit*.
4   All of these maps can be found on the excellent website http://mapco.net.
5   Dickens, *Little Dorrit*, p 787.

This essay is an extract from Rattenbury's book-in-progress, provisionally called *Another Country: On the Architecture of English Novel*.

CHAPTER 25

On 'Sachlichkeit': Some Additional Remarks on an Anglo-German Encounter

LAURENT STALDER

The oeuvre of Hermann Muthesius (1861–1927) has long been associated with the notion of 'Sachlichkeit'. Karl Scheffler named Muthesius a 'maestro of Sachlichkeit' as early as 1908, while Nikolaus Pevsner appraised Muthesius's contribution to the rise of modern architecture in similar terms some two decades later in his classic work, *Pioneers of the Modern Movement* (1936).[1] Pevsner therein defines 'sachlich' as meaning 'at the same time pertinent, matter-of-fact, and objective'. He carefully distinguishes between two meanings of the word 'Sachlichkeit' in the writings of Muthesius, speaking firstly of 'reasonable Sachlichkeit' to denote the pragmatic objectivity which Muthesius saw reflected in English architecture and decorative arts; and, secondly, of an 'almost scientific Sachlichkeit' which manifests itself solely in 'railway stations, exhibition halls, bridges, steamships, etc'. It is this second definition of 'Sachlichkeit' which Pevsner would come to associate with the origins of the 'Maschinenstil' of his day. Stanford Anderson, in two noteworthy articles on Muthesius's notion of 'Sachlichkeit', moves beyond this teleological reading and posits the importance of reading the term in the intellectual context of the period. In particular he highlights the fact that there are correspondences – but no similitude – between Muthesius's demands for Sachlichkeit in industrial design, on the one hand, and in design tasks such as those posed by domestic interiors, on the other. He notably demonstrates that these two meanings of 'Sachlichkeit' correspond to the definitions of 'realism' developed by Richard Streiter in 1896.[2] Streiter – whose correspondence with Muthesius shows them to have been in close contact, and whose suggestion it was that Muthesius approach the English house from a historical perspective[3] – was also the first person to link the notion of 'Sachlichkeit' with the English house and thus to associate it explicitly with concrete architectural practice.[4] Muthesius continues in the same vein in the foreword to his 1904 study, *Das Englische Haus* [The English House], stating that his research is grounded in the particular architectural history of England in order to better show the close relationship between 'external design features' and 'natural given circumstances'.[5]

The term 'Sachlichkeit' or 'sachlich' is used repeatedly in *Das Englische Haus*. However, in only three cases does Muthesius discuss the subject at sufficient length to merit an entry in the book's general index. The first such passage is found in the general introduction to Volume I, the other two in Volume II: one at the end of the chapter 'The Structure of the English House'; the other, a mere summary of the previous two, in the conclusion.[6]

In Volume I, which is devoted to the historical evolution of the English house, Muthesius offers the following definition under the subheading 'Exemplary Qualities of the English House': 'English houses, as we can see, are wisely reduced to essentials and adapted to given circumstances; the point that is worth copying from them, therefore, is the emphasis laid on purely objective requirements [*rein sachliche Forderungen*].' The author then proceeds to list the finer attributes of the English house: firstly, 'Sachlichkeit in the design', which is achieved through rejecting all forms of representation and following the example of simple rural dwellings; secondly, 'Sachlichkeit in the placement of the house on its lot and in its relationship to its natural surroundings'; thirdly, the 'simplicity, sachliches, sobriety and discreet comfort' which characterise its interior; and, finally, 'a very extensive knowledge of sanitary conditions'.[7] Even if Muthesius, elsewhere in his critique of the contemporary house, describes interior planning as 'scientific work'[8] and sanitary facilities as 'purely scientific' issues 'without national particularities',[9] his distinction between scientific and reasonable Sachlichkeit does not seem entirely clear-cut, especially as these factors are evidently considered to be as important for 'Sachlichkeit' as the design of the house or its placement on its lot.

The difficulty of providing unambiguous definitions is even more apparent in the second passage, which addresses the 'overall appearance' of the English house under the heading 'Sober Sachlichkeit'.[10] Here, Muthesius develops a two-pronged argument. Firstly, he contrasts the 'puritan attitude' of contemporary English architecture with the 'pretentiousness' and 'external impact' of the Palladian movement. Secondly, and in more general terms, he contrasts the contemporary search for a 'modern style' with a more fundamental notion of modernity: 'These advocates of the modern style are generally shocked to find this sober and sachliche simplicity in England, which they presume is the home of all things "modern".'[11] He concludes: 'These qualities [of the English house – refined sobriety, quiet reserve, appealing honesty] are the legacy of old English vernacular architecture, whose simple sentiment, once reclaimed, is wed to the spirit of modernity in order to forge the artistic character that distinguishes the English house of today.'[12] Thus, in place of a normative or stylistic concept of modernity, Muthesius foregrounds his claim that architecture is indissolubly bound to its environment and proposes to underpin this claim through the study of two major components of the English house: the wall and the roof.

The chapters dealing with these two elements may initially appear to be little more than a catalogue of building materials and techniques, since they list English construction methods exhaustively: 'cut stone construction', 'brick construction', 'half-timber construction', 'old construction techniques' and new 'concrete-based construction techniques', along with 'brick roof', 'slate shingles', 'stone roof' or even 'thatched roof', etc. At first glance, the list may seem trivial, yet it serves to clarify the notion of 'Sachlichkeit' as defined above. In the case of stone construction, for example, Muthesius observes that ordinary dressing is used most commonly in urban contexts, while dry stone remains more popular in the North of England as it is readily available there. He notes that brick is the material best adapted to conditions in the country, even if it was originally imported from Holland; and also that the traditional English half-timber construction recently revived by modern architects reflects a 'common national character' which distinguishes it from German architecture. He further maintains that contemporary architects will continue to revive old construction techniques through the study of local examples.[13] The various categories listed – city, countryside, England, Holland, tradition, climate, as well as function, construction, etc – attest to Muthesius's desire to sketch out a range of architectural criteria, and to understand their characteristics and potential as a means of responding to a particular cultural context in the most complete and differentiated manner possible.

Various other passages demonstrate that this notion of 'Sachlichkeit' is by no means limited to various construction techniques and building materials, but encompasses formal questions too. Muthesius therefore discusses affective qualities at one point: 'The broad peaked roof is, in the North at least, a fundamental emblem of the dwelling; it stands for a sense of home and consequently evokes in us familiar and comforting sensations.'[14] 'Sachlichkeit' is also a means to imbue a building with character, as revealed in another passage where Muthesius credits Philip Webb, William Eden Nesfield and Richard Norman Shaw with having 'turned away from the study of castles, palaces, and cathedrals' in order to find 'a creative freedom that is respectful of functional, material, and purely sachliche factors' similar to those found in the English cottage.[15] Moreover, this formal approach to 'Sachlichkeit' is not limited to matters of exterior design. It is expressed also in the plan, as can be seen in another passage dealing with the evolution of the English house from the reign of Elizabeth I through to the 19th century. Recalling the 'perfect fusion of comfort and representation' evinced by the Elizabethan period, the 'regularity' of Palladian layouts, and (to his mind) the equally questionable 'irregularity' of the first half of the 19th century, Muthesius concludes: 'In short, Sachlichkeit has suffered here too from an archaeology on the rampage, from that excessive scholarship which has prevented this most recent period of architectural evolution from realising its full potential.'[16]

Numerous other passages could be quoted in order to similarly show that the term 'Sachlichkeit' persistently evades precise definition, to say nothing of stylistic attribution. Indeed, use of the term, which by 1900 was popular in architectural circles yet still far from being commonly understood,[17] served merely to describe various constellations. That which Muthesius proposes is not a set of normative rules for architecture regarding such factors as proportion, architectural *ordonnances*, principles of composition or even architectural types, but differentiated responses to a series of natural givens – such as climate, geography and topography – and social givens – such as conventions, customs and traditional construction techniques.[18] In the writings of Muthesius, 'Sachlichkeit' is thus a means to paraphrase any number of circumstances in any number of constellations, whenever these have an impact on the design of a house and its individualisation: from the properties of a lot to the qualities of the light, from the particular view to the formal qualities of an evocative landscape. It was no accident that Muthesius, in the introduction to his book, spoke of the house as an organism whose evolution could be apprehended through the history of the English house. For with this biological metaphor he clearly rooted the qualities of architecture in the discipline's interdependence with its environment. Therein lay the novelty of his methodology. Its scientific legitimacy derived from the historical and ethnographic research of its day. It found its expression in the notion of 'Sachlichkeit'.

Notes

Translated from the German by Jill Denton, Berlin

1   Karl Scheffler, 'H Muthesius: Das Englische Haus' [Review], *Kunst und Künstler*, Vol VI (1908), p 530; Nikolaus Pevsner *Pioneers of the Modern Movement, from William Morris to Walter Gropius*, Faber & Faber (London), 1936, p 35.

2   Stanford Anderson, 'Sachlichkeit and Modernity, or Realist Architecture', in Harry Francis Mallgrave (ed), *Otto Wagner: Issues and Debates – Reflections on the Raiment of Modernity*, Getty Center (Santa Monica, California), 1993, pp 338–41. Stanford Anderson, 'Introduction' in Hermann Muthesius (ed), *Style-Architecture and Building-Art: Transformation of Architecture in the Nineteenth Century and its Present Condition*, Getty Center (Santa Monica, California), 1994, pp 14–19. Anderson quotes in this text a passage from Richard Streiter, 'Aus München', *Pan*, Vol 2, 1896, p 249. In *Stilarchitektur und Baukunst*, Muthesius evokes within a single paragraph the 'Sachlichkeit' of architecture, the 'realist tendencies' of decorative art and the 'naturalism' of painting. See Hermann Muthesius, *Stilarchitektur und Baukunst*, Karl Schimmelpfeng (Mühlheim-Ruhr), 1902, p 66. See also: Alfred Lichtwark, *Palastfenster und Flügelthür*, Cassirer (Berlin), 1899/1901. In the second edition Lichtwark renamed his essay 'Realistische Architektur' in 'Sachliche Baukunst'.

3   See correspondence of Richard Streiter with Hermann Muthesius from 29.5.1894 to 11.2.1905. Werkbundarchiv Berlin, estate of Hermann Muthesius.

4   Richard Streiter, 'Das deutsche Kunstgewerbe', *Illustrite Kunstgewerbliche Zeitschrift für Innen-Dekoration*, Issue 7, 1896, pp 106–15, here in particular p 114.

5   Hermann Muthesius, *Das Englische Haus*, Vol I, Wasmuth (Berlin), 1904, p 10.

6   Ibid, pp 168, 237.

7   Ibid, p 9.

8   Ibid, p 93.

9   Hermann Muthesius, *Das Englische Haus*, Vol II, Wasmuth (Berlin), 1904, p 214.

10 Ibid, p 168.

11 Ibid, p 169.

12 Ibid, p 170.

13 Ibid, pp 171–212.

14 Ibid, p 165. Muthesius seems to refer in this passage to John Ruskin, 'Lectures on Architecture and Painting, etc, delivered in Edinburgh in November, 1853', in *The Works of John Ruskin*, George Allen (London), 1904, p 33.

15 Muthesius, *Das Englische Haus*, Vol I, p 100.

16 Ibid, p 92. On this subject, see: Robert Kerr, *The Gentleman's House; Or, How to Plan English Residences, from the Parsonage to the Palace*, J Murray, (London), 1871, p 380. Here, Kerr distinguishes between the different ideas expressed in the symmetry of 'classical' plans and the irregularity of 'gothic' ones.

17 Herman Hirt (ed), *Deutsches Wörterbuch von Fr. L. K. Weigand*, Alfred Töpelmann (Giessen), 1910, p 633, lists the adjective 'sachlich' and its variant 'sächlich' as early as 1820. While Daniel Sanders, *Wörterbuch der Deutschen Sprache*, Vol II, Otto Wigand (Leipzig), 1876, p 830, notes under the entry 'sachlich' the use of the noun 'Sachlichkeit' by Jeremias Gotthelf, the noun did not feature in the pertinent dictionaries until the 1930s, despite being already in common use among art historians, in the compound term 'Neue Sachlichkeit'. See: Richard Pekrun, *Das Deutsche Wort. Rechtschreibung und Erklärung des deutschen Wortschatzes sowie der Fremdwörter*, Georg Dollheimer (Leipzig), 1933, p 831, and also *Das grosse Brockhaus: Handbuch des Wissens in zwanzig Bänden* (15), completely revised edition of *Brockhaus' Konversations-Lexikon*, Vol XVI, Brockhaus (Leipzig),1928–1937, p 280 (with a reference there to 'Neue Sachlichkeit'). On the emergence and proliferation of the term 'Neue Sachlichkeit', see: Fritz Schmalenbach, 'The term neue Sachlichkeit', *The Art Bulletin*, Vol 22, No 3, September 1940, pp 161–5.

18 See on this Michel Foucault, '11 January 1978', in *Security, Territory, Population: Lectures at the Collège de France 1977–78*, Palgrave Macmillan (New York), 2007, pp 35–6; first published as Michel Foucault, *Sécurité, territoire, population: Cours au Collège de France 1977–1978*, Gallimard/Seuil (Paris), 2004, pp 16–38.

CHAPTER 26
Double Vision
MARK SWENARTON

Although not published until 1986, Adrian Forty's first book, *Objects of Desire*, was completed in 1980, the same year as my first book, *Homes fit for Heroes* (published in 1981). Both were commenced in the early 1970s and were largely produced at The Bartlett. And both arose from a shared intellectual endeavour, namely to uncover the hidden forces at work in shaping our material world – consumer goods in the one case, housing and the urban environment in the other.

With hindsight, we can see this interest as a very 1970s concern. This was a traumatic period, when what Eric Hobsbawm called the golden age of postwar affluence gave way to the era of crisis.[1] The naive optimism that had sufficed in the golden age (including, in architectural history, simple-minded accounts of the rise of modernism as a story of good versus evil) no longer seemed adequate; instead the critical approach associated with Roland Barthes, whose *Mythologies* was published in English in 1972, and other French theorists suggested a more satisfactory way of understanding what was happening. To many people in the 1970s it felt as though something was fundamentally rotten in the state, if not of Denmark, then of Britain and Western society in general; and the history of architecture and design could not be studied without reference to this fact. Architecture and design, it seemed, was in some way complicit in this condition and the job of the historian was to find out what was happening.

Adrian Forty and I had a lot in common intellectually. We were both Oxford-trained historians (Adrian a few years earlier than me) who had then moved to The Bartlett to undertake doctoral work under Reyner Banham – Adrian initially on interwar radio cabinets, myself on homes fit for heroes (it was in fact through Adrian that I first approached Banham). Adrian was appointed as a lecturer there in 1973 and me (following Banham's departure for the USA) three years later. Thanks to our previous training as historians we were both interested in historical rigour: ie making verifiable statements about the past on the basis of evidence rather than, as so often was the case in architectural and design history, on the basis of unsubstantiated assertion or even, dare it be said, mumbo-jumbo.

At The Bartlett we worked closely together developing these ideas about architectural history in both teaching and research. If I recall correctly, we each read and commented on every chapter that we produced for our respective projects; in both *Objects of Desire* and *Homes fit for Heroes* the debt that each owed to the other is explicitly acknowledged.[2] And, in teaching, the fruits of our labour came in 1981 with the launch of the History of Modern Architecture (later Architectural History) Master's course, which we co-wrote

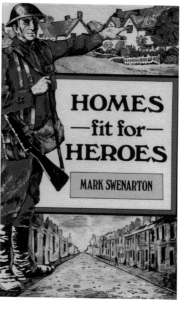

Adrian Forty, *Objects of Desire*, Thames & Hudson (London), 1986.

Mark Swenarton, *Homes fit for Heroes*, Heinemann Educational (London), 1981.

and co-taught for six years and which, under Adrian's direction for more than three decades, has proved to be one of the most successful architectural history courses in the world.

The subtitle of *Objects of Desire* was *Design and Society since 1750*. The subject was the design of consumer goods in the modern (industrial) era, with an emphasis on Britain and especially the 20th century. The book argued that these mass-produced goods embodied social myths – about class, gender, work, home, housework etc – and their design was therefore embedded in much more profound, and much more important, social processes than previous accounts had admitted. Although design for workplaces was not excluded, the focus was on 'the world of consumer goods':[3] radio cabinets, household goods, cookers, vacuum cleaners etc (today he would doubtless have included laptops and iPhones). The coverage was wide-ranging but not comprehensive. As Adrian wrote in the introduction, 'the book could have contained a different set of designs and yet retained its argument intact' and while the focus was on consumer goods, as he said elsewhere 'its argument was no less applicable to architecture'.[4]

The subtitle of *Homes fit for Heroes* was *The Politics and Architecture of Early State Housing in Britain*. The subject was the introduction of large-scale state housing at the end of the First World War and the adoption as an integral part of that programme of a new type of housing, based on the Garden City model as set out by Raymond Unwin and the Tudor Walters Report. In the existing studies of housing history, housing policy was generally separated from housing design; but with homes fit for heroes, as the name made clear, the new kind of design was a central part of the new policy. I wanted to know why that was, and what it told us about design and architecture more widely; and the release under the 50-year rule of hitherto-unseen government papers meant that it was possible for the first time to find out. In contrast therefore to *Objects of Desire*, you could definitely not have changed the subject matter but left the argument intact.

In both cases thus the interest was twofold. There was the substantive interest in finding out, in certain places and at certain times, what had happened and why, and seeing how design in these specific historical instances contributed to broader social or even political and ideological processes. And there was the parallel historiographical interest in uncovering and explaining the blindnesses and lacunae of previous studies, and seeing why they had come about. This dual interest, in history and historiography, would be fundamental to the History of Modern Architecture Master's course.

At the time, the similarity in terms of approach and method that we had each adopted was obvious. But it never occurred (at least to me) that there was much in common between the subject matter of the two investigations. Looking back today however it strikes me that the two were in fact connected, and in a perhaps surprising way.

This changed perception arises from the work I have been doing recently, with colleagues from Delft and elsewhere, on architecture and the welfare state in a cross-European perspective.[5] Looking back from today, it is apparent that the golden age of the postwar boom ('you've never had it so good') and the social provisions of the welfare state ('from the cradle to the grave') were two sides of the same coin. The great innovations of the welfare state (health, social security, housing, education ...) in the aftermath of the 1942 Beveridge Report, and the consumer boom of the 1950s and 1960s (television, cars, washing machines ...), were the twin progeny of the Keynesian macroeconomic policies established as part of the postwar political settlement – the settlement that for two decades seemed to have found the key to ever-increasing prosperity and social justice. As Helena Mattsson's work has shown, both the welfare state and consumerism were central elements of the phenomenal postwar boom (the *Trente Glorieuses*) which lasted from the 1940s to the 1970s: the European country with arguably the most advanced welfare state, Sweden, was also the one most attuned to the logic of the new consumerism.[6]

This relationship between consumer goods and welfare state was not one that occurred to me (nor I suspect to Adrian) at the time. But with hindsight we can see that in their subject matter *Objects of Desire* and *Homes fit for Heroes* were complementary. Both were looking at the role of design and the material world in the era of the welfare state and seeking to understand the part played by design in the operation (or what we would probably have called the reproduction) of society: one from the point of view of consumer goods and the other from the point of view of state housing. Hence while one deals with all kinds of products other than buildings, and the other with buildings but not any other kind of products, they might perhaps now usefully be read, as they were written, one alongside the other.

Notes

1   Eric Hobsbawm, *The Age of Extremes: The Short Twentieth Century, 1914–1991*, Abacus (London), 1995, p 403.

2   Adrian Forty, *Objects of Desire: Design and Society since 1750*, Thames & Hudson (London), 1986, p 4; Mark Swenarton, *Homes fit for Heroes: The Politics and Architecture of Early State Housing in Britain*, Heinemann Educational (London), 1981, p 4.

3   http://iris.ucl.ac.uk/research/personal?upi=JAFOR22, Prof Adrian Forty Profile (accessed 1 August 2013).

4   Forty, *Objects of Desire*, p 9; http://iris.ucl.ac.uk/research/personal?upi=JAFOR22, Prof Adrian Forty Profile (accessed 1 August 2013).

5   Mark Swenarton, Tom Avermaete and Dirk van den Heuvel (eds), *Architecture and the Welfare State*, Routledge (London), forthcoming, 2014.

6   Helena Mattsson and Sven-Olof Wallenstein (eds), *Swedish Modernism: Architecture, Consumption and the Welfare State*, Black Dog (London), 2010.

CHAPTER 27

Modernism

MARY MCLEOD

Among Adrian Forty's many gifts to architectural historians was to make us all much more conscious of the words we use and to recognise that they have a rich and complex history, in which meanings and usage change significantly over time. One word that Adrian does not include in his lexicon in *Words and Buildings: A Vocabulary of Modern Architecture* (2000) but which appears with some regularity in that wonderful book is 'modernism'. These days, we use the word 'modernism' when we refer to modern architecture or the Modern Movement, or to what German and Dutch practitioners used to call *Neues Bauen* or *Nieuwe Bouwen*. Now, we even say 'early modernism' (pre–World War I) and 'late modernism' (post–World War II), and even occasionally 'high' and 'classic' modernism (a seeming oxymoron). The question is why. Although this shift in vocabulary seems to have occurred almost unconsciously, it might be seen as indicating how the notion of modern architecture itself changed during the 20th century: from a living movement committed to specific values and aspirations to a codified style and cultural period of the past, usually the two decades between the world wars.

The word 'modern' has a long and varied genealogy. From the 16th to the late 19th century, however, it usually meant 'contemporary' or 'of the present', and its meaning varied considerably depending on the circumstances and period. It was not until the emergence of Art Nouveau in the 1890s that the word 'modern' was widely used to designate a specific new stylistic tendency, one that stood as a radical break with past historical styles. While different countries referred to Art Nouveau by different names – *stile floreale* in Italy, *Sezessionstil* in Austria, *Jugendstil* in other German-speaking areas – all of them claimed this new movement as 'modern'.

Even this important break, which is often seen as marking both the end of 19th-century historicism and the beginning of the Modern Movement, is not as critical to subsequent usage of the word 'modern' in architecture as Otto Wagner's seminal book *Moderne Architektur* [Modern Architecture] of 1896. Like the German literary magazines of the early 1890s, Wagner's text was filled with phrases such as 'modern life' (often capitalised), 'modern man', 'the modern eye', and 'modern social conditions'; and by the second edition of his book (1898), the phrase 'Modern Movement' appears with insistent repetition (a total of eight times in the two-page preface). Without question, it is Wagner's book that led to the association of functionalism, rationalism, and the elimination of 'useless' decoration with the words 'modern architecture' (even if his own buildings were still a far cry from the stripped-down forms we associate with 1920s modern architecture). In other words, Wagner gave the phrase 'modern architecture' specific ideological content.

In central Europe, Wagner's vocabulary persisted into the 1920s but, as Rosemarie Haag Bletter has documented, by the mid-1920s German and Dutch architects began to prefer the adjective *neues* or 'new' to 'modern'.[1] Bletter explains that this choice might have been influenced not only by the phrase *neue Sachlichkeit* and titles of newspapers such as *Die neue Zeit* but also – because 'new' implied change – by a desire to suggest an emerging process rather than a fixed style.[2] In France, where the word 'modern' had for so long been used, Le Corbusier and André Lurçat shied away from using it at all, preferring to say either simply 'architecture', as in the former's *Vers une architecture* [Towards an Architecture] (1923) and the latter's *Architecture* (1929), or else 'new', as in Le Corbusier and Pierre Jeanneret's 'Les 5 points d'une architecture nouvelle' [Five Points of a New Architecture] (1927). Like Wagner and Adolf Loos before them, they sought to make the modern both new and timeless; in this respect, their image of modernity is exactly the opposite of Charles Baudelaire's in his 1863 essay 'Le Peintre de la vie moderne' [The Painter of Modern Life], which extols fashion and emphasises the changing, fleeting nature of modernity.

The phrase 'modern architecture' gained the most currency in England and the United States – in fact, just at the moment when the word 'modern' was loosening its hold in Germany and Austria. Examples that immediately come to mind are Henry-Russell Hitchcock's *Modern Architecture: Romanticism and Reintegration* of 1929 and the so-called 'International Style' exhibition of 1932 at New York's Museum of Modern Art, the official title of which was actually 'Modern Architecture: International Exhibition'.³ More important, Nikolaus Pevsner's early history *Pioneers of the Modern Movement: From William Morris to Walter Gropius* (1936) brought Otto Wagner's phrase to England, and it is undoubtedly due to Pevsner's influential book that the term 'Modern Movement' joined the more general term 'modern architecture' as the standard designations in Britain for progressive architecture until about 1970.

Despite the plurality of terms for modern architecture in the 1920s and 1930s and the diversity of examples in the early surveys, the word 'modernism' was rare in architectural circles during this period. American author and critic Sheldon Cheney used it as a general descriptive term in his book *The New World Architecture* (1930), a book that was widely read in the States; but in Britain, 'modernism' seems to have been primarily a literary term, employed to describe the work of TS Eliot, James Joyce and Virginia Woolf. When the word was occasionally applied to architecture in Europe before the Second World War, its meaning was often derogatory, as was the case in Reginald Blomfield's *Modernismus* (1934).

So when did our vocabulary change and why? How did the word 'modernism' suddenly become so ubiquitous in architecture? In hindsight, it appears the present-day usage can be traced to three phenomena: first, the gradual realisation that modern architecture itself could no longer be seen as a collective ongoing project, sharing common goals and a unified aesthetic; second, the widespread influence of other fields on architectural writing and criticism from the 1970s to the present; and third, the increasingly international dissemination of architectural theory – more specifically, the increasing hegemony of American and British architectural history and theory in shaping historical narratives and ideas, and by extension our architectural language.

Many architectural historians would trace the first of these generating tendencies, what might be called 'modern architecture's self-critique', back to the 1930s and early 1940s, with its new attention to regionalism and monumentality. But for the profession at large, the dissatisfaction with the dogma of the heroic first generation emerged full-scale in the 1950s, after the tragedies of World War II, when architects became increasingly aware of the Modern Movement's failure both to generate social reform and to create a formal language with broad popular appeal. A whole new set of 'isms' and styles (the New Empiricism, the New Humanism, Brutalism, Regionalism, Neo-Liberty, etc) came to the fore, along with a critical examination of the limits of functionalism by younger members of the Congrès Internationaux d'Architecture Moderne (CIAM), such as Alison and Peter Smithson and Aldo van Eyck, who would go on to form Team 10.[4] During the 1950s, the word 'modernism' was rarely used. Clearly, though, modernist dogma no longer comprised the only mode, or even the dominant mode, of making architecture. This reaction against the universalist doctrine and reductive aesthetic of modern architecture intensified in the 1960s with the publication of Robert Venturi's *Complexity and Contradiction in Architecture* and Aldo Rossi's *L'Architettura della città* [The Architecture of the City], both 1966, gaining further momentum from an even earlier public critique. It culminated in the

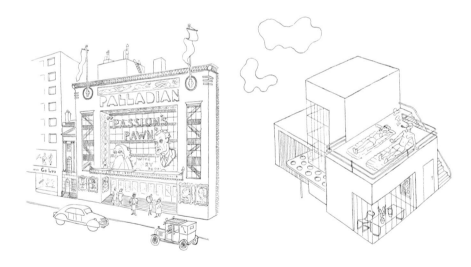

'Modernistic' versus 'Functional'.
Osbert Lancaster, the brilliant English cartoonist, captured in his book *Pillar to Post* (1939) the differences between fashionable 'Modernistic' architecture and 'Twentieth-Century Functional' architecture. Lancaster called the former 'revolting', whereas he saw the latter as having an 'excellent and revivifying' effect, although it too was subject to ridicule (to wit: sunbathing was 'frequently rendered impossible' in the British climate).

arrival of 'postmodern' architecture, which soon became seen as part of a more general cultural transformation dubbed 'postmodernism'.

The increasing currency of the term 'modernism' correlates directly to this sense that the Modern Movement was no longer a vital, ongoing development, but instead something past. Modernism by now connoted a historical movement and style. The term was most prevalent in the United States and, already in the late 1950s and 1960s, 'modernism' was heard in revisionist contexts, such as the second Modern Architecture Symposium, held at Columbia University in May 1964. The young Robert AM Stern was one of the speakers who employed it with most ease (though still within quotation marks in his written text); as did architectural historian William H Jordy, who used it in the title of a survey book, *American Buildings and Their Architects: The Impact of European Modernism in the Mid-Twentieth Century* (1972). Kenneth Frampton recalled that when he arrived at Princeton University from England in 1965, he kept wondering 'where all this "modernism" was coming from'.[5] However, by the early 1980s, the word gained wide currency on both sides of the Atlantic. In *The Language of Post-Modern Architecture* (1977), Charles Jencks still primarily used the capitalised adjectives 'Modern' and 'Post-Modern', although the nouns 'modernism' and 'post-modernism' slipped occasionally into the text. In the second edition of Jencks's *Modern Movements in Architecture*, published in 1985, they are everywhere.

A second source of the word 'modernism' in architectural writing is art criticism and cultural theory. The writings of art critics such as Clement Greenberg, of literary figures such as Irving Howe, Renato Poggioli, Matei Calinescu, Peter Bürger, and Andreas Huyssen, and of philosophers such as Theodor Adorno and Jürgen Habermas all influenced architectural critics and historians, and soon, in turn, architects. The meanings of the word 'modernism' varied widely from individual to individual. Greenberg defined it as essentially artistic self-critique – that is, art that focused on the aesthetic properties of its medium to criticise itself.[6] Michael Fried, Bürger and Huyssen generally followed his usage, although both Bürger and Huyssen distinguished it from another cultural tendency: in Bürger's case, from the avant-garde which he conceived as artistic currents that sought to destroy the institutions of art; and in Huyssen's, from art forms that embraced mass culture. Whether modernism was embraced (as Greenberg and Adorno did) or criticised for its political

189

and social withdrawal (as Bürger and Huyssen did), both positions linked modernism to formalism and the autonomous pursuit of a discipline. But for others, such as philosophers Henri Lefebvre and Jürgen Habermas and political theorist Marshall Berman, modernism was a more encompassing term: it was the cultural expression of modernity (the experience of modern life), which in turn was a product of modernisation, arising from the forces of rationalisation in capital and technology. In architectural writing, these manifold theoretical constructs of 'modernism' soon began to blur, making its meaning vague and ambiguous. In fact, the very ambiguity of the term may have led to its popularity and broad usage, giving it an applicability beyond the terms 'Modern Movement' or *Neues Bauen*, which were typically associated with a specific programmatic agenda.

Thus, as postmodernism and cultural theory began to coalesce in writings about architecture, the word 'modernism' began to be used regularly by a younger generation of historians and critics, especially in Britain and the United States, supplanting 'modern architecture' or 'Modern Movement'. By the early 1990s, at the height of the theory wave in American academic circles, the word 'modernism' began to appear in titles of architecture books, and within a few years with regularity – for example, in K Michael Hays's *Modernism and the Posthumanist Subject: The Architecture of Hannes Meyer and Ludwig Hilberseimer* (1992), Robert Bruegmann's *Modernism at Mid-Century: The Architecture of the United States Air Force Academy* (1994), and Sarah Williams Goldhagen's *Louis Kahn's Situated Modernism* (2001). The wide-ranging content of these three books reveals the very malleability of the term: from a theoretical construct indebted to neo-Marxist periodisation (Hays), to a straightforward monographic account (Bruegmann), to a revisionist reading of a major postwar architect, who is seen as perpetuating the legacy of modern architecture while transforming it (Goldhagen). If the meaning of the word remains nebulous today, its usage is now ubiquitous, with the Victoria and Albert Museum exhibition 'Modernism' in 2006 evidence of its widespread acceptance.

Related to but not quite synonymous with the rise in usage of the word 'modernism' was an increasing understanding of modern architecture as a diverse and varied phenomenon. While early historians of modern architecture often spoke of distinct tendencies or strains and acknowledged national differences, the canonical histories such as Sigfried Giedion's and Nikolaus Pevsner's stressed modern architecture's shared and unifying characteristics – notably functionalism, structural rationalism and simplicity – rather than its geographical or cultural differences. Again, it was in the postwar period that this unified vision began to fracture, owing to an increasing recognition of, and value placed on, local traditions and customs, on the one hand, and personal expression, on the other. With the advent of postmodernism and poststructuralist theory, critics began to celebrate this plurality and heterogeneity, although they debated at times whether these qualities were characteristics of modernism (Berman and the early Charles Jencks) or of postmodernism (Jencks after 1975). More recently, the awareness of architectural pluralism has coalesced with the somewhat awkward use of 'modernisms' in the titles of books, such as Sarah Williams Goldhagen and Réjean Legault's *Anxious Modernisms: Experimentation in Postwar Architectural Culture* (2000), and in the 2006 Docomomo conference, titled 'Other Modernisms'.

The use of the plural raises questions about the word 'modernism' itself. As this brief chronology shows, the adoption of 'modernism' to characterise the Modern Movement and modern architecture largely emerged in the English-speaking world. The ascendance of English in publications, teaching and conferences, the proliferation of American doctoral programmes in architecture, and the growing numbers of foreign students in British and American schools, have all led to a form of globalisation – an English-dominated globalisation – not only of architectural culture but also of architectural history itself. One issue to consider is whether the rapid and widespread dissemination of the word 'modernism', despite its new plural form, might not risk being another form of homogenisation wiping out the linguistic diversity that characterised the original names given to the Modern Movement itself, and with them some of the movement's distinctive national and regional aspects that those names signified. Has the term given modern architecture a universalism that it never initially had? Or, more positively, does the very generality of the term 'modernism' and its many different connotations encourage us to consider a much broader range of modernist architectural work, alerting us to the richness and variety as well as the wide geographical influence of the Modern Movement's forms and ideas? As Adrian reminds us throughout his eloquent study of words, there are gains as well as losses.

Notes

1 Rosemarie Haag Bletter, Introduction to Adolf Behne, *The Modern Functional Building*, Getty Research Institute (Santa Monica, California), 1996, pp 2–3.

2 Ibid.

3 The accompanying exhibition catalogue had the same title as another book by the same authors, the *International Style: Architecture since 1922* (1932), immediately became better known giving the show its popular name. One might also mention the numerous English primers of the 1930s and 1940s, such as: Howard Robertson, *Modern Architectural Design*, (1932); FRS Yorke, *The Modern House* (1934); and JM Richards, *An Introduction to Modern Architecture*, (1940).

4 The Congrès Internationaux d'Architecture Moderne [International Congresses of Modern Architecture] was an organisation formed by a group of modern architects in 1928 to discuss and exchange ideas, and to promote the dissemination of principles of modern architecture and urbanism. It was disbanded in 1959 with the increasing dissent of a group of younger members who formed Team 10.

5 Kenneth Frampton, comments to the author, especially in September 2006.

6 See especially Clement Greenberg's oft-quoted essay, 'Modernist Painting', originally delivered as part of Voice of America's Forum Lectures in 1960 and then published the following year in *Arts Yearbook*, No 4, 1961, pp 101–8. A revised version was published in *Art and Literature*, No 4, Spring 1964, pp 194–201.

CHAPTER 28

Yes, And We Have No Dentists

MICHAEL EDWARDS

'I am shocked by the scaffolding. Your scaffolding in London is so heavy, so dangerous. It shows human labour is cheap here, and human life too.'

— FIRST-YEAR UNDERGRADUATE STUDENT, FROM DENMARK, AFTER A FIRST LECTURE AT THE BARTLETT,

RESPONDING TO THE LECTURER'S REQUEST FOR FIRST IMPRESSIONS OF LONDON (ABOUT 2004)

'Why don't we build housing? That's a good question but the answer is simply that we don't get asked to.'

— RICHARD ROGERS, ANSWERING A QUESTION FROM A STUDENT AFTER A LECTURE AT THE BARTLETT (1988)

The last four decades of education at The Bartlett, University College London (UCL) have seen a counter-revolution of professions and disciplines in which the early promise of a fertile dissolution of boundaries has been almost totally suppressed.

When Richard Llewelyn Davies merged the UCL schools of architecture and planning and assorted research centres in 1970, adding scientists, engineers and social scientists to the mix, it was part of a project to weaken the inherited division of labour among built environment practitioners and foster innovations. It brought with it new freedoms and responsibilities for individual students to select and mix their topics of study. These changes met with some active resistance from staff, but primarily with inertia and passive aggression. The time-honoured curricula of distinct professions were being replaced with nothing but a supermarket. In a highly effective bid to help students and staff deal constructively with these dissolving boundaries, Llewelyn Davies recruited the eminent group analytic psychotherapist Jane Abercrombie. Announcing this at a faculty board meeting, he observed that the school had no psychologists on its staff and was met with a *sotto voce* comment from Dr Bruno Schlaffenberg (planning officer of Camden and a visiting teacher): 'Yes, and we have no dentists.'

The experimental syllabus operated for perhaps a decade, gaining some momentum from the simple fact of colocating the factions in the new Wates House in 1976 (though still segregating them floor by floor) and surviving for a while after Llewelyn Davies himself lost interest. The two people who could have kept up some momentum disappeared – Duccio Turin to die on the autostrada after launching UN Habitat, and Reyner Banham to profess in California. From that point onwards the professions and disciplines began to strengthen, regroup and assert themselves.

If some future historian tests these recollections against documentary evidence, I think they'll find that by the late 1980s there were distinct curricula for architecture, planning and construction with virtually no overlap and even more tightly circumscribed curricula for master's students. Teaching styles too had substantially reverted, with students of Planning doing essays and group projects, Architecture students working individually in the competitive creative culture of 'crits' and 'juries', and Construction students visiting sites, assimilating bullet points and passing exams.

Two safety valves survived to enable difficult individuals to escape the silos of the packaged programmes: undergraduates remained free to opt out of the professionally accredited compulsory programmes and mix their own diet; a small minority continue to do so. And, at postgraduate level some master's programmes offered critical and highly intellectual material which could be taken instead of or as well as the narrower professional packages.

For the last two decades the undergraduate programme has contained just one course aiming to build some understanding of the built environment as a social product, shared among all the student body, and this survives despite some active and passive denigration and is still the only faculty-wide activity for most students.[1] This course has often started with a provocation from Adrian Forty: a micro-lecture arguing that professional identities are essential to the learning process and the effective social division of professional labour – right down to the self-referential private languages, dress codes and contemptuous stereotyping of the other professions. It is a good debate but there is nowhere to hold it beyond a first-year classroom.

This history is a great defeat for those of us who have always hoped that a university education would enable society to be continuously self-critical, enabling students to combine specialised skills with a good grasp of the world they are making. The problem has been exacerbated by the marketisation of universities and the pressure on marketable subject fields to grow and grow. Since the production of the built environment plays a central role in the capital accumulation strategies of the wealthiest one per cent across the world, it is no surprise that our 'product' is selling so well. But the challenge of maintaining and developing a critical debate on what we are collectively achieving is ever harder. Furthermore the UK's stance on the Bologna Declaration – to standardise master's-level study at one year while the rest of Europe settled for two years – has surely tended to dumb down what can be achieved and cut out breadth and adventure in the choice of subjects.

This string of reminiscence has so far been entirely negative: the grumpy old man speaks. However, I do consider that there are some gleams of hope.

Within UCL, we have in recent years seen a great flowering of cross-cutting initiatives, mainly affecting research but with some influence on teaching. One example is the UCL Urban Lab which brings together staff and postgraduates not just from all parts of The Bartlett but from other departments and faculties for discussions, joint projects, film screenings and research initiatives. It has proved to be instrumental in getting the UCL 'management' to listen to scholars in its deliberations on whether and where to establish a second London campus, and claims some credit for the decision not to choose a site which displaces a settled community.

Within The Bartlett, we see the launch of an interesting new programme which enables students to draw upon the hitherto segregated strands of teaching about urban design which take place in four sections of the faculty.

Finally, I am cheered by the strong and spontaneous interest shown by students volunteering to work alongside and for community groups and activist networks in London, contributing to public debates and decision-making at City Hall, borough and neighbourhood levels. This activity, supported in part by UCL's Public Engagement Unit, reframes the city through the experiences, priorities and organisations of Londoners struggling with the intensifying attacks on material conditions and social life. Students discover in this work which of their skills and which areas of their intellectual apparatus are most useful in new contexts. It may be mapping or statistics or air quality monitoring but it may equally be a strong historical grasp of London's social geography. Among these students I commonly have to ask (if I want to know) whether an individual is based in Geography, Architecture, Planning or Engineering, and that feels like progress.[2]

A unified social science remains elusive. The quest for an integrated social understanding of the production of the built environment, which preoccupied many of us in the 1980s, fizzled out in the 1990s.[3] The society and the city are fraught with contradictions and so it's no surprise that within our own institution we find retrograde and emancipatory tendencies side by side.

Professions and academic disciplines continue to drift apart and become further removed from any shared understanding of their social role. We have achieved very little.

Notes

1   Michael Edwards, Ben Campkin and Sonia Arbaci, 'Exploring Roles and Relationships in the Production of the Built Environment', *Centre for Education in the Built Environment (CEBE) Transactions*, Vol 6, No 1, 2009. Publisher's version at http://www.cebe.heacademy.ac.uk/transactions/index.php.

2   UCL Just Space (2009), http://ucljustspace.wordpress.com [accessed 30 September 2013].

3   Bartlett International Summer Schools on the Production of the Built Environment, Proceedings (1979-1996) London.

CHAPTER 29

Reyner Banham's Hat

MURRAY FRASER

The first and only time that I saw Reyner Banham's hat – in the flesh, as it were – was in June 1982. I remember this because he had come to give a talk on Anglo-American interchange in the Arts and Crafts Movement to us students in the first cohort of the Master's programme in the History of Modern Architecture, a course which had just been set up by Adrian Forty and Mark Swenarton. Both had been PhD students and protégés of Banham's while he was at the Bartlett School of Architecture. Adrian and Mark knew how he dressed. We didn't.

Of course we had all read Banham's work, and greatly admired his energetic and vivid style. But none of us expected the person entering the rather drab seminar room in UCL to look like a cowboy. No sir, no way. For all his glittering reputation and undoubted skill with words, I have to report that the lecture was not that substantial. Banham didn't really make enough out of the transatlantic connection to grab our attention. And we were probably too fascinated by his attire.

Looking back now, however, I realise that this was one of the impetuses that later prompted me to research a book published in 2007 as *Architecture and the 'Special Relationship'*, on which Joe Kerr also worked in the initial years. The book charts the complex hybridisation of British architecture in the decades after the Second World War as it came to terms with the USA's new-found hegemony in all matters economic, political, military and cultural.

How then had Reyner Banham – the boy from Norwich, Nikolaus Pevsner's PhD student, the eager young staffer on the *Architectural Review* in

WILL ROGERS
Out of the plains he came
A homely man
With lariat twirled.
A hitch on our hearts he gained
This kingly man
As he rounded up the world.
T. W. Hurst

Vitruvian cowboy.
An old postcard showing Will Rogers, the most celebrated Hollywood cowboy of the 1920s and 1930s, performing his trick roping act. Reyner Banham, born in 1922, was one of millions of British schoolboys who idolised heroes like Rogers after watching them in the Saturday morning 'penny pictures'.

the 1950s, a star Bartlett academic from 1964 up to 1976, after which he moved to teach at the University at Buffalo in New York and then the University of California, Santa Cruz – turned into this cowboy we saw before us? Earlier photos of Banham show someone who obviously looked like a typical London intellectual living in Hampstead, or more accurately in his case, in Aberdare Gardens in Swiss Cottage, just down the hill from Hampstead's elite enclave. He had a bushy beard, wore suitably thick glasses and pedalled around town on a mini-bicycle, and held sought-after Sunday soirées attended by those in the up-and-coming generation. The young Archigrammer, Peter Cook, happened to live on the same road, and would pass copies of new editions of their now-legendary magazine to Banham so the latter could spread them across America whenever he went to lecture there.

Banham's initial visit to the USA was in 1961, following the immediate global success of his book *Theory and Design in the First Machine Age* (1960). He went over for a single weekend in New York City. The invitation came from

Philip Johnson, who for decades acted as the power broker and reputation maker in American architecture. Banham joined Johnson in a public forum sponsored by the Architectural League of New York and *Architectural Forum* journal, discussing the future of 'International Style' modernism. Johnson even paid for Banham's air fare, the only reason the latter could afford the trip at a time when transatlantic flights were out of most people's reach.[1]

Banham also got a chance to lecture at Yale University in the 1960–61 academic year. Many other visits to the USA followed, including as a semi-regular speaker at the annual international design conference in Aspen, Colorado. In 1964 Banham gave a paper at a conference at the Cranbrook Academy of Art on how history and theory should be taught in architectural courses; the following year he was funded by the Graham Foundation of Chicago to research into environmental servicing in American buildings. Banham used this money to visit Los Angeles, his first trip to a city that he fell in love with instantly. He was delighted when in 1968 he was asked to coordinate the Aspen Design Conference, this event acting as the trigger for when the cowboy dressing began.

There are a few accounts left by participants at the 1968 Aspen conference, but perhaps none are quite as revealing as that of the young Austrian architect, Hans Hollein – a somewhat bristly architect who was closely involved in the Viennese artistic avant-garde, and fascinated by space rockets and environmental control measures like helmets, pills, sprays and smart spectacles. Hollein was also someone who, like Banham and Archigram, was fixated with – indeed, in love with – America and its culture. Hollein had spent a year in the USA back in 1958–9, travelling thousands of miles by road and infusing himself with its buoyant spirit.

Hollein subsequently wrote a short piece titled 'Nuts and Bolts' for the 'Cosmorama' section of *Architectural Design* in September 1968. A photograph shows Hollein, Banham and others at the Aspen conference, with Banham wearing a rather fine Stetson. Hollein observed:

> Design is important, and to find out more about the state of design, its definitions, intentions and problems – on this and the other side of the Atlantic – Reyner Banham was made programme chairman. He set out by buying a Western outfit complete with cowboy hat ...[2]

Hollein wrote another, less reverential review in German for his natural habitat of *Bau* magazine, and again one of the key points he mentioned was that Banham 'bought a cowboy hat and suit' in order to preside at Aspen. He also explained Banham's intentions as the event organiser:

> To juxtapose Europe and America, to discuss the hard facts of realization, and finally to give an understanding of the things that designers and architects should expect in a time in which everything has to become architecture.[3]

Hollein's comment on everything now having to become architecture was of course an observation Banham often made himself. It was to surface again in the iconic, if highly staged, photographs that Tim Street-Porter took of Banham on his small-wheeled bike in the Californian desert for the latter's 1982 classic book, *Scenes in American Deserta* – a brilliant early example of psychogeography. These are images I took pains to deconstruct in *Architecture and the 'Special Relationship'* since they so clearly demonstrate the culturally hybrid image of Banham as a combination of sensitive North London intellectual and that tough-guy-academic-in-the-field, Indiana Jones. 'Swooping and sprinting like a skater over the surface of Silurian Lake, I came as near as ever to a whole-body experience equivalent to the sheer space that one enjoys in America Deserta,' Banham wrote breathlessly in his text.[4] Also crucial was the absence in the photographs of anything which remotely smacks of 'fine' architecture, or indeed any buildings at all; instead the emphasis is on the elemental and primitive forms of the desert that engulf the cycling figure. Banham today is probably best remembered for his promotion of advanced technology in architecture, but the point is he was always far more than that. Ultimately, it was to create a British understanding of America – and especially of American architecture of many different varieties (pueblo-style, Arts and Crafts, concrete factories and warehouses, Case Study houses, etc) – that was his real intellectual project.

I mention all this about Banham because it also reflects on the unique intellectual contribution that Adrian Forty has made. Adrian greatly admired Banham but was also far too aware of the latter's blind spots and weaknesses. He took so much from Banham, possibly in part subconsciously, something that was to become more evident over the years. I would contend there are two main infusions from the Banham influence which shaped Adrian's writings: firstly, the realisation that, due to the interconnection of industrial capitalism and 20th-century modernism, everything is now intrinsically related to architecture (or as Hollein expressed it in his 1968 mantra, 'Everything is Architecture'[5]); and secondly, that architecture is a profoundly cultural creation and can only ever be understood in such terms.

Taking the first point, in this sense Banham's cowboy hat is an obvious contender as an 'Object of Desire'. It serves as a material witness in itself, in having been bought in the USA, and by possessing a functional basis for its existence, keeping off the sun and flies in dusty western plains, while also being clearly styled as a design artefact. The hat also tells us about the social relations of its wearer and his attempt to escape what Banham regarded as the third-rate environment of British architecture and culture, along with his pressing desire to become an actor in his own tales – or what Robert Maxwell memorably described as 'the plenitude of presence' in Banham's writings.[6] Hence in Adrian's own classic book of design history, *Objects of Desire* (1986), the discussion is able to move seamlessly from a Wedgwood teapot to a Lucky Strike cigarette packet to a 1930s London Underground map. Each, in its own way, has to be considered in relation to architecture, just as architecture has to be considered in relationship to them within the capitalist constructs of production and meaning and experience.

The second point, that architecture is a profoundly cultural creation, is something that emerged more slowly from the course set up by Adrian and Mark. Initially the course's rationale, which we all repeated dutifully, was that it was the first attempt – certainly in British circles – to bring an economic and political interpretation to architectural history. Indeed, in many respects it has been Adrian's lifetime intellectual goal to explain what happened to Western architecture as a consequence of the development of industrial capitalism from the mid-18th century. But reflecting back now, while of course we talked in the 1980s of economics and politics, we never actually studied those subjects in any detail. Also revealing is the fact that in a period during the 1980s and 1990s when so many young architects were reading critical theory from Roland Barthes or Henri Lefebvre or Gilles Deleuze, the Bartlett Master's course always had more affinity with the British left tradition of cultural studies, as founded by Raymond Williams. It was culture – that is, how people lived every day – which could illuminate abstract economic and political ideas. Architecture in this sense genuinely matters as a physical entity and ideological construct, with its essence being cultural. Adrian's latest book, *Concrete and Culture* (2012), is in my view his coming to terms with this realisation.

I took my own cue from the approach I had learned at The Bartlett, looking to the likes of Edward Said and Stuart Hall to stimulate my interest first in postcolonial theory, then cultural hybridisation, and more recently the processes of globalisation. Using the formulation – as mediated through Adrian – that all things are interconnected with architecture and also need be investigated as cultural constructs, it has been possible to avoid the two weaknesses of contemporary architectural history: on the one hand, an escape into meta-theory among East Coast US academics, in some bizarre kind of modern neo-idealist thinking that apparently allows them to avoid any discussion of actual problems in the world; and on the other hand, the ultra-empirical approach found in Britain and elsewhere whereby facts-in-themselves are regarded somehow as holding self-evident truths, despite all evidence to the contrary.

Following on from Adrian's lead, we became the generation which fully opened up architectural history as a cultural subject. Whether future generations will thank us for this remains uncertain, but it certainly accorded well with the parallel infusion of cultural theory into architecture by the more interesting practitioners of our time, be they as diverse as Rem Koolhaas or Bernard Tschumi or Liz Diller or Teddy Cruz.

Notes

1   Adrian Forty, 'Reyner Banham and his Context', conference paper, for 'The Special Relationship: American and British Architecture since 1945', Architectural Association/Paul Mellon Centre, London, 29–30 October 1998; see also: *Architectural Review*, Vol 135, No 807, May 1964, p 315; Robert AM Stern, Thomas Mellins and David Fishman (eds), *New York 1960: Architecture and Urbanism between the Second World War and the Bicentennial*, Monacelli Press (New York), 1995, p 1207; Robert Stern, 'The Impact of Yale' reprinted in D Jenkins (ed), *On Foster … Foster On*, Prestel (Munich, London and New York), 2000, p 354; Nigel Whiteley, *Reyner Banham: Historian of the Immediate Future*, The MIT Press (Cambridge, Massachusetts and London), 2002, pp 28–9.

2   Hans Hollein, 'Nuts and Bolts', *Architectural Design*, September (No 9), 1968, p 397; see also: Reyner Banham (ed), *The Aspen Papers: Twenty Years of Design Theory from the International Design Conference in Aspen*, Pall Mall Press (London), 1974.

3 Hans Hollein, '18th International Design Conference in Aspen: America and Europe', *Bau*, No 4, 1968, p 83: this translation from German to English was kindly provided by Eva Branscome as part of the research for her PhD thesis on 'Hans Hollein and Postmodernism: Art and Architecture in Austria 1958–1985', Bartlett School of Architecture, UCL.

4 Reyner Banham, *Scenes in American Deserta*, The MIT Press (Cambridge, Massachusetts and London), 1982/89, p 18.

5 The mantra first appeared in Hollein's essay 'Alles ist Architektur', *Bau*, No 1–2, 1968, pp 1–32.

6 Robert Maxwell, 'Reyner Banham: The Plenitude of Presence', *Architectural Design*, No 6/7, 1981, pp 52–7.

CHAPTER 30

Situated Architectural Historical Ecologies

PEG RAWES

Although many contributors to this book, and its readers, will know Adrian through discussions of buildings, my conversations with him frequently revolve around the history of ideas. Recently, we've talked about non-standard biological thinking and his work on the geopolitics of concrete and the politics of the commons. We also talk a good deal about art. And, while Adrian does not personally express himself through these particular vocabularies, the role of the historian in 'taking care' of understanding the co-mutual relationship between the individual and his/her environmental, cultural and technological contexts, and the consequent impact of these for human and non-human relations are, for me, vibrant throughout his work. I also see his work as contributing to the 'care of the self and others' that defines those thinkers and practitioners who also, perhaps more explicitly than Adrian, examine our ethical, poetic and ecological architectural relations.

Broadly, throughout this kind of discussion, there is a sustained focus upon the cultural and material production of life that enable different modes of expression in, and for, the individual, society and the built environment. In addition, unequivocally, there is a renewed urgency to examine how beneficial or damaging these relationships are for the human and the non-human built and 'natural' environments that we inhabit.

I would like to suggest that these kinds of practices might be called 'biopolitical ecologies', and I would wish to situate Adrian's work within this milieu. I also use this conjunction of terms because these are examinations of situated beings, spaces and cultures that come after Ernst Haeckel's 1866 definition of 'ecology', which he identified as the study of the 'household of nature'.[1] In addition, it acknowledges the tension between regulatory and determining societal modes of constructing concepts of life in and for the individual (which Michel Foucault famously analysed in his 'Birth of Biopolitics' lectures in 1978–79[2]), yet also affirms the more recent and positive expressions of life (*zoe*) as ethical, poetic and situated difference that have been developed by feminist philosophers (such as Donna Haraway, Rosi Braidotti or Luce Irigaray),[3] and in Félix Guattari's thought-provoking social, mental and environmental 'eco-logical praxis' of *The Three Ecologies* (1989).[4]

These latter, affirmative, biopolitical practices are distinct from the pathological regimes of exclusion, or normative self-management that Giorgio Agamben and Roberto Esposito derive from Foucault's lectures, and I draw attention to them as especially relevant now because of the complex challenges that human and environmental relations pose for the political and poetic constitution of our corporeal selves, our homes, our urban environments, as well as for the planet's resources more broadly. For those communities who are not recipients of the life-opportunities that tend to be available only to those who can afford them (for example, high-end medical care or high-quality urban housing), such 'biopolitical poetics' designate 'another way of entering into relation with oneself, with the world, with ... other(s)'.[5] And, because these are inherently relational 'states of affairs', they might also be conceived as ecological habits and habitats that situate the subject, and his/her others within human and non-human, built and natural, local and global, environments.

In recent years, I've explored how these questions operate in the work of feminist philosophers such as Luce Irigaray, especially because of her emphasis on the cultivation of diverse human relations between cultural and natural social forces, and the places and patterns of inhabitation which reflect contemporary critiques about the rights given to or withheld from communities in these relations. These approaches are also powerfully critical modes of imagining and building diverse psychophysical ecologies for individual women, men, communities and societies, and for enabling understandings about how ecologies of life contribute to the formation of positive and negative expressions of difference in the past, the present and the future.

My discussion here also follows Alison Stone's helpful identification of Irigaray's later work as 'realist essentialism' in which male and female sex differences are real, naturally existing expressions that are independent of a society's particular cultural expression of sexual difference, and which consequently also construct relations between women and men, and their respective environments.[6] Irigaray defines these relations as 'sexuate' difference (rather than her earlier formation of 'sexual' difference), and here we find that difference defines an *ethics or 'care'* of non-pathological human–human and human–nature relations. Consequently, I would suggest, this expressive biodiversity of care can also inform thinking about the sustainability of human and natural resources in the process of designing and inhabiting built environments.

The feminist philosopher, Lorraine Code, has named the explicit undertaking of these relations as 'ecological thinking' that draws attention to the political need to protect existing, and create future, sexuate ecological *relations* between women, men and their natural, cultural and built environments.[7] She writes:

> Ecological thinking is not simply thinking about ecology or about the environment: it generates revisioned modes of engagement with knowledge, subjectivity, politics, ethics, science, citizenship, and agency, which pervade and reconfigure theory and practice alike. First and foremost a thoughtful practice, thinking ecologically carries with it a large measure of responsibility. [… As to] how it could translate into wider issues of citizenship and politics, [...] the answer, at once simple and profound, is that *ecological thinking is about imagining, crafting, articulating, endeavoring to enact principles of ideal cohabitation.*[8]

Code's elegant definition of ecological thinking shows how feminist conceptualisations of ethically sustainable relationships question prioritising large-scale governmental and private industrial investment in market-driven eco-technologies and sciences (such as the contemporary contexts of biofuel manufacturing and fracking technologies). Instead, feminist environmental and ecological philosophy value the overlooked historical, political and ethical practices of life which concern the enduring life of society as a whole, as well as our stewardship of the natural environment, rather than the short-term, shallow, profit-led benefits which technocratic environmental markets gain for the privileged few. Informed by these approaches, architectural ecologies might then constitute the complex interrelationship between culture and nature, on the local spatiotemporal scale of everyday domestic and community inhabitations, as well as on the global or planetary scales of environmental relations and communities.

A cultivation of built ethical ecologies is also present in Irigaray's discussions of dwelling where ecological relations are poetic psychophysical modes of inhabitation:

> To construct only in order to construct nevertheless does not suffice for dwelling. A cultivation of the living must accompany a building of that which does not grow by itself. [...] To cultivate human life in its engendering and its growth requires the elaboration of material and spiritual frameworks and constructions. These should not be opposed to the becoming of life, as they have too often been, but provide it with the help indispensable for its blossoming.[9]

Here, an architectural ecology is both the cultivation of poetic sense and physical matters which are directed towards the invention of new ecological relations, as well as the retrieval of forgotten or repressed relations. Irigaray's examination questions the belief that energetic relations can only be effectively defined through the techno-scientific disciplines, which currently dominate debates about environmental resources and energy provision. In *Thinking the Difference* (1993) she suggests that women's psychophysical nature highlights how human–nature relations can be cultivated through low-impact energetic durations, which correspond with the conservation of energy of low-impact technologies, and contrast with the damaging psychophysical tendency towards unsustainable cycles of highly unstable energy consumption and expenditure which underpins some advanced technologies, such as nuclear power.[10]

TECHNICAL ETHICS OF CARE

However, in the end, Irigaray's overall tendency to reject the value of technology raises significant issues for contemporary architectural, feminist and ecological thinking, especially when physical models of energy are also still so necessary towards establishing critical models of ecological education and transformation in society. In addition, her approach imposes an obstructive and often exclusive division between the arts and sciences, and upon architecture, thereby also ultimately constraining women's and men's positive and transformative powers to express sexuate difference in all disciplines – architecture, the arts, as well as in engineering and the sciences. Instead, work by feminist-scientists since Rachel Carson's pioneering research on DDT (*Silent Spring*, 1964) has shown that ethical and situated understandings of ecology and technology are essential: for example, Isabelle Stengers and Karen Barad's ethical situated feminist critiques of chemistry and particle physics,[11] or Donna Haraway and Rosi Braidotti's future-focused 'sympathetic critiques' of advanced technology which argue that the survival of our human and non-human lives require this especially nuanced kind of 'care' *for all.* As Haraway noted over thirty years ago, the individual's, the community's and society's habits and respective habitats can only be ethical and non-exclusionary when advanced technology is 'situated' *and* sexed.[12]

Such approaches also 'have a care' with Gregory Bateson's 'ecology of mind', and Guattari's 'ethico-political' inquiry into the consequences of 'Integrated World Capitalism' for the future survival of biodiverse *altérité* (that is, the right to positive differentiation) across the mental, physical, technical, aesthetic and biological spheres.[13] And, although these men do not identify themselves with a conceptualisation of difference that is developed through Western feminist philosophy's traditions, each critiques the resulting pathological relations that shallow forms of technological thinking result in, and the obstruction of such approaches towards cultivating real ethical, poetic and political difference.

Notes

1   Haeckel develops the term in *Generelle Morphologie der Organismen*, 1866.

2   Michel Foucault, *The Birth of Biopolitics: Lectures at the Collège de France, 1978–1979*, Palgrave Macmillan (Basingstoke), 2010.

3 For instance, see Rosi Braidotti, *The Posthuman*, Polity Press (Cambridge), 2013; Rosi Braidotti, *Transpositions: On Nomadic Ethics*, Polity Press (Cambridge), 2006; Donna Haraway, *When Species Meet*, University of Minnesota Press (Minneapolis, Minnesota and London), 2008; and Luce Irigaray, *Thinking the Difference: For a Peaceful Revolution* (1989), translated by K Montin, Continuum-Routledge (London and New York), 1993.

4 Félix Guattari, *The Three Ecologies* (1989), translated by I Pindar and P Sutton, Athlone Press (London), 2000.

5 Luce Irigaray, *Key Writings*, Continuum (New York and London), 2004, p x.

6 Alison Stone, *Luce Irigaray and the Philosophy of Sexual Difference*, Cambridge University Press (Cambridge), 2000, pp 18–19.

7 There are many others in this tradition including Val Plumwood, Vandana Shiva and Verena Andermatt Conley.

8 Lorraine Code, *Ecological Thinking: The Politics of Epistemic Location*, Oxford University Press (Oxford), 2006, p 24.

9 Luce Irigaray, *The Way of Love*, Continuum (New York) 2002, p 144.

10 Irigaray, *Thinking the Difference*, pp 7–8.

11 Karen Barad, *Meeting the Universe Halfway: Quantum Physics and the Entanglement of Matter and Meaning*, Duke University Press (Durham, California), 2007; and Isabelle Stengers, *Power and Invention: Situating Science, Theory Out of Bounds*, Vol 10, University of Minnesota Press (Minneapolis, Minnesota and London), 1997.

12 Donna Haraway, *Simians, Cyborgs and Women: The Reinvention of Nature*, Free Association Press (London), 1991.

13 Gregory Bateson, *Steps to an Ecology of Mind*, University of Chicago Press (Chicago, Illinois), 2000; Guattari, *The Three Ecologies*.

CHAPTER 31

Objects

PENNY SPARKE

I was introduced to Adrian Forty by Peter (Reyner) Banham in the mid-1970s. At that time the discipline of design history was still in its infancy. Both Peter and Adrian were intensely involved in the development of the new discipline. They attended the early subject conferences held at Newcastle and Middlesex Polytechnics and gave papers.[1] Although he is best known as an architectural historian, Adrian Forty's intervention into design history has proved to be hugely significant. His book on the subject, *Objects of Desire: Design and Society since 1750*, published in 1986, has become hugely popular. Widely read by Design and Design History students, among others, and included as recommended reading in academic institutions across the globe, it has become a key text, sold many thousands of copies and been extremely widely cited.[2] However, most students read it primarily as a source of invaluable research material relating to design's history in the period in question and are probably unaware that, when it was published, it transformed the, then-still-emerging, discipline of design history irrevocably.

Up until the 1980s the debate around design history and its methodology had largely focused on whether the new discipline belonged to Art History or to Architectural History. In both cases the emphasis was upon 'great men' and their visualising skills. The only difference was which 'great men'? With only a very few exceptions the idea that design was more dependent upon economic, ideological and social forces than upon the creative choices of individuals had not been given serious consideration. *Objects of Desire* changed all that. Suddenly the debate was less about Raymond Loewy's input into the design of the Lucky Strike cigarette pack and more about the interwar period's obsession with hygiene and 'whiteness'. In forming his highly persuasive argument,

Adrian was responding to the kind of designer-celebrity syndrome that Stephen Bayley had promoted in his 1979 book, *In Good Shape: Style in Industrial Products, 1900–1960*, in which industrial designers were described as the new Leonardo da Vincis of their day, transformers of the everyday world into a better and more beautiful place through design.

Adrian was not party to that utopian vision, one incidentally that had been promulgated by the designers themselves back in the 1930s as part of the modernist dream. He positioned himself, rather, as a neutral academic historian, keen to analyse and explain rather than to exalt. Most importantly he used his training as a historian to think about the ways in which different forces interact with each other to bring about change and how, to a significant extent, we, as mere mortals, are powerless to alter things. His overt irritation with the progress of design history to that point and its obsession with style was expressed in strong language. 'The study of design and its history has suffered from a form of cultural lobotomy which has left design only connected to the eye, and severed its connections to the brain and to the pocket,' he wrote.[3] Architectural historians, Mark Girouard among them, also got a beating for making social generalisations. Adrian compared those generalisations to the 'weeds and gravel around a stuffed fish in a glass case'.[4]

Adrian set up his powerful argument by explaining that 'designers' (the word itself was not necessarily used at the time) began their lives as lowly employees of manufacturing companies. Indeed, in the early mass-producing companies, Josiah Wedgwood's ceramics works among them, designing involved a range of anonymous individuals each of whom performed a highly specialised task. The following section of the book dug beneath the variety of styles presented by designed objects to address the more profound notion of the requirement for diversity in the marketplace. The latter, Adrian argued, had a clear economic rationale, albeit with inevitable aesthetic manifestations. This discussion led him to address in some detail two designed and inhabited environments, those of the home and the office. In both of those spaces he focused on the links between design and ideology and on their role in the formation of identities. Throughout the text he was adamant that objects were important mechanisms of ideological transfer rather than mere communicators of visual content, and that designers' statements about design were of no more significance than anyone else's.

On one level Adrian probably took his argument too far. Of course designers' choices, including visual ones, are important. Indeed, as my 1978 article – 'From a Lipstick to a Steamship: The Growth of the American Industrial Design Profession' – demonstrated, I am one of the design historians from that era who felt the need to recover the influential pioneer designers and recognise their contribution. They, and, more particularly, their backgrounds in commercial art, I contended, had previously been overlooked and were important factors in understanding why designed artefacts look as they do and mean what they mean.[5]

The strength of Adrian's argument needs to be seen in context, however. Back in the mid-1980s, such was the growing adulation (led by Terence Conran and others and supported by Margaret Thatcher) for the new heroes of the day – designers, that is – that strong arguments against their burgeoning omnipotence were much needed. Adrian's voice was, back then, a rare but important antidote to the 'designer culture' that was fast becoming a defining characteristic of Britain's consumer culture. Only recently, in the early 21st century, have we begun to reject that concept as not offering a sustainable way of life; begun to think seriously about design as a social phenomenon with the potential to transform lives; and to understand the designer as just one agent among others in the realisation of that goal.

Although he didn't dwell on it, Adrian was more interested in the idea of 'taste', a social concept that relates to the values held by different groups, defined by, among other categories, class, gender or nation, than in that of 'style', which leads, more naturally, to an art historical analysis. In spite of the fact that, unlike Adrian, I considered the input of designers to be an important part of design historical knowledge that needs to be unpacked in order to be able to discover what objects have meant in the past, my own trajectory in design history from the late-1980s onwards, also focused on the concept of taste.[6] Although I had a different agenda from Adrian, my reason for addressing it, like his, emanated from a desire to understand design, not only in the context of production, but also in that of consumption. My mission, however, was not, like Adrian's, that of a scholar-historian setting out to address the limitations of existing design historical studies that had not understood the workings of the deep forces of change but, rather, to show how, from a feminist perspective, design of the modern period had been aligned to the values of masculine culture with the result that it had contributed to the marginalisation of feminine culture.

In that project, which ended up as my 1995 publication, *As Long as It's Pink: the Sexual Politics of Taste*, I was indebted to the rigorous scholarship in *Objects of Desire* on a number of levels. Firstly, the idea, proposed by Adrian, that design and cultural values are closely linked was fundamental to my study. Secondly, the space of the home became a very important place for me as the location within which feminine culture was embedded, and I found myself working with many of the same sources that Adrian had unearthed in his case study of the domestic sphere. I also realised that I was treading in his steps in my work on the ideological underpinnings of modernism.

I am only one of the many design historians who discovered that Adrian had got there first. Not only did he provide a methodological object lesson to the discipline as a whole by demonstrating that we have to ask more far-reaching questions of our material, he also undertook pioneering research in areas that have subsequently been readdressed from many different perspectives and offered many different readings. Adrian is a true pioneer of the discipline of design history as it has developed, and continues to develop, today. As a result of his work, design historical scholarship has finally found itself a secure place in the academy alongside art and architectural history.

Notes

1   The first Design History conference was held at Newcastle Polytechnic in 1975. Entitled 'Design 1900–1960: Studies in Design and Popular Culture of the 20th Century', the conference included papers by Reyner Banham and Adrian Forty. The second Design History conference was held at Middlesex Polytechnic in the following year. It was entitled 'Leisure in the Twentieth Century' and Reyner Banham delivered a paper.

2   733 citations on Google Scholar, 27 August 2013.

3   Stephen Bayley, *In Good Shape: Style in Industrial Products, 1900–1960*, Van Nostrand Reinhold (London), 1979, p 6.

4   Ibid.

5   Penny Sparke, 'From a Lipstick to a Steamship: The Growth of the American Industrial Design Profession', in Terry Bishop (ed), *Design History: Fad or Function?*, Design Council (London), 1978.

6   See, for example, Penny Sparke, *Italian Design: 1870 to the Present*, Thames & Hudson (London), 1988 and Penny Sparke, *Japanese Design*, Michael Joseph (London), 1988, both of which acknowledge the importance of designers.

CHAPTER 32

Richard Llewelyn Davies, 1912– 1981: A Lost Vision for The Bartlett

SIR PETER HALL

Richard Llewelyn Davies (1912–1981), Baron Llewelyn-Davies of Hastoe, was one of the very few people of whom you could truly say: you could never make him up. He was simply *sui generis*: Professor of Architecture at The Bartlett from 1960 to 1969, Professor of Urban Planning and Head of the School of Environmental Studies from 1970 to 1975, founder and head of Llewelyn-Davies Weeks, co-designer of Milton Keynes, one of the very few architects to have ever been invited to reside at the Institute for Advanced Study in Princeton, his life was a unique blend of Celtic Romanticism and alleged upper-class skulduggery. His father, Crompton, was a respectable Edwardian Welsh lawyer and civil servant; his mother, née Moya O'Connor, was the daughter of James O'Connor, the Irish Fenian leader, who was in Kilmainham Gaol when she was born. Logically enough she grew up to become one of the closest associates (and possible lover) of the Irish revolutionary Michael Collins; following inimitable family form, she was in Mountjoy Prison on gun-running charges when Richard was a child. His four cousins, sons of Sylvia Llewelyn Davies, daughter of cartoonist/writer George du Maurier, were the inspiration for JM Barrie's *Peter Pan*. At Cambridge, Llewelyn Davies was a member of the 'Apostles' and an associate of the Soviet spies, Guy Burgess and Anthony Blunt, as well as Victor Rothschild, later accused of being the 'Fifth Man', who became a lifelong friend as well as a fellow Lords Peer. Married to Patricia Parry, who became a Life Peeress, they were one of the few couples who both held titles in their own right.

With a Diploma in Architecture from the Architectural Association (AA), Llewelyn Davies was briefly in partnership with Peter Moro from 1938, and was elected an Associate of the Royal Institute of British Architects (RIBA) in 1939. After the Second World War he became celebrated for his research at the Nuffield Foundation on the design and planning of hospitals, before his appointment to the Bartlett Chair of Architecture in 1960 and to the Chair of Planning in 1970, succeeding William Holford – thereby becoming the first to combine these two titles in the Bartlett's long history. His mission, he wrote, was 'trying to bring architecture into closer touch with developments in the natural and social sciences', and consistent with this the architecture school under his aegis became the School for Environmental Studies.

In his inaugural lecture as Professor of Architecture, on 10 November 1960, he recalled that in that very month, 300 years earlier, the Royal Society had been born. Christopher Wren, one of its founders, had been a mathematician, astronomer and architect. As Llewelyn Davies pointed out:

> [Wren] saw no conflict between his work as an artist and as a scientist; it would not have occurred to him to draw a line between art and science. But this distinction, which became firmly established in the nineteenth century, is now entrenched in our thinking. It has split our concept of the architect down the middle [...] We therefore have to review the whole pattern of architectural education, to consider the range of knowledge which an architect needs, and the methods by which he can be trained to use his knowledge as a creative designer.[1]

Llewelyn Davies concluded that the entire architectural curriculum needed to be reshaped to incorporate a much wider range of essential knowledge, including 'the sciences which deal with the human being – both as an individual and as a member of a group'.[2] He wrote:

To understand what he is doing when he designs a building, an architect must know how it will affect people. Therefore he must be taught something of anatomy, physiology, and the psychology of the special senses. He must also understand enough physics to predict the physical conditions which will be produced within his buildings by his design. In our present courses some consideration is given to these questions, but they are dealt with in the wrong way and at the wrong time. Instead of presenting the physics, psychology, and physiology of the human environment at the very beginning of the course as part of the theoretical basis of architecture, we usually give the student a short account of the practical problems of heating, lighting, and acoustics towards the end of his training. He naturally forms the conclusion that these environmental factors are something additional to the architectural design – something to be solved by calling in a technical expert. This is a striking example of the consequences of the false opposition of art and science. Perhaps the extreme physical, psychological, and aesthetic discomfort which you are suffering this evening in this lecture room can be attributed to the mal-education of its architect in this respect.[3]

Evidently – as Llewelyn Davies usually did – he was making his point in a highly effective way. He went on:

The social sciences are equally important, as they provide the means whereby we can fit buildings to the needs of human beings as a group. Modern society is too complex for the architect to have an automatic understanding of what is wanted in a building; the client does not know this either, although he sometimes thinks he does. For many modern buildings, there is no single client. Many people are concerned with the functioning of a hospital or a college, each may understand the workings of some part of it but no one understands it completely, as a whole. Again, the long life of buildings when compared with the rate of change of human organisation, means that people often adjust their pattern of life or work to fit an old building. If they are asked to specify their needs for a new one they think in terms of an old and familiar environment, they cannot break out to see what they really want. Therefore the client's brief is nearly always wrong, and a bad brief inevitably results in disastrous architecture. The solution lies in the joint study of building function by architect and client. The techniques for study are those of the social sciences, and the architect's education must equip him to understand and use these methods.

The idea that these sciences are related to architecture is fairly new and we have still to work out how best to teach them. In doing so we shall be greatly helped by the development of research.[4]

Here we see that behind the James Bond quality – the black Mercedes with the leather-clad female chauffeur, the whirlwind arrivals from Heathrow – he was a desperately serious man with a desperately serious purpose. That was to build research – across the whole gamut of the natural and the social sciences – as the foundation of the work of architects, planners and other professionals in the built environment, and in doing so to educate them in common practices and common values, so that they would in effect become subdivisions of a single unified profession. In other words, he wanted all architects and all planners to become like Richard Llewelyn Davies. That was a tall order, and he did not succeed; not because there never was anyone quite like Richard Llewelyn Davies, but because the contrary forces were just too strong.

True, over thirty years after his death and over forty years after he restructured The Bartlett, it celebrates his memory with an amazing proliferation of taught Master's courses: more than twenty-five MSc programmes and a number of research-focused MRes programmes in a variety of disciplines, as well as specialist Master's programmes for students of Architecture and Architectural History, the last led with such distinction by Adrian Forty. But they remain separate and self-contained entities. The broad-based undergraduate and postgraduate courses in Architecture and Planning, which form the core of The Bartlett's work, remain quite separate. Attempts over the decades to achieve a small degree of integration – especially through common first-year classes and overseas field classes – have produced misunderstanding and even hostility among the student participants.

There is at least one good reason and one bad reason why this should be so. The good reason is that professional education has become so overloaded, so dense and in-depth, that there is no room, no time for integration. I personally saw the truth of this in 2008, when the then government appointed a 15-strong Eco Towns Challenge Panel, chaired by Milton Keynes new town veteran John Walker and including such luminaries as that year's RIBA President, Sunand Prasad. They found themselves engaged in a massive programme of mutual education: we none of us knew more than a fraction of what was needed to build sustainable urban spaces. The bad reason is that the folkways of the relevant professionals remain deeply different, even contraposed. In particular, while planning education was restructured in the 1960s along precisely the lines that Richard was seeking to achieve, as a result of the momentous 1950 Schuster Report[5] – a strong foundation in the social sciences, especially geography, sociology and economics – no such change occurred in architectural education, which – no matter the ferocity of the battles between different schools – continued to be based firmly on the atelier or studio tradition, in which students learned in small groups around an individual master: an artistic–creative, not a research–scientific tradition.

Worse, at precisely this time, one perverse result of Schuster was that the architectural content of planning, the urban design tradition, was steadily reduced to an absolute minimum. By the 1990s it was possible to become a qualified planner without any architectural knowledge or sensibility at all. Symbolic of this was the fact that down to Llewelyn Davies, all the Bartlett Professors of Planning were architect-planners; afterwards, none were. And the few places which tried to keep integration alive, such as the distinguished small school at Nottingham University, were dismembered in a brutal reorganisation; one small consolation being that one of the reluctant academic refugees, Matthew Carmona, came to The Bartlett, there to build a respectable reputation in urban design.

You could argue, I would argue, that the results for the quality of our built environment have been catastrophic. Our planning system has lost the capacity to plan good urban places, and is supine in the face of proposals for low-grade development backed by repeated legal appeals. The main argument of Richard Rogers's Urban Task Force report, fifteen years ago – that we should promote three-dimensional masterplans for new and redeveloped urban areas – has been bypassed. Other countries – Sweden, Germany, the Netherlands – have surged ahead of us. In a new book, *Good Cities, Better Lives: How*

Europe Discovered the Lost Art of Urbanism (2014), I chronicle just a few of their remarkable successes: new towns such as Stockholm's Hammarby Sjöstad and Malmo's Västra Hamnen, suburban satellite towns at Ypenburg outside the Hague and Vathorst outside Amersfoort, or the brilliant Freiburg suburbs of Vauban and Rieselfeld. All of them display the same common features: strong, well-equipped city planning departments or agencies with the will and the capacity to draw up bold masterplans, the ability to work with private developers or building cooperatives to achieve them, and adequate financial mechanisms.

We could and should build a campaign to achieve developments of similar quality in the United Kingdom. But where are the professional teams that could generate them? I doubt that even The Bartlett is up to the job of producing them. The reason, I am certain, is that these other countries have radically different traditions of professional education. Specialists they may be, but they share a common base of understanding that enables them to work effectively in multidisciplinary teams, in a way that we would find difficult. Here, as in so many other respects, we have fallen behind our European neighbours and we need to learn from them.

Notes

1   Richard Llewelyn Davies, *The Education of an Architect: An Inaugural Lecture, Delivered at University College London, 10 November 1960*, published for University College London by HK Lewis & Co (London), 1960, p 1.

2   Ibid, p 9.

3   Ibid, p 9.

4   Ibid, p 10.

5   Great Britain Committee on the Qualifications of Planners, *Report* (Cmd 8059), HM Stationery Office (London), British Parliamentary Paper, 1950, p 14.

CHAPTER 33
Things Ungrand
SARAH WIGGLESWORTH

To a practitioner like myself, words are tangible things: textures, symbols, techniques and space. None of our actions exist outside of language. Commentators who have the time and the intellectual discipline can, through their writing, help us to explore and interpret the meanings of our work. These are writers who, though holding a disinterested position, are nonetheless interested in what is practised and produced. Without theorising

Sarah Wigglesworth Architects, Cremorne Riverside Canoeing Club, London, UK, 2008. Corten Steel cladding.

Sarah Wigglesworth Architects, Sandal Magna Primary School, Wakefield, West Yorkshire, UK, 2010. Timber deck meets cedar cladding.

design and forms, we designers are more likely to be victims of powers we do not comprehend; moreover we are unlikely to command the outcomes we desire if we don't understand how they come about.

While the dominant media discourse concerns itself with product and brand, less attention is directed to analysing the cultural matrix that gives rise to the creation of desire. Through their familiarity, the daily objects that surround and define us are often overlooked or taken for granted, so their potency is neutralised. Yet these products don't come out of nowhere: they are the result of cultural forces and preferences guided towards specific purposes. To think and write about this context is to raise to consciousness both how things are done and why this is important, which is essential to any act of creativity.

So thinkers and critics who know that designing and making are both forms of knowledge have things to say to practitioners, and are to be cherished. By pointing out what we are not aware of, we are awoken to new sensibilities. The measured pace of the thinker contrasts with the urgency of the builder,

Sarah Wigglesworth Architects with Jeremy Till, 10 Stock Orchard Street, London, UK, 2000. Fraying cement bags.

reminding us that although buildings may be produced in haste, they will almost certainly outlast the present and have something to say to the future. Directly referencing examples and details in support of the argument, Adrian Forty has helped us speak our own language more clearly. We are opened up to complex and original ideas through the beauty, directness and accessibility of his writing.

Adrian's method is to select, examine, enquire, analyse and illuminate. A strong element of his work concerns scrutinising phenomena over time, recording and describing. His observations are unique and precise and have a critic's eye. Sometimes they take the form of photographs, which he takes himself. On several occasions he arrived at our house with a long ladder accompanied by one of his daughters. He climbed the ladder to photograph our decaying cement bags. Many years later, one of these photos found its way into his book *Concrete and Culture: A Material History* (2012). In some of the images reproduced therein, a child appears too. Such evidence provides a

Sarah Wigglesworth Architects, Sandal Magna Primary School, Wakefield, West Yorkshire, UK, 2010. Infants and brick bonding.

fleeting glimpse of the context to the author's own methods; Adrian is not afraid to show us his own process. So, the research trips that coincide with outings to interesting sites and conference invitations that create an opportunity for family holidays demonstrate how, in his work, the personal and the professional so easily conjoin.

The objects of Adrian's attention are startling for their very familiarity. They are the overlooked things. Everyday things. Domestic things. Ordinary things. Things that fall through the cracks. The minor narratives. The un-grand. The verbs rather than the nouns. Through his interpretation of the how in relation to the what, Adrian connects the twin actions that are at the heart of the architectural process – thinking and doing – with their consequences. By revealing the ethic and purpose of our praxis he has made a profound and original contribution to our discipline.

CHAPTER 34

'Minor' Spaces in Officers' Bungalows of Colonial Bengal

TANIA SENGUPTA

In their guide to setting up a household in India, published in 1888, the authors Flora Annie Steel and Grace Gardiner – writing about their lived experience as wives of British civil servants based in provincial towns of India – observed that they '[did] not wish to advocate an unholy haughtiness; but an Indian household can no more be governed peacefully without dignity and prestige, than an Indian empire'.[1] What is interesting is the authors' apparently audacious suggestion that housekeeping of colonial officers' residences in India was no less important than governing the empire, embodying the values and efficiency of worthy rulers.

Indeed, underpinned by such grandiose ideological aspirations, and being epitomised in the British officer's bungalow, these households constituted an everyday domain where colonial relationships were continuously reconfigured.[2] I will reflect here upon the 'minor' spaces and 'paraphernalia' within bungalows in provincial Bengal, which were mostly dominated by large drawing rooms, dining rooms, bedrooms and home offices. Often virtually unknown to European inhabitants, or else viewed as secondary or incidental, areas such as kitchens, storerooms, toilets, bathrooms and anterooms were where much of colonial housekeeping, bodily rituals and other day-to-day activities took place. Similarly, ordinary elements like doors, windows or furniture also embodied integral aspects of colonial lifestyle.

Despite the broad split between dominant and subservient spaces in provincial bungalows based on race, privilege and social hierarchy,[3] the territorial relationships on the ground were far more complex in reality. Minor spaces, and their daily practices, routinely intersected with the major spaces of bungalow life. And as a result, various aspects of life and living in India continued to be 'discovered' by the British at a domestic level, as well as the other way round.[4] Representing at once an intimacy and estrangement between the European inhabitants and native staff, these minor spaces can tell us much about colonial social and power relationships, the dominant thrust of postcolonial critique. Equally, they help to reinstate the value of 'mundane' aspects of everyday life and spaces in historical studies, which are not always possible to discern through engagement with meta-structures of power and space alone.

COUNTRY LIVING AND BEING SERVED

Filtered initially through their experience of appointments in the colonial headquarters at Calcutta – the epicentre of colonial rule in India up to the early 20th century – subsequent postings out to provincial areas of Bengal were largely perceived by British officers as a move to the countryside. Poised between geographical isolation and natural abundance, the provincial officer's bungalow represented a denial of metropolitan amenities and the luxury as well as vulnerabilities of being 'close to nature'. Typically, it would sit within a vast enclosure called the 'bungalow compound', enjoying extremely generous internal space-standards[5] and a large retinue of servant staff. Designed to counter 'tropical' weather, it also offered a familial refuge from exposure to Indian life and people that the officers' work in the provincial revenue office, or *cutcherry*, involved on a daily basis.

The officer's bungalow consisted of a core-and-envelope arrangement drawn largely from the Bengal rural hut, but also referring at least partly to small neo-Palladian villas in Britain.[6] At its simplest, the core comprised a three-by-three arrangement of spaces for living, dining or sleeping, all shaded by an enveloping verandah which was enclosed in parts to form service spaces such as storerooms, bathrooms or toilets. Bungalows had a profusion of doors and windows to help deal with the hot-humid climate of Bengal and these made them, in effect, highly porous and low-privacy environments, filled with native

Officer's bungalow, Bankura, 1870s.

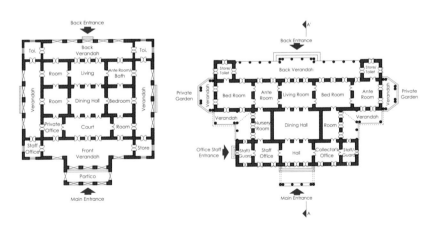

Early and late 19th-century bungalow plans, Bengal.
Plan (a) shows the Circuit House, Bankura, 1808; plan (b) is of a collector's residence, Bankura, 1860s/1870s.

servants. Over the course of the 19th century, however, the officer's bungalow developed more complex forms with multiple other spaces being plugged onto the same basic 'core'.

Above all, the provincial officer's bungalow was a service-heavy environment. It could not exist in isolation, but relied upon a number of subsidiary structures within the compound. A typical Circuit House[7] compound, for instance, would comprise the main dwelling, 'cook-room', stable block and well. By the end of the 19th century, officers' bungalows had expanded in size to include servants' quarters, out-offices and outhouses – with almost 50 per cent of the building cost going on these numerous secondary structures.[8]

SPACES FOR FOOD AND COOKERY

A typical space that aided the functioning of the main bungalow was the 'cook-room', or kitchen, built as a detached structure behind it. Attempts to keep the 'messy' life of the kitchen away from the perceptual world of the bungalow were common, with few Europeans being aware of activities inside it. One officer's wife, Mrs Clemons, observed:

> We have certainly improved them ['native' Indians] in the art of cooking, for there is scarcely anything which they cannot prepare in a superior manner. Few people however, think it necessary to visit the cook-room and as this is some distance from the house, none of the disagreeables of that department are ever seen. Perhaps the sight of the place and of the manner in which many a dainty dish is prepared, might affect the delicate stomachs of our country-women.[9]

The cook-room also became a site for hybrid practices like the development of Anglo-Indian cookery, whereby European recipes were modified by native cooks to suit Indian ingredients.[10] This was all done by servant staff in less than sumptuous circumstances, with Herbert Compton, a civil judge in the late 19th century, making the comment that: 'The kitchen is a detached building erected as far away as possible from the bungalow [… and] the cooking arrangements are primitive.'[11] So was its architecture modelled on local building practices – the cook-room was usually a 2.4- to 3-metre (8- to 10-foot) deep linear structure with thatched roof on mud walls, few openings, and a continuous verandah in front, almost identical to a traditional Bengali kitchen.[12]

Storerooms and other spaces then made up the rear service layer of the officer's bungalow, acting as an interface between the cook-room and the main dwelling (which was the domain of the House-Lady). Accidental connections between the bungalow and the cook-room were not unknown, as observed again by Mrs Clemons:

> On one occasion [...] I determined just to peep into the cook-room [...] On putting my head within the door, I found everything dished and placed on the ground without covers, in regular order, as if on the table, and the butler and the cook disputing in high terms. On my inquiring the reason of all this, they told me they always laid the dishes thus, to see which way they would look best when placed on the table![13]

This narrative reveals how, in the absence of any 'real' physical place within the official residence itself, the cook-room was used to simulate the anticipated spatial arrangement and presentation of food in the dining room. Evidently, such mimicking of situations and spaces were efforts to bridge the gaps in comprehension between apparently diverse cultural practices, but – despite all attempts by the British rulers to maintain the sanctity of their cultural practices – there were inevitable slippages that allowed Indian sensibilities about food preparation and arrangement to seep into the European tables inside.

SPACES OF BODILY RITUAL

In climatic conditions that Europeans found ever difficult to naturalise to,[14] massive value was placed in the provincial officer's bungalow on bodily rituals like bathing, morning walks and a regular diet – as heavily recommended in private accounts, travel guides or lifestyle manuals meant for East India Company and later British Crown staff working in India.[15] Another piece of advice by Mrs Clemons to officers embarking on a career in India encapsulated the role of such bodily rituals:

> I have mentioned that early rising is required on account of duty [...] But should this not be the case, it is essential to health that you should

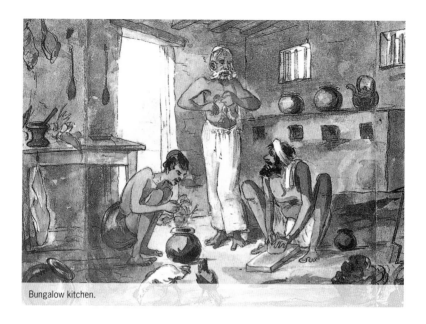
Bungalow kitchen.

rise at this hour, for the purpose of enjoying cool refreshing morning air [...] Bathing is also another essential in the preservation of health. The best time for using the bath is an hour or two after breakfast, when the atmosphere becomes hot, and you begin to feel a lassitude creeping over you. All the houses have baths attached to them, which are daily filled, and you will always find that the plunging into the cold water and remaining in it for five minutes will refresh you for some hours afterwards. [...] I have known many who regularly bathed twice a day during the very hot seasons.[16]

In spatial terms, these rituals to keep the body in reasonable order caused officers' bungalows to develop elaborate areas for toilets, washing, bathing and walking. Not only were significant proportions of space dedicated to these functions, but crucially, the temporal rhythm of the bungalow – its spatial use at different times of the day – was largely determined by them. Such cycles of rituals were intrinsically bound with distinct physical experiences – including the early-morning walk in the vast bungalow grounds, breakfast on the shaded

Bungalow storeroom.

verandah, morning bath, afternoon nap in the cool dark bedrooms, and retiring to the cool, breezy verandah for drinks after dinner. These domestic cycles also directly moderated the temporal rhythm of 'official' work. The need to take a bath two hours after breakfast meant either a trip home at noon, combined with lunch and a handy afternoon nap, or else staying at home at what would be regarded as 'office time' in Britain, or even in Calcutta.

ANCILLARY SPACES

Provincial bungalows also contained a range of intermediate spaces as anterooms, nurseries, or multipurpose rooms usually attached to bedrooms, or located close to the service spaces at the rear. Sometimes the sequence of rooms functioned together as composite cluster-units such as 'bedroom-nursery-anteroom-bathroom-toilet', or 'home office-staff office-toilet-storeroom'. The factor that most aided this functional clustering was the characteristic spatial porosity of bungalow environments. Fanny Parks, a travel writer, noted in the second quarter of the 19th century:

The style of Indian [i.e. Anglo-Indian] houses differs altogether from that of one in England [...] The windows and doors are many; the windows are to the ground, like the French [full-height glazing]; and on the outside, they are also protected by Venetian windows of the same description. All the rooms open into one another, with folding doors.[17]

Herbert Compton also wrote in the late 19th century:

Every room has direct access to a verandah, and all enter one into another, for there are no passages [...] Each bedroom has its own bath and retiring room [...] A room with a single door in it is unknown; all have two, and many three, four, and even six.[18]

The absence of corridors to mediate between rooms, and the need to access one room through others, also reveal a more flexible notion of privacy within the domestic setup of the provincial officer's bungalow, mandated by climatic requirements as well as the deep dependence of the European inhabitants on Indian staff. It would be misleading, however, to assume that the numerous doors implied a freely connected, non-hierarchical, spatial scheme. Instead, its very potential lay in the possibility of a range of spatial relationships – of clusters and hierarchies – through a selective opening or closing of doors. Thus it was the combination of non-deterministic, flexible spaces that could be adapted to a range of functions on the one hand, and the potential connectivity created by multiple doors on the other, which accounted for the provisional, ever-changing character of bungalow environments.[19]

FURNITURE AND PROVINCIAL TRANSIENCE

This provisional nature also stemmed from the use of furniture within officers' bungalows. Up to the mid-19th century, the interiors of provincial officers' bungalows appear to have been rather sparse, with few pieces of furniture. One visitor observed: 'The interior appears to the new comer to be quite unfurnished, for there are neither curtains nor fireplaces, and seldom is a carpet to be seen.'[20]

In fact, rather than any fixed furniture layout, rooms were left free to absorb temporary or provisional arrangements. While by the late 19th century bungalow interiors became more crowded,[21] their essentially flexible and ever-changing character remained.[22] This was directly due to the working culture of colonial governance. An official posting to a provincial town was typically short-term and transient, with the maximum duration being around two years.[23] In describing a colleague's house, a provincial civil servant noted that its furniture was simply handed down from one officer to his successor:

> One feature that particularly struck me in my visit, was the incongruous nature of the furniture [...] the articles had been got together as they could be purchased from persons leaving the station from time to time; and as these had previously been obtained in a similar fashion, the general result can be imagined.[24]

The outcome was a chance-collection of often 'old-fashioned' items – very different from the conception of 'good living' back home in England, where interiors increasingly aspired towards stylistic consistency.[25] It was also very distinct from the colonial lifestyle in Calcutta, which was sent the 'finest' furniture from across Europe and had many native copies thereof.[26] The

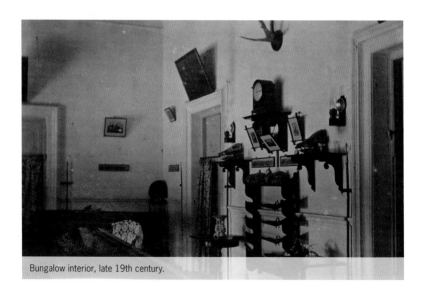

Bungalow interior, late 19th century.

provincial bungalow, by contrast, was an ad-hoc assembly of fragments from different officers' family lifestyles and intrinsically heterogeneous and assimilative in character.

This adaptability and flexibility – with its inevitable linkages or accidental overlaps between the 'major' and 'minor' spaces – was created by the fundamental dependence of colonial officers on Indian staff for their daily needs. It was also an outcome of the transient and provisional nature of provincial official life, located as it was within mobile circuits of colonial governance. Much of the spatial relationships arose, if by default, also from the porous and interconnected nature of bungalow spaces, originally driven by climatic needs. And in the end, these varied imperatives drew minor spaces and their paraphernalia right into the very core of colonial provincial life.

Notes

1   Ralph Crane and Anna Johnston (eds), *Flora Annie Steel and Grace Gardiner: The Complete Indian Housekeeper and Cook*, Oxford University Press (Oxford), 2010, p 18.

2   See for example Anthony King's seminal work on the bungalow and Elizabeth Collingham's deliberations on Indian bungalows as mediating between the body, the family and the household: Anthony D King, *The Bungalow: The Production of a Global Culture*, Oxford University Press USA (New York), 1995; Elizabeth M Collingham, *Imperial Bodies: The Physical Experiences of the Raj*, Wiley-Blackwell (Oxford), 2001.

3   Typically, kitchens, stores or ante-rooms were used mostly by servants and support staff while the primary rooms more by the European family members.

4   See Cecilia Leong-Salobir's observation that cookery involved the intimate nurturing of the coloniser by the colonised: Cecilia Leong-Salobir, 'Morality and Servants of Empire: A Look at the Colonial Kitchen and the Role of Servants in India, Malaysia and Singapore, 1858–1963', in Susan R Friendland (ed), *Food and Morality: Proceedings of the Oxford Symposium on Food and Cookery 2007*, Prospect Books (Oxford), 2007, p 162.

5   The typical plot-sizes ranged from 2 to 4 hectares (5 to 10 acres), and internal spaces were 4.9 to 6.1 metres by 6.1 to 12.2 metres (16 to 20 feet by 20 to 40 feet) for the major rooms and 2.4 to 3.7 by 2.4 to 9.1 metres (8 to 12 feet by 8 to 30 feet) for ancillary spaces.

6   This lineage is explained in King, *The Bungalow*. For a detailed spatial analysis, see also Chapter 6 of Tania Sengupta, *Producing the Province: Colonial Governance and Spatial Cultures in District Headquarter Towns of Eastern India, 1786–c. 1900*, unpublished PhD thesis, University of Westminster, London, 2011.

7   Circuit Houses were residence-cum-courts, generally in the early 19th century, for the use of officers who moved between towns to settle legal matters.

8   WBSSLC, *Register of Buildings Borne on the Books of Public Works Department, Bengal, 1884*, Vol 2, p xxiii.

9   Mrs Major Clemons, *The Manners and Customs of Society in India*, Smith, Elder & Co (London), 1841, pp 187–8.

10 For detailed works on colonial culinary history, see for example: David Burton, *The Raj at Table: A Culinary History of the British in India*, Faber & Faber (London), 1993; David Burnett and Helen Saberi, *The Road to*

Vindaloo: Curry Cooks and Curry Books, Prospect Books (Totnes), 2008.

11 Herbert Compton, *Indian Life in Town and Country 1853–1906*, George Newnes (London), 1904, p 158.

12 In Bengali houses, the detached kitchen stemmed from the religious association of food with 'contamination'. While in the bungalow this feature was adopted, it also helped to separate out the servants' areas (as was similar in 19th-century British houses).

13 Clemons, *The Manners and Customs of Society in India*, p 188.

14 Emerging racial theories in the late 19th century proposed that adjusting to 'tropical' conditions was virtually impossible due to the 'constitutional' difference between European and Indian bodies.

15 The discipline, management and display of bodies also played a crucial role in the movement from British mercantile colonialism to imperialism, as shown by Elizabeth Collingham in *Imperial Bodies*.

16 Clemons, *The Manners and Customs of Society in India*, pp 316–7. See also Herbert Compton's comment: 'the Anglo-Indian is, or should be, an early riser. To lie late in bed is called a "Europe morning",' in Compton, *Indian Life in Town and Country 1853–1906*, p 164.

17 Fanny Parks, *Wanderings of a Pilgrim in Search of the Picturesque, During Four and Twenty Years in the East; with Revelations of Life in the Zenana*, Pelham Richardson (London), 1850, p 21.

18 Compton, *Indian Life in Town and Country 1853–1906*, p 157.

19 These pose a radical contrast to 19th-century British domestic architecture, which had strong functional designation of spaces in the dwelling and a highly controlled circulation pattern arising from the limited number and careful positioning of doors.

20 Clemons, *The Manners and Customs of Society in India*, p 10.

21 This refers to a trait drawn from domestic aesthetics in Victorian England of drawing rooms crammed full of furniture, intensive use of fabrics and knick-knacks drawn from imperial territories.

22 An art historian, Prasannajit De Silva, has shown how the sparse and controlled 'order' of the early 19th-century colonial house interior seems to break loose with more crowded furniture in the late 19th century. P De Silva, 'Representing Home Life Abroad: Lifestyle Manuals for Company Men', paper presented at the conference on *Britain and India: Intersections in Visual Culture, 1800–1900* held at the Department of Art History, University of York, 2009.

23 See for example a civilian officer's comment in the 1860s: 'for in most parts of India it is even more necessary to "speed the parting" than "welcome the guest"'. Anonymous, quoted in George Graham, *Life in the Mofussil, Or, The Civilian in Lower Bengal*, CK Paul & Co (London), 1878, pp 56–7.

24 Graham, *Life in the Mofussil, Or, The Civilian in Lower Bengal*, pp 111–12.

25 As begun by leading architects like Robert Adam or William Chambers in the 18th century, stylistic consistency was still highly valued in Victorian England despite the increasing mix of objects gathered from across the world. The Arts and Crafts Movement was a classic example of attempts to maintain aesthetic consistency amid a plethora of commodities.

26 Parks, *Wanderings of a Pilgrim in Search of the Picturesque*, p 21.

CHAPTER 35

Memoirs of Adrian

THOMAS WEAVER

> I had governed a world infinitely larger that that of Alcibiades's time, and had kept peace therein; I had rigged it like a fair ship made ready for a voyage which might last for centuries; I had striven my utmost to encourage in man a sense of the divine, but without at the same time sacrificing to it what is essentially human. My bliss was my reward.[1]

This is the Roman emperor Hadrian (AD76–138) writing, with an equal measure of bombast and reverie, on the legacy of his 21 years of imperial rule. Or rather, to be more precise, these are actually the words of the Belgian novelist Marguerite Yourcenar, whose own *Memoirs of Hadrian* rcreates the life and death of one of antiquity's most influential and compelling characters. Taking the form of a long valedictory letter to his successor, Marcus Aurelius (its opening begins 'My dear Mark …'), and pairing an adoring reminiscence of his lover Antinous with a series of meditations on the things that have most pleased and defined him, the book stems from a writing project that Yourcenar first began in the 1920s, only to burn the resulting manuscript in despair. Following the publication of another novel and several stories and essays she began to look again at Hadrian in the 1930s, but these efforts, too, met with the same unceremonious end. Unable to fully abandon the idea, she returned to it ten years later in the winter of 1949, on a journey from New York to Taos in New Mexico. Sitting down to write first in a train carriage from New York to Chicago, and then in a restaurant at Chicago's Union Station while she waited out a snowstorm, and then further in a Santa Fe railway observation car as she passed through the Colorado mountains, she managed to complete a large part of the book to her satisfaction. Published to immediate critical acclaim in 1951, it has remained in print ever since.

Each year, when the architectural historian Adrian Forty packs for his annual summer holiday with his wife and daughters he carries in his suitcase a number of books – the usual assortment of histories, biographies and novels – but among them is always a copy of *Memoirs of Hadrian*, which he ritualistically rereads and rediscovers every August. This repetition may simply reflect a personal fondness for the Roman emperor and for Yourcenar's impeccably researched prose, but it could also suggest that there is more to this book than first meets the eye. Architectural history tells us that the definitive work on antiquity is Vitruvius's *De architectura* [Ten Books on Architecture] (*c* 15 BC), architecture's own Book of Genesis. But in his reading habits if nothing else, this particular architectural historian appears to be telling us that there is an alternative rival genesis, which just like Leon Battista Alberti's 15th-century championing of 1st-century BC Vitruvius, could be at the same time both ancient and modern.

'In the second century of the Christian era,' Edward Gibbon writes in the very first line of his six-volume *History of the Decline and Fall of the Roman Empire* (1776), 'the Empire of Rome comprehended the fairest part of the earth, and the most civilised portion of mankind.' Warming to his theme, he continues, 'If a man were called to fix the period in the history of the world, during which the condition of the human race was most happy and prosperous, he would, without hesitation, name that which elapsed from the death of Domitian to the accession of Commodus.'[2] Almost a century later, in a letter to his friend, Madame Roger des Genettes (later cited by Yourcenar as the inspiration for her novel), Gustave Flaubert wrote:

> The melancholy of the antique world seems to me more profound than that of the moderns, all of whom more or less imply that beyond the dark void lies immortality. [...] Just when the gods had ceased to be and the Christ had not yet come, there was a unique moment in history, between Cicero and Marcus Aurelius, when man stood alone. Nowhere else do I find that particular grandeur.[3]

And of course the figure who occupies the historical midpoint between both Gibbon's Domitian and Commodus and Flaubert's Cicero and Marcus Aurelius is Hadrian, whose reign came to represent the very apogee of worldly civility and urbanity, and who in this focal position can in many ways be seen to represent an emblematic figure far more tangible and quantifiable than the diagrammatic abstraction of Leonardo da Vinci's *Vitruvian Man* (c 1490).

Hadrian therefore seems fundamental because he inhabits the centre of a world more advanced than any other, and the *Memoirs* goes to some length to detail the component parts – or architecture – of his good governance, highlighting in particular the value of astronomy, mathematics, rhetoric, logic, poetry, art, etc. The book in this sense is also a kind of manual for learning and self-improvement, instilling an educational model that leans heavily (good Hellenist that Hadrian was) on the didacticism of Plato's Academy and Aristotle's Lyceum. Establishing something of a cliché for so many absolute rulers who succeeded him, Hadrian is also revealed to fancy himself as something of an architect, marking a transition from the metaphorical to the literal that sees the narrative of the *Memoirs* punctuated by one building project after another. As the historian James Morwood has noted, in travelling across the Roman world one feels like echoing the inscription to Christopher Wren in St Paul's Cathedral, '*si monumentum requiris, circumspice*' ['if you are seeking a monument, look around you'], for all across Europe, Asia and North Africa you can find architectural traces of Hadrian's life and empire.[4] The flames of Hadrian's architectural ambitions, however, were not simply fanned by this expansiveness, or by all those ceremonial gates and memorials his reign spawned, but by three projects in his layman's architectural portfolio against which all subsequent architectural endeavours came to be judged: a house (Hadrian's Villa at Tivoli), a temple (his remodelling of the Pantheon in Rome) and a border (Hadrian's Wall demarcating the northernmost limit of his empire) – three prototypes that immediately established not just a canon but a whole discipline. Moreover, in their materiality as much as their meaning, these buildings offer an umbilical connection to a contemporary world, for it was with the huge celestial dome of the Pantheon and the constellation of smaller domes at Tivoli that Hadrian mixed quicklime paste, volcanic ash and tufa into antiquity's own version of concrete. This, then, is an architecture of both things and ideas, an imprint for a way of thinking about the buildings and builders around us that is both actual and ideological.

Of course, the writing of this history is not Hadrian's but Yourcenar's. And yet here, too, *Memoirs of Hadrian* reveals more than it first suggests, for alongside the erudition and lyricism of Hadrian's farewell address, the novel contains another book within a book – a 20-page 'Reflections on the Composition', placed immediately after the main narrative, that recounts the impulses behind its writing – so as to present the whole as both biography and autobiography, the essential incompleteness of the latter following on from the inevitable finality of the former (autobiographies, unlike biographies, have to end before the end). Moreover, within the story of the composition of the book, Yourcenar also smuggles in a series of aphoristic instructions as to how to write a scholarly work of this kind ('learn everything, read everything, enquire into everything'; 'keep one's own shadow out of the picture; leave the mirror clean of the mist of one's own breath'; 'one has to go into the most remote corners of a subject in order to discover the simplest of things'; and 'we write in order to attack or defend a view of the universe, and to set forth a system of conduct which is our own'). Offering something more than the *De architectura*, then, *Memoirs of Hadrian* becomes a template not just for the practice of architecture but for its historicisation, for what is a memoir, after all, if not a work of history? And if the good historian, even more than the good emperor, is the ultimate truth behind the book, then Yourcenar's Hadrian is in so many ways analogous to The Bartlett's Adrian. For here is the guardian of architecture's immediate past, a figure at the centre of it all, whose trilogy of couplets – objects and desires, words and buildings, concrete and culture – perfectly captures a way of presenting the world through both things and ideas, one half incomprehensible without the other, and whose economy, modesty and above all clarity of expression presents its own kind of pantheon. To engage with this historian is to find within his histories a source of insight and contentment quite unlike any other. Our bliss is our reward.

Notes

1   Margaret Yourcenar, *Memoirs of Hadrian* (1951), translated by Grace Frick, Penguin (London), 2000, p 144.

2   Edward Gibbon, *The History of the Decline and Fall of the Roman Empire* (1776), abridged edition, edited by David Womersley, Penguin (London), 2000, p 9.

3   Gustave Flaubert, undated letter to Madame Roger des Genettes, quoted by Marguerite Yourcenar, 'Reflections on the Composition of Memoirs of Hadrian', *Memoirs of Hadrian*, p 269.

4   James Morwood, *Hadrian*, Bloomsbury (London), 2013, p 32.

CHAPTER 36

All That Glitters

TOM DYCKHOFF

'Earth has not anything to show more fair ...'

— WILLIAM WORDSWORTH, *UPON WESTMINSTER BRIDGE*, 1802

The sun is glinting off the bubble carriages of the London Eye observation wheel as it slowly, almost imperceptibly rises on one side, and falls the other. But every other second, these blazing reflections are matched by momentary flashes from second suns within, as the occupants of the bubbles photograph the views all about, and their little camera flashbulbs, which they have forgotten to turn off, attempt in vain to illuminate the enormity of the world below. The London Eye sparkles like a gigantic silver bracelet.

It is a curiously modern phenomenon: a building (can we call this giant bicycle wheel that?) designed to be looked at, and looked from. We have built such buildings throughout our history, but never in such numbers. These days they are commonly called 'icons': spectacular buildings that we visit in droves, simply to experience something. We go expecting to be transformed by the experience, to leave seeing the world a little differently.

The London Eye has been called iconic since it was first proposed. And it has gone on to fulfil this prophecy. It is world famous. Rare is the day when there is not a queue at its entrance morning, noon and night. The building has performed for the nation, as the framework for fireworks displays at significant events, the scene-stealer of famous films and modern acrobatics, such as the unfurling of political banners by those brave enough to scale its high wires, or, in 2003, the balancing upon one of its carriages by the popular magician David Blaine, to advertise his upcoming antic, during which he suspended himself in a plastic cage for 44 days without food on the banks of the Thames. The London Eye, though only 14 years old, has received the ultimate accolade of modern celebrity: being cloned all around the world. Facsimiles also appear in miniature, a modernist interloper beside familiar olde worlde retainers such as the Tower of London within snowdomes or on porcelain plates commemorating historic London, sold in the tourist shops beneath it.

All around me, on the pavements of Westminster Bridge, tourists are hustling for the best position to photograph it. There is quite a throng among the hustlers from Peru selling trinkets and the bagpiper busker who pipes *Auld Lang Syne* most days. There always is. For this is the very epicentre of spectacular London. There is a sweet spot on the bridge, about halfway across, where the canny photographer can get the best shot of both it, and, if he or she nimbly swivels, that other, older tourist icon, Big Ben, without shifting position. The tourists wisely ignore the more unpicturesque prospect to the south, of luxury apartment complexes that have sprouted upriver during the economic boom of the late 1990s. These buildings are also here to take advantage of the view, only they offer more permanent access to it for those able to pay for the privilege. Indeed, their very architectural form is moulded by the views offered from within that they can then sell to prospective buyers of their apartments. St George Wharf, for instance, comprises towers of many heights, like a Hydra in glass and steel, each craning higher than its neighbour to peer that little bit further, its flanks ridged and stepped and folded so as to maximise the surface area of windows and balconies. The views from within, the marketing brochures puff, are, of course, 'spectacular'.

So thick are the crowds on Westminster Bridge on some days that tutting Londoners bustling to get to important meetings at the Houses of Parliament or St Thomas's Hospital spill onto the road to get past, swerving to avoid the buses and lorries. The pavements on the bridge become the sole habitat of the tourists who, left alone, en masse, if you stand back and observe them, enact a curious kind of performance beside the busking bagpipers. The photographer of the party crouches, or stands on one leg like a flamingo, bends this way and that trying to squeeze into the image both the view and their friend, their mum, their entire family or school party – who, in turn, strike whatever witty pose comes to mind, which must make sense viewed through the camera lens, but looks utterly odd to the rest of us watching them from outside the camera. One man is trying to line up the London Eye so that it forms a halo around his friend's head: 'Left a bit … That's it, that's it, ha! Now, look like a saint.'

In recent years, Westminster Bridge has become less a crossing, and more a promenade or seaside pier suspended over the Thames from which to look and experience. The London Eye is, I suppose, nothing more or less than a promenade, too, only circular and constantly rotating. Indeed, during the two decades I have lived in London, the promenade evident here seems to have unfurled itself eastwards from this spot along the entire south bank of the Thames to Tower Bridge. A vast landscape of spectacle and amusement has been built, entirely given over to encouraging you to experience stuff: taste, touch, smell, sight, sound. It is a route of permanent *passeggiata*. A tide of humans-with-cameras flows from here downriver with the water from dawn till dusk and into the night, experiencing the thrills human and architectural put on for their benefit, set against the picturesque background, like those painted backdrops from film sets, of the sights of London on the other side of the river, obligingly lit by the southern sun.

One could, perhaps, date the emergence of such a landscape back to the 1951 Festival of Britain, which turned a bombed old industrial neighbourhood here on the South Bank into a jaunty festival of modern design, illustrating new directions for the country after the Second World War in this or that pavilion on agriculture or industry. In fact, a key part of the future direction of the country turned out to be not what was contained inside the pavilions – new efficient modes of sheep farming and coal mining, etc – but what was created outside them, in the act of visiting and experiencing: the very act of festival itself.

The river, when I arrived in the city, was mostly ignored, unsure of its role now that the clippers and gantries of the trading heart of the British Empire had disappeared. Well-meaning articles in newspapers would beseech us to use the river better. The famous architect, Richard Rogers, in 1986 even came up with plans for piazzas and promenades and café-bars, called 'London As It Could Be'.[1] And now it is. It has been the policy of local and national governments to encourage this promenade, and extend it, ever since Margaret Thatcher sold the historic seat of London's administration beside the London Eye, County Hall, to the Japanese that same year. County Hall now houses the kind of souk of attractions you might find on a seaside pier: an aquarium, pubs, a McDonald's, amusement arcades, bowling alleys, shops selling trinkets and sweet fatty treats, bumper cars and Death Trap, a 'Live Horror Show'. Only a Japanese teahouse offering a 'Zen Universe' seems somewhat out of place.

But the unexpected is ordinary in this landscape. Indeed it is expected.

These visitors haven't come all this way for the kind of humdrum they can get in their ordinary lives. How about a giant, upturned inflatable purple cow housing comedy events? Of course. Outside it, living statues (would Gilbert and George be proud?) dressed as Captain Jack Sparrow from *Pirates of the Caribbean* and other popular shows entertain the crowds; one dressed as Yoda from *Star Wars* tickles ladies dressed in burqas with his light sabre; a half-dressed Cyberman, off duty, off his makeshift stage, smokes a cigarette; a headless giant fluffy duck, sweating in the sunshine, is groomed by her partner.

We have all manner of kiosks and pop-up installations sponsored by this or that company offering entertainment temporary and permanent for this or that festival – world poverty, dance, 'poetry bombing'. We have food from every corner of the world. We have coffee, of course, however you want it. We have lurid banners encouraging you to 'Touch. Explore. Play', or offering visitors' smartphones websites to augment their promenade with virtual, multimedia fun. Bollards and the latest in avant-garde paving stones have a theatrical edge. Even alienated urban youth has its moment of public theatre. A cave of concrete beneath the Queen Elizabeth Hall is home to things which in most places are now actively discouraged – graffiti, skateboarding, Brutalist architecture – but which here, officially sanctioned by the cultural elite, are, for a moment, permitted. A crowd of adoring tourists watches the twists and shouts of skaters and parkour free runners.

At moments the melee of festival reaches fever pitch, say lunchtime on a Saturday outside the Royal Festival Hall. But it's only ever a street or two deep. The cruddiness of ordinary life, kept at bay by this new urban skin, surges forth once more: say when the Thames is at low tide, revealing its riverbed of rubble, shopping trolleys, traffic cones and mud, or when those tourist cameras catch an occasional view of buildings dating from one of London's gloomier periods, such as the 1970s, when the city seemed destined for a future of motorways and concrete, until a brighter, shinier future was fixed upon.

Note

1   'London As It Could Be', exhibition at the Royal Academy of Arts, London, 1986; see project details on Rogers Stirk Harbour + Partners website: http://www.richardrogers.co.uk/render.aspx?siteID=1&navIDs=1,4,22,562 (accessed 15 January 2014).

CHAPTER 37

A Response to
Words and Buildings

TONY FRETTON

The origins of this article lie in my polite refusal to give a short exposition on the subject of 'the wall' to the MA students in Adrian Forty's programme at The Bartlett. I did not think I could speak abstractly about something that is experiential for me. This and subsequently reading Adrian's *Words and Buildings: A Vocabulary of Modern Architecture* (2000) made me keenly aware of how differently writers and designers use words, concepts and arguments.

For architectural writers, words, concepts and arguments need to be precise to bear scrutiny on the page or in a lecture. For designers they need to be slack to allow conflicting practical and material factors to be fitted together with issues of power, ideology, ethics, cultural norms and the designer's own architectural formation, and for the project to be presented to a client in understandable terms. Design thinking is associative and its arguments operate between reason and rhetoric. Ultimately it is just a means to an end, which is the production of buildings.

I am not being diffident when writing this: I believe in design. It is a very great form of verbal and non-verbal knowledge and a state of being from which to produce things in the material world – design's natural habitat – that are culturally innovative and other people can use and enjoy. Equally, I believe in architectural writing, particularly that of Adrian Forty, Alan Colquhoun and Robin Evans, writers with careful, well-founded styles of thought, who feel ideas very keenly while acknowledging their hypothetical nature, and who above all are conscious that writing should have a productive relationship

Tony Fretton Architects, Fuglsang Art Museum, Lolland, Denmark, 2008.
Entrance sequence.

Tony Fretton Architects, Fuglsang Art Museum, Lolland, Denmark, 2008.
Encounters between strangers.

Tony Fretton Architects, Fuglsang Art Museum, Lolland, Denmark, 2008.
The spaces for art.

Tony Fretton Architects, Fuglsang Art Museum, Lolland, Denmark, 2008.
Views of the surrounding agricultural landscape.

245

with design. But that relationship is not straightforward. Architectural writing cannot provide the means to make buildings, and design thought is often inchoate. Designers have to absorb what occurs in writing into the processes I have described. Characteristically they do that in highly selective ways according to their sensibility and interests, and the result is a transformation. My response to *Words and Buildings* will be like that – that is, not a critical examination, but a new piece of writing stimulated by some of the issues raised in this wonderful book, a reciprocation by a designer to a writer.

LANGUAGE AND DRAWING

The primacy given in early modernism and the tradition of orthogonal projection over perspective has been completely reversed by digital drawing. Like many others, my office makes three-dimensional digital models of projects at the outset of design. Among other things, these allow constructional issues and conventional associations of materials to be simultaneously understood, details to be situated within the project as a whole, and understanding of how the building will be seen as people will move through and around it and how it will relate to the surrounding world. Above all it provides a way of showing the design to our clients, ourselves and other interested parties in rendered drawings, as if the building were real.

DESCRIBING THE SOCIAL

I am an advocate of social democratic society in a time when less well-meaning ideologies have the upper hand. Consequently I seek to create conditions for productive sociability and social awareness in the buildings that I design. I look for configurations when designing that are surprising and have a wide appeal to the basic ranges of pleasure, political dimensions that can be experienced bodily, and the capacity to allow artistic exploration and the development of ideas. I find many of these qualities in buildings that already exist, in the physical changes that people make to them and the meaning they acquire through word of mouth, film, television and literature. In the Fuglsang Art Museum in Lolland, Denmark (2008), the entrance sequence brings strangers temporarily into contact before they disperse into the spaces for art. Among the galleries they can find a room where they can come together again to appreciate views of the surrounding agricultural landscape, which like the collection of art in the museum is an artefact, but one made anonymously by successive generations of local people.

FUNCTION

I would like to argue positively for functionalism as a formative aspect of early modernism and a continuing technique in contemporary architecture. Its historic achievement within modernism was to provide a means of generating original architecture for mass democratic industrialised society from the most representative uses, and to purge architecture of social hierarchies so that it could play a part in the development of a fairer society. Functionalism in contemporary architecture allows design to proceed from analysis rather than custom, whether of complex uses and their conjunction, the realpolitik of a project, or to establish rules in building restoration. It was never and is not simply the rule of utility, because architecture by its very nature has always been both useful and sensory.

TRUTH

Science, of all practices, has the greatest claim to truth, but it offers no overall system by which to live. We rely instead on faulty but very sophisticated common sense to coexist and communicate with each other, to locate ourselves and to feel a degree of certainty. Design operates here using its ability to resolve large numbers of issues into intelligible form. Unlike science and other practices that seek finely drawn abstract knowledge, design is profligate, naturally containing social and cultural purpose, and producing things and ideas that people make their own.

NATURE

There is a strong sense for me of nature in human-made things, through the fact that the people who made them and the raw materials they used came into being through natural processes that cannot be fully understood. In conceptualising that sensibility I am drawn to American transcendentalism, which I find in the objects made by artists like Donald Judd, Sol LeWitt and Dan Graham. But most telling for me is the relationship that is made between natural and human-made objects in Fernando Távora and Álvaro Siza's work in the park at Quinta da Conceição near Porto (1958). The industrial dockland that is overtly on view from the park, the architects' new buildings and the buildings they chose to keep, and the dense trees are presented in a way that points out the co-dependence of human folly, creative thought and other life forms.

USER

The term 'user' that arose in the 1960s was, in my experience, not disenfranchising or the affront to individuality as would be felt today. It has to be understood as part of a general feeling at the time of inclusiveness and purpose, and of the commitment by successive governments to provide buildings for dwelling, health and education as the outcome of postwar social democracy. Architects working in the public sphere were understood to be acting in the public interest, and the term 'user' was an acceptable way of conceptualising people as members of society with collective needs.

I want to finish by returning to modernism, the locus of *Words and Buildings*, and its relation to the ideas and values of the present time. Problematisation that has become something of a technique in recent architectural writing, and fractiousness in British architecture's relationship to its public role should tell us something: that it was not modernism that was wrong, but its unreasonable rejection.

CHAPTER 38

Material Culture: 'Manchester of the East', Le Corbusier, Eames and Indian Jeans

VICTORIA PERRY

drian Forty's Thursday-morning lectures to first-year architectural students at The Bartlett, University College London first awoke me to the delights of material culture. History was a subject I had abandoned early at school (too many wars and laws). However, the story of buildings and objects was clearly different; sensual and immediate as well as intellectual and analytical. Indeed architectural history became, for me, like time-travel; I began to see everything in four dimensions.

Throughout my architectural training and career, Adrian's visionary thinking proved a constant thread – and diversion from architectural practice. Some years after completing the pioneering Bartlett Master's in History of Modern Architecture, I returned part-time to embark on a doctorate with Adrian as my supervisor. Seven years later, my thesis *Slavery, Sugar and the Sublime* (on the influence of colonial Caribbean plantation profits on British landscape, art and architecture) won the 2010 RIBA President's Award.

Back, once again, in practice – but teaching at The Bartlett – I was, therefore, honoured to be asked if I would like to contribute a piece to a publication marking Adrian's retirement. The request came at a moment that was at once inconvenient and opportune: inconvenient as I was about to fly to Ahmedabad in India, to speak at the Design History Society's annual conference 'Towards Global Histories of Design'; opportune in that Adrian's 1986 book *Objects of Desire: Design and Society since 1750* had long established his status in design history circles, while Ahmedabad was a city with a legacy of iconic concrete architecture – the subject of his latest publication *Concrete and Culture: A Material History* (2012). Moreover, I also discovered that Ahmedabad, a city of which I had little previous knowledge, had strong links with my previous work on the transatlantic colonial plantation economy. Rather than a piece about the material legacy of the Caribbean, then, this piece focuses on another part of the former British Empire and attempts to link West and East in a global, postcolonial story.

Ahmedabad is a sprawling, rapidly growing megacity of six million people; a city that, for anyone new to India, epitomises the title of Amartya Sen and Jean Drèze's recent book *An Uncertain Glory: India and its Contradictions* (2013). Certainly, the city's contradictions and complexity are what make it so beguiling for those interested in architecture and design. A textile town of medieval origin, once renowned for its lustrous silver and gold cloth and indigo dyes, Ahmedabad was also one of India's first industrial cities. Indeed, until Indian independence in 1947, the city was known in Britain as the 'Manchester of the East' on account of its numerous cotton mills. Ahmedabad's first mill entrepreneurs had purchased British machinery in the late 1850s intending to supply Asian customers. However, they had made rapid, unexpected fortunes supplying printed cotton fabrics to British traders during the Lancashire mill strikes and anti-slavery cotton blockades of the American Civil War. Ahmedabad's merchants (who had previously supplied British traders with opium for Chinese buyers) quickly saw new opportunities. By the latter part of the 19th century, the skyline of a city once famed for its minarets had been transformed.[1]

The compact nature of the original walled town, coupled with its sudden industrialisation, means that the historic Anglo-American influence on

Ahmedabad's development is visible today. Moreover, the city's importance at the time of independence means that an architectural trip in a three-wheeled auto-rickshaw not only gives glimpses of the city's history, but also provides an insight into the foundations of modern India. Just to the south of the exquisitely carved temples and *haveli* (merchants' houses) that line the choking, polluted lanes of Ahmedabad's old town, you can still see a few smoking factory-chimneys and a built landscape that the idiosyncratic Lancashire artist LS Lowry – or, perhaps, the Gothic Revival pioneer and polemicist AWN Pugin – could have drawn. Within a minute's walk of the magnificent, 16th-century Sidi Syed Mosque with its celebrated *jaali* (pierced-stone screen) lies Electricity House, a 1930s cement-rendered Art Deco electrical showroom designed by the British architects Gregarth and Claude Bartley – a reminder of the city's strong Anglo-American connections.

On the opposite bank of the broad Sabarmati river, however, lies a very different building from the same era. Once set in open country at the edge of Ahmedabad's urban development, Mahatma Gandhi's humble, whitewashed bungalow and its compound were the nerve centre of India's early 20th-century struggle against British imperial rule. It was here that Gandhi and others developed political ideas of economic self-sufficiency or *swadeshi* and the promotion of the village as an economic unit. Gandhi's Ashram is now a museum, and a site of pilgrimage for visitors from throughout the country. At the side of the terrace where you remove your shoes, a woman sits cross-legged on the floor spinning cotton thread with an old, Indian-style spinning wheel; a demonstration of the laborious task made redundant by the import of the British-designed, mechanised 'spinning jenny' to Ahmedabad.

Gandhi's vision of a new India predicated on the manufacture of homespun cloth (*khadi*) had an extraordinary symbolic power (the spinning wheel is the centre of modern India's national flag). Understandably, however, it had limited appeal to Ahmedabad's outward-looking industrialists. Indeed, in 1954 the Ahmedabad Textile Mills Association commissioned the fashionable Swiss-French architect Le Corbusier (then working on the new Punjabi city of Chandigarh) to design a majestic, new reinforced-concrete headquarters. The Mill Owners' Association Building is also on the western side of the river, a little way to the south of the Ashram and past a slum settlement marked by vivid blue polythene sheeting. The bright sunlight and luxuriant planting of the

Mill Owner's Building (as it is generally known in the West) softens the grey, board-marked facade, creating an icon of International Modernism that is a built riposte to Gandhi's ideals.

Le Corbusier designed other buildings in Ahmedabad, including the red-brick and concrete Sanskar Kendra city museum (1954) and two large houses, one of which, the Sarabhai House (1955), was for the descendants of one of the city's first mill owners. The Sarabhai family were also instrumental in the patronage of the American architect Louis Kahn, who designed the poetic red-brick and concrete Indian Institute of Management (1962), and the creation of the National Institute of Design, set up following the publication of Charles and Ray Eames's *India Report* of 1958.[2]

Just across the road from Le Corbusier's city museum and constructed using the same architectural language of handmade red Gujarati bricks and in-situ concrete, the Institute is set in lush, walled grounds. It is a calm oasis set apart from the frenetic traffic, street hawkers, wandering cows, camels and elephants in the streets beyond. However, the building's tasteful modernist isolation seems, like many of the products in the Institute's shop, to have been removed a step too far from the apparent chaos of the city outside the walls. It takes a visit to Sarabhai's rambling former mansion – now the home of Ahmedabad's renowned Calico Museum – where American-style 'log-cabin' patchwork quilts of modest, floral-sprigged cotton lawns[3] are displayed together with sumptuous silk textiles, to rediscover the visual and historical complexity of the manufactures that underpinned the growth of the 'Manchester of the East'.

Like Manchester, most of Ahmedabad's 19th-century textile mills are now closed and the city's economy has diversified. Like Manchester, too, regeneration and heritage tourism are starting to play a part. Opposite Sidi Syed Mosque lies the House of Mangaldas Girdhardas, an eclectically-designed textile magnate's mansion from the 1920s, now a hotel and restaurant. The hotel's founder, scion of the Mangaldas family and son of an architect, is a pioneer of heritage conservation in the city. As we talked over lime sherbets, he told me how, unusually for India, Ahmedabad's Municipal Corporation had taken a strong lead in envisioning how the conservation of the old town could be integrated with contemporary development. Indeed, the city's politicians were aiming to apply for UNESCO World Heritage Site status for the old town – the first city in India to do so.[4] We also spoke of the hotel and how he had partially rejected his father's precise modernism in favour of creating something more complex, locally rooted and historically nuanced. I laughed, agreed, but pointed out that much of the hotel was floored with coloured Minton Hollins encaustic tiles once manufactured in my husband's hometown of Stoke-on-Trent.

As we got up and shook hands, I noted that Mr Mangaldas was wearing jeans, the only person I had seen in the city doing so. In India, wearing jeans is mark of wealth and education,[5] but in Ahmedabad, the indigo-dyed American origins of the garment had particular resonance. Indeed, the few remaining textile mills in the city were now producing denim fabric for jeans manufacturers.[6] A discussion of the symbolism of the hotel owner's trousers, however, seemed inappropriate and I kept my thoughts on this aspect of material culture to myself.

All these opinions are my own but I must thank Tanishka Kachru, Suchitra Balasubrahmanyan, Tapati Guha Thakurta, Dipti Baghat, Tanvir Hasan, Vivek Nanda and Abhay Mangaldas for helping me to see and understand.

Notes

1   See Achyut Yagnik and Suchitra Sheth, 'Chimneys and Chaalis', in *Ahmedabad: From Royal City to Megacity*, Penguin (New Delhi), 2011, pp 156–76.

2   Charles and Ray Eames, *India Report*, 1958, available to download at http://nid.edu/Userfiles/Eames___India_Report.pdf [accessed September 2013].

3   See Adrian Forty, *Objects of Desire: Design and Society since 1750*, Thames & Hudson (London), 1986, pp 76–9, for a discussion of British printed cotton designs in the 19th century.

4   See Paul John and Ashish Vashi, *Ahmedabad Next: Towards a World Heritage City – Connecting Ahmedabad to its People*, Bennett, Coleman & Co (Ahmedabad), 2011.

5   See: Daedal Research, *Indian Denim Jeans Market: Trends and Opportunities (2012–2017)*, December 2012, http://www.researchandmarkets.com/reports/2359106/indian_denim_jeans_market_trends 110053100039_1. html; Kalpesh Damor and Vinay Umarji, 'Ahmedabad Denim Makers Gear Up for Expansion', May 2010, http://www.business-standard.com/article/companies/ahmedabad-based-denim-makers-gear-up-for-expansion-110053100039_1.html [both accessed October 2013].

6   Yagnik and Sheth, *Ahmedabad: From Royal City to Megacity*, pp 289–306.

CHAPTER 39

Mr Mumford's Neighbourhood

WILLIAM MENKING

My first seminar presentation in The Bartlett's History of Modern Architecture Master's course focused on the concept of 'neighbourhood' as it appeared in the writings of Lewis Mumford, particularly his texts for the Regional Planning Association of America (RPAA) in the 1920s. I will never forget the look of nearly complete mystification on the faces of the two course tutors, Adrian Forty and Mark Swenarton, when I concluded the presentation to the class. Adrian went on to gently describe 'neighbourhood' as an American notion that was not accepted on the UK side of the Atlantic because it was a concept so unclear as to be unworthy of productive analysis. I had recently graduated from a Master's programme in City and Regional Planning where the concept had been the basic unit for designing functional, self-contained, and desirable neighbourhoods that satisfied all the requirements for satisfactory urban existence. While it was criticised by some planners, myself included, who questioned its ability to entirely solve all urban issues, it had never occurred to me at the time (1982) that anyone would dispute entirely the validity or efficacy of the notion – even given the imprecise nature of its metric, definition, and ambiguous early 20th-century sociological heritage.

I had gone to the new Bartlett's Master's programme (its second year of operation) led by Forty and Swenarton with the intention of writing a thesis about Mumford's early championing of modernism both because the programme focused solely on modern architecture and because so many of the American's ideas came from British figures like Patrick Geddes and the Garden

City movement of Ebenezer Howard, Raymond Unwin and Barry Parker. In addition, it was almost forty-five years since the publication of the influential *New York City Guide* (1939) and I had been working on a reissue of the book. This guide was undertaken by the Federal Writers' Project, and the authors found 'neighbourhood' a precise and useful enough definition of urban form to arrange the entire city into these divisions and then described them in great detail.

But more importantly, 1982 was the 50th anniversary of Henry-Russell Hitchcock and Philip Johnson's landmark 'International Exhibition of Modern Architecture' at the Museum of Modern Art in New York. This exhibition was one of the defining moments of the modern architecture movement in the 20th century, but many scholars – even those who in 1982 were rediscovering the show's importance – overlooked Mumford's contribution to the exhibition. In fact Mumford was not only the organiser of the Housing section of the exhibition (assisted by Catherine Bauer, Henry Wright and Clarence Stein), but he authored a catalogue essay on the topic which did not specifically mention the neighbourhood unit but spoke instead about the proper 'community' size or scale as critical to the definition of what made habitation modern.[1] This focus on community scale was an explicit attack on the formalism of the rest of the exhibit and part of his ongoing project to create a social argument for modern architecture.

Mumford argued against the individual house or isolated mansion (the subject of most of the rest of the exhibition) as being outdated since modern technology now connected all residences below the ground with utility lines into an integrated community. But above ground the major issue for Mumford was always density, scale and community size, and it was the neighbourhood unit that he thought ideal. His attempt to create a specifically American architecture and an alternative 'social' architectural criticism – something he thought necessary because of the corporatisation of every aspect of American life – went back to an analysis of the social organisation of the first European settlements in New England. He idealised life in these cities but made the point that 'for a hundred years or so after its settlement, there lived and flourished in America a type of community which was rapidly disappearing in Europe' and called them the 'dying embers of a medieval order'. In these small villages grouped 'around [a] meeting house the rest of the community crystallized in a definite pattern,

A print of Lewis Mumford.

tight and homogeneous' and it did 'not continue to grow at such a pace that it either becomes overcrowded within or spills beyond its limits into dejected suburbs'.[2] He compared these 'medieval' villages favourably to New York City where 'all the land on Manhattan Island was privately owned, although only a small part of it was cultivated so eagerly had the teeth of monopoly bitten into this fine morsel that there was already a housing shortage'.[3] These New England villages adopted a basic plan where 'attention was paid to the function the land was to perform, rather than the mere possession of property'.[4] They were organised around a traditional town green or square where every essential communal facility (church, meeting hall, and store) and housing were located.

Mumford brought this small tightly organised typology forward in his writings in the 1920s, calling for a similar development typology for today's modern settlements. Indeed, all of the RPAA unit developments created interior block neighbourhoods: New York's Sunnyside Gardens and California's Baldwin Hills and cul-de-sac residential pods in Radburn, New Jersey. In his 1954 essay in the *Town Planning Review*, 'The Neighborhood and the Neighborhood Unit', he could not have been more clear about the value of this unit of development, writing that:

During the last two decades the idea of planning by neighborhoods
has been widely accepted [...] At the same time, a counter-movement
has come into existence; the critics of neighborhood planning identify
it with many practices that have nothing to do whatever with the
neighborhood principle, such as segregation by race or caste or
income; and they treat the city as a whole as the only unit for effective
planning. Much of the argument on this subject has only served to
confuse the issues that should be defined [...] By accident, I began
this paper in Paris and revised it in Venice. Within these two urban
environments the [...] question of whether neighborhoods actually
exist, particularly in great cities, seems a singularly academic one,
indeed downright absurd in the suggestion that neighborhoods are
the willful mental creation of romantic sociologists. Paris, for all its
formal Cartesian unity, is a city of neighborhoods, often with well-
defined architectural character as well as an identifiable social face.[5]

The Parisian neighbourhood is not just a postal district or a political unit,
but an area which has grown historically; and the sense of belonging to a
particular *arrondissement* or *quartier* is just as strong in the shopkeeper, the
bistro customer, or the local craftsman as the sense of being a Parisian. Indeed,
in Paris the neighbourhood attachment is so close, so intense, so narrow that
it would have satisfied the soul of Adam Wayne, GK Chesterton's Napoleon of
Notting Hill.[6]

It is clear that Mumford believed in the notion of neighbourhood scale
as the principal building block of the modern community. While he turned
against modernism after the 1930s, he never gave up on this scale as the basis
of residential design. I was hoping in my Bartlett seminar not just to highlight
Mumford's overlooked pre-1930 critique and nuanced support for modernism,
but to bring his argument forward as a still-relevant and useful social critique.
I recognised that the RPAA's focus on neighbourhood design – and particularly
greenswards behind and around residences – contributed in some ways to
the evolution of the anti-urban suburb, but the concept was still useful as
an analytical tool as well as a valuable unit of development. Today, city and
regional planning has moved away from an interest in physical analysis and
design towards public policy. I left the planning field for this reason and enrolled

in The Bartlett's Architectural History programme – which explains my shock when I ran up against this push back on my interest in neighbourhood. Forty is of course a great scholar and I recognise he was simply trying to get me to be more precise and critical in my writing and thinking, and though I have not abandoned my belief in the concept I have a finer understanding of its limitations and unique American lineage.

© William Menking

Notes

1   Lewis Mumford, 'Housing', in *Modern Architecture*, Museum of Modern Art (New York), 1932, pp 179–92.

2   Lewis Mumford, *Sticks and Stones: A Study of American Architecture and Civilization* (1924), revised edition, Dover Publications Incorporated (New York), 1955, p 1.

3   Ibid, p 2.

4   Ibid, p 3.

5   Lewis Mumford, 'The Neighborhood and the Neighborhood Unit', *The Town Planning Review*, Vol 24, 1954, pp 256–70 (p 256).

6   GK Chesterton, *The Napoleon of Notting Hill*, Bodley Head (London), 1904.

CHAPTER 40

Banyan Tree and Migrant Cities: Some Provisional Thoughts for a Strategic Postcolonial Cosmopolitanism

YAT MING LOO

'Place is security, space is freedom: we are attached to the one and long for the other. There is no place like home.'

— YI-FU TUAN, *SPACE AND PLACE* (1977)[1]

Human beings are nowadays migrating urban beings. They are shaping and being shaped by increasingly diverse cities. More than half of the world's population of seven billion are now urbanised. Nearly 200 million people now live outside their countries of origin, a figure that has leapt up by 25 per cent since 1990.

Migration within nations is also increasing. Of China's 1.35 billion people, more than 50 per cent now live in urban areas. In experiencing the largest mass migration in human history, Chinese urbanites today amount to twice the total US population.

MIGRANT CITIES

Hence we now live in a world of migrant cities. Cosmopolitan cities, hybrid cities or mongrel cities are all, in essence, migrant cities. The interconnected transnational and transcultural network of migrant cities in the world are changing our cultural values, worldviews and built environments.

Most of us are now migrants to a certain degree. It is a common fate for

A 'banyan-place' in Hong Kong, photographed in 2013.

all. In this increasingly diasporic intercultural and interracial life-world, there is an urgency in contemplating a form of rooted cosmopolitanism. Plurality of identity, culture, society, economy and modernity are irreversible. The diverse societies resulting from the influx of migrants, who belong to a variety of ethnic groups, intensify the need for recognition for these minority migrant communities.

BORROWED TIME AND PLACE

Whenever I visit Hong Kong, I love to look at the banyan trees. They are everywhere. With their aerial and prop roots – hanging, mingling, spreading and floating – they live in between cracks of concrete slabs and in between buildings. They seem to be fluid and unpredictable, and yet also rooted.

I have taken many photos of these banyan trees. No two of them are the same. They look like urban octopuses, freely grasping onto the land or any footholds they can find. They live in between either iconic or, more often, nondescript modernist buildings. Together with the man-made environment of Hong Kong, every banyan tree individually forms a mongrel 'banyan-place' – a combination of tree, human and building; a hybrid of Britain, Hong Kong, China and others; a mixed memory of modern, postmodern, colonial and postcolonial eras. Each is a hybridised place.

To me, every banyan-place symbolises the desire, struggle, beauty, creativity, resilience and life-energy of this city. My friends remind me that these urban banyan trees epitomise the life of Hong Kong people – living in a 'borrowed time and place',[2] uncertain of their future. This metaphor which applied to colonial Hong Kong still continues after the British withdrawal in 1997: life is left 'hanging in the air', and people's sense of home is still elusive, although their hearts are deeply rooted in this place.

This of course is not just the fate of the Hong Kong people, but also that of the drifting migrants elsewhere: living in a borrowed time and place, finding a foothold of existence, making a home between two worlds – that is, between the place of origin and the adopted place.

The migrant life-world is a banyan-place.

THE DISCONTENT OF MIGRANT CITIES

My first introduction to migrant spaces as a child was a visit to my uncle's house in a squatter settlement in the centre of Kuala Lumpur. It was a squalid place full of wooden shanty houses. There were no sanitation facilities and no lamps to light up the dark nights when I had to walk in the narrow alleyways between the houses. My impression of a modern city was a human place squeezed by urban development and tall buildings, struggling to breathe.

This imprint of a binary-city stays with me still.

Every city has its shanty spaces. Frantz Fanon described in *The Wretched of the Earth* this generic colonial binary-city or divided city as being an entity with two irreconcilable parts:

> The zone where the natives live is not complementary to the zone inhabited by the settlers. The two zones are opposed, but not in the service of a higher unity [...] No conciliation is possible [...] The settler's town is a strongly built town, all made of stone and steel. It is a brightly lit town [...] is always full of good things [...] The town belonging to the colonised people [...] is a hungry town, starved of bread, of meat, of shoe, of light.[3]

This colonial othering of spaces is being reproduced in today's postcolonial migrant cities. The world now is still divided between the few who are rich and the many who are poor, between the free and the oppressed.[4]

The place of the first historical occurrence of the multicultural city was linked to colonialism, which has long pioneered its methods of dealing with ethnically, racially and culturally different societies. Many lessons can be drawn from (post)colonial cities. The world today is still plagued by mythologies, racial and cultural prejudice constructed during the past 300 years of colonialism, coupled with capitalist urbanisation. These prejudices have their material consequences, in that they have architectural, spatial and geographical implications for the migrant groups and their spaces. Today, the sight of shantytowns, ghettoes, slums and segregated spaces are commonplace in migrant cities. Fanon's vision of 'The Wretched of the Earth' has become 'The Wretched of the Cities'.

Faced with the rapid change of globalisation, issues of race, religion and culture are being exploited as tools for regressive political agendas. The danger of politically correct multiculturalism is that it also can fuel cultural isolationism and fundamentalist nationalism in a way that kindles ethnocentrism, xenophobia and enmity towards others. Yet, people also need a sense of rootedness, identity and belonging. This search for existential being is like searching for the eponymous castle in Franz Kafka's 1926 novel: unreachable, and yet desirable as it seems so close.[5]

This human predicament can be seen as similar to the urban banyan-place in Hong Kong – attached to a borrowed time and place, yearning for a home.

STRATEGIC POSTCOLONIAL COSMOPOLITANISM AND ENCOUNTERING THE OTHER

One cannot know oneself fully, without encountering the 'Other'. Everyone is an 'Other' in the view of 'Others'.

Encountering the 'Other' is one of the biggest challenges of the 21st century.[6] The increasing interconnectedness of migrant cities provides an opportunity that never existed before: an opportunity to imagine being a world citizen through encountering those who are culturally and racially 'Other'.

Different cultures have their versions of cosmopolitanism.[7] In contrast to adopting an acultural approach, I contend that a new form of Strategic Postcolonial Cosmopolitanism is needed to recognise the role of different modernity, life-world and social imaginary associated with a particular person and culture. This strategy aligns with Gayatri Chakravorty Spivak's notion of Strategic Essentialism.[8] It dares to provisionally essentialise self, culture and community. It dares to imagine flexible citizenship. It rethinks the idea of nation. It speaks in recognition of universalism and particularity. It supports the self-determination of the Third World and the recovery of self of the subaltern. It is concerned about alleviating injustice in poor countries and at home. It questions instant hybrid culture. Its position is provisional.

It is about questioning, replacing, dismantling and transgressing the previous containments and hierarchies of space, power and knowledge that divided racial, ethnic and cultural groups.

The main target of a Strategic Postcolonial Cosmopolitanism is power. There is little meaning to reach across the lines of race, class, gender, culture and faith that divide cities and nations, if we do so without sharing power more equally.

MIGRANT CITIES AND THEIR ARCHITECTURE AS A POSITIVE FORCE

To see contemporary cities as migrant cities is to cure a cultural amnesia that forgets the key contribution of migrants in constructing this intercultural civilisation. Cities and architecture are machines both for remembering and forgetting history.[9] A shared collective memory and history of cities may help assert minority migrants' cultural right in the urban movement of 'right to the city' and in the making of the urban commons. We need to treat the migrant people or place not as hostile aliens or objects of study, but as full partners sharing responsibility for the fate of humankind.

Strategic Postcolonial Cosmopolitanism celebrates situation-specific spatial tactics in seeing, thinking and making architecture. It aligns strategically with the vision of fluid topographies. It celebrates complexity and heterogeneity. It embraces the specific lived experience and emotion of an individual and a society.

With Strategic Postcolonial Cosmopolitanism, migrant cities can become a positive force to inspire us to imagine being a world citizen, to help to liberate ourselves and others from our own conditioned culture, and to dwell poetically with many 'Others'.

ARRIVING

'We shall not cease from exploration
And the end of all our exploring
Will be to arrive where we started
And know the place for the first time.'
— TS ELIOT, *LITTLE GIDDING* (1941)[10]

Notes

1   Yi-Fu Tuan, *Space and Place: The Perspective of Experience*, University of Minnesota (Minneapolis), 1977, p 3.

2   Richard Hughes, *Borrowed Place, Borrowed Time: Hong Kong and Its Many Faces*, André Deutsch (UK), 1976.

3   Frantz Fanon, *The Wretched of the Earth*, Grove (New York), 1971, p 29.

4   See Carl H Nightingale, *Segregation: A Global History of Divided Cities*, University of Chicago Press (Chicago), 2012, for a discussion on divided cities.

5 Franz Kafka, *Das Schloss*, Kurt Wolff (Munich), 1926; first published in English as *The Castle*, translated by Willa and Edwin Muir, Martin Secker (London)/Alfred A Knopf (New York), 1930.

6 See Ryszard Kapuscinski, *The Other*, Verso (London), 2008, for some essays on the ethics of encountering Others.

7 For a discussion on cosmopolitanism, see Kwame Anthony Appiah, *Cosmopolitanism: Ethics in a World of Strangers*, WW Norton (New York), 2006.

8 Applying the idea of Strategic Essentialism to a postcolonial writing of architecture has been explored in Yat Ming Loo, *Architecture and Urban Form in Kuala Lumpur: Race and Chinese Spaces in a Postcolonial City*, Ashgate (London), 2013.

9 See Adrian Forty and Susanne Küchler (eds), *The Art of Forgetting*, Berg (Oxford and New York), 2001, for a discussion of the relationships between architecture and memory.

10 TS Eliot, 'Little Gidding' (1941), *The Complete Poems and Plays*, Faber and Faber (London), 2004, p 197

Author Biographies

ADRIAN FORTY joined the Bartlett School of Architecture at University College London in 1973, subsequently becoming Professor of Architectural History. In 1981, with Mark Swenarton, he set up what is now the MA Architectural History. He is President of the European Architectural History Network and globally renowned for his books *Objects of Desire: Design and Society since 1750* (Thames & Hudson, 1986), *Words and Buildings: A Vocabulary of Modern Architecture* (Thames & Hudson, 2000) and *Concrete and Culture: A Material History* (Reaktion, 2012).

ANDREW SAINT has been General Editor of the *Survey of London* since 2006. He has written a number of books including *Richard Norman Shaw* (Yale University Press, 1976/2010), *The Image of the Architect* (Yale University Press, 1983), *Towards A Social Architecture* (Yale University Press, 1987) and *Architect and Engineer: A Study in Sibling Rivalry* (Yale University Press, 2007). From 1995 to 2006 he was Professor of Architecture at Cambridge University.

ANNE HULTZSCH teaches at The Bartlett, University College London as well as at Queen Mary University of London while specialising in the histories of architectural criticism and visual perception. Author of *Architecture, Travellers and Writers: Constructing Histories of Perception 1640–1950* (Legenda, 2014), Anne has also published on the relationship between early photography and art history, 17th-century travel writing and the use of metaphor in architectural writing.

ANTHONY VIDLER is Professor of Architecture at the Cooper Union School of Architecture in New York. He served as Dean of that school from 2001 to 2012, before which he taught at the University of California, Los Angeles (UCLA) and Princeton University. Among his most recent books are *Warped Space* (MIT Press, 2002), *James Frazer Stirling: Notes from the Archive* (Yale University Press, 2010) and *The Scenes of the Street* (Monacelli Press, 2011).

BARBARA PENNER is Senior Lecturer in Architectural History at the Bartlett School of Architecture, University College London. She is author of *Bathroom* (Reaktion, 2013) and *Newlyweds on Tour: Honeymooning in Nineteenth-Century America* (University Press of New England, 2009). She has co-edited several book collections and has contributed chapters and journal articles to other publications.

BEN CAMPKIN is the author of *Remaking London: Decline and Regeneration in Urban Culture* (IB Tauris, 2013) and co-editor of *Dirt: New Geographies of Cleanliness and Contamination* (IB Tauris, 2007, paperback 2012). He is the Director of the University College London Urban Laboratory and Senior Lecturer in Architectural History and Theory at the Bartlett School of Architecture.

BRIAN STATER is a journalist and lecturer who studied for a master's degree in the History of Modern Architecture under Adrian Forty at The Bartlett, University College London. He taught at The Bartlett from 1996 to 2014.

BRIONY FER has been married to Adrian Forty since 1983. She is Professor in the History of Art Department at University College London. She has published extensively on 20th-century and contemporary art, such as her books *On Abstract Art* (Yale University Press, 1997) and *The Infinite Line* (Yale University Press, 2004). She has written on individual artists including Ed Ruscha, Rachel Whiteread and Eva Hesse.

DAVID DUNSTER, sometime Roscoe Professor of Architecture at the University of Liverpool, has also taught in London at Kingston Polytechnic, University College London and South Bank University. He chaired the RIBA Research Trust Awards, was the founding editor of the *Journal of Architecture* and contributes regularly to the *Architectural Review*.

DAVIDE DERIU is a Senior Lecturer in Architecture at the University of Westminster. He took his master's and PhD at The Bartlett, University College London, and his work has been published in several books and periodicals, including the *Journal of Architecture*, *Architectural Theory Review* and the

London Journal. He has recently co-edited the volume *Emerging Landscapes: Between Production and Representation* (Ashgate, 2014).

ELEANOR YOUNG is Executive Editor of the *RIBA Journal*. Before jumping to architectural journalism, she studied at The Bartlett, University College London where Adrian Forty showed her the value of moments of silence, told her the stories of two hundred years of select British buildings and got her to seriously analyse architectural writing. She lives in a 1953 London County Council-designed block in north London.

GRISELDA POLLOCK is Professor of Social & Critical Histories of Art and Director, Centre for Cultural Analysis, Theory & History at the University of Leeds. Recent publications include *After-Affects / After-Images: Trauma and Aesthetic Transformation* (Manchester University Press, 2013) and *Art in the Time-Space of Memory and Migration: Sigmund Freud, Anna Freud and Bracha Ettinger in the Freud Museum* (The Wild Pansy Press, 2013).

HILDE HEYNEN is Full Professor and Chair of the Architecture department at the University of Leuven. Her research focuses on issues of modernity, modernism and gender in architecture. She is the author of *Architecture and Modernity: A Critique* (MIT Press, 1999) and co-editor of *The SAGE Handbook of Architectural Theory* (Sage, 2012).

IAIN BORDEN is Professor of Architecture & Urban Culture at the Bartlett School of Architecture, University College London, where he is also Vice-Dean for Communications. His books include *Drive: Journeys through Films, Cities and Landscapes* (Reaktion, 2012) and *Skateboarding, Space and the City: Architecture and the Body* (Berg, 2001, revised edition forthcoming).

IRENA ŽANTOVSKÁ MURRAY is a Prague-born architectural historian and curator. She holds a PhD from McGill University in Montreal, and has been active as a translator of Karel Teige and editor of *Le Corbusier and Britain* (Routledge, 2009). Her particular interests are in language and the transnational dissemination of architectural ideas. Until 2013 she was Sir Banister Fletcher Director of the RIBA British Architectural Library.

JAN BIRKSTED (MA Soc Anth, PhD Art History) is editor of *Landscapes of Memory and Experience* (Spon Press, 2000) and *Relating Architecture to Landscape* (E & FN Spon, 1999), and author of *Modernism and the Mediterranean: the Maeght Foundation* (Ashgate, 2004) and *Le Corbusier and the Occult* (MIT Press, 2009) and *An Architecture of Ineloquence: José Lluis Sert's Carmel de la Paix* (Ashgate, 2012).

JANE RENDELL is an architectural historian and art critic who has developed her position on critical spatial practice and site-writing through books such as *Site-Writing* (IB Tauris, 2010), *Art and Architecture* (IB Tauris, 2006) and *The Pursuit of Pleasure* (Athlone Press, 2002). Recent texts have been commissioned by artists such as Jasmina Cibic, Apolonija Susteric and transparadiso. She is Professor of Architecture & Art at The Bartlett, University College London. www.janerendell.co.uk

JEAN-LOUIS COHEN holds the Sheldon H Solow Chair for the History of Architecture at New York University's Institute of Fine Arts. His recent publications include: *Le Corbusier: An Atlas of Modern Landscapes* (Thames & Hudson, 2013); *Interférences / Interferenzen: Architecture Allemagne–France 1800–2000* (Éditions des Musées de Strasbourg, 2013 – with Hartmut Frank); *The Future of Architecture Since 1889* (Phaidon, 2012); and *Architecture in Uniform* (Hazan, 2011).

JEREMY MELVIN studied architecture and architectural history at The Bartlett, University College London. He is consultant curator for architecture at the Royal Academy of Arts, where he curated 'Richard Rogers Inside Out'. He is also curator for the World Architecture Festival. He is author of *...isms: Understanding Architecture* (A & C Black, 2005), *FRS Yorke and the Evolution of English Modernism* (Wiley, 2002), and many articles in professional, academic, national and international publications.

JEREMY TILL is an architect, educator and writer. He is Head of Central Saint Martins and Pro Vice-Chancellor, University of the Arts London. His written work includes *Flexible Housing* (Elsevier/Architectural Press, 2007 – with Tatjana Schneider), *Architecture Depends* (MIT Press, 2009) and *Spatial*

Agency (Routledge, 2011 – with Nishat Awan and Tatjana Schneider). All three of these have won the RIBA President's Award for Outstanding Research.

JOE KERR is a writer, broadcaster, teacher, and Head of the Critical & Historical Studies Programme at the Royal College of Art. His most recent book, edited with Andrew Gibson, is *London From Punk to Blair* (Reaktion, 2012). He is currently writing a book on London's wartime Lenin Memorial designed by Berthold Lubetkin. He is also a London bus driver working from Tottenham Garage.

JOHN MACARTHUR is Professor of Architecture at the University of Queensland, Australia, where he directs the ATCH (Architecture, Theory, Criticism, History) research group. He writes on the cultural history and aesthetics of architecture. His book *The Picturesque: Architecture, Disgust and other Irregularities* (Routledge) was published in 2007. He is currently working on projects including the 20th-century reception of baroque architecture.

JONATHAN CHARLEY is Director of Cultural Studies, Department of Architecture, University of Strathclyde. He has taught across the world, was Project Director for Scotland at the 2012 Venice Biennale, and alongside exhibitions and media projects writes mainly about the political and social history of architecture and cities. His most recent book is *Memories of Cities: Trips and Manifestoes* (Ashgate, 2013). www.jonathancharley.com

JONATHAN HILL, an architect and architectural historian, is Professor of Architecture & Visual Theory at the Bartlett School of Architecture, University College London, where he directs the MPhil/PhD Architectural Design programme. Jonathan is the author of *The Illegal Architect* (Black Dog, 1998), *Actions of Architecture* (Routledge, 2003), *Immaterial Architecture* (Routledge, 2006) and *Weather Architecture* (Routledge, 2012).

KESTER RATTENBURY is Reader in Architecture in the Department of Architecture at Westminster University, where she runs a postgraduate design unit and also the Centre for Experimental Practice (EXP). She is known for her journalism and books like *This is Not Architecture* (Routledge, 2002) and

Architects Today (Laurence King, 2004). She co-created the online Archigram Archival Project and organised the acclaimed 'Supercrit' series.

LAURENT STALDER is associate professor at ETH Zurich. His research focuses on the intersection of architectural history and theory with the history of technology, from the 19th century onwards. He is the author of *Hermann Muthesius, 1861–1927: Das Landhaus als kulturgeschichtlicher Entwurf* (Gta, 2008), and co-editor of *Valerio Olgiati* (Walther König, 2008), *Der Schwellenatlas* (Arch+, 2009), *God & Co. François Dallegret: Beyond the Bubble* (Architectural Association, 2011), and *Atelier Bow-Wow* (Walther König, 2013).

MARK SWENARTON is James Stirling Professor of Architecture, Liverpool University. From 1976 to 1987 he worked closely with Adrian Forty at The Bartlett, University College London, together setting up the History of Modern Architecture master's in 1981. He was co-founder/co-editor of *Architecture Today* from 1989 to 2005 and Head of Oxford Brookes School of Architecture from 2005 to 2010. Books include *Homes fit for Heroes* (Heinemann Educational, 1981), *Artisans and Architects* (Macmillan, 1989) and *Building the New Jerusalem* (IHS BRE Press, 2008).

MARY MCLEOD is a Professor of Architecture at Columbia University. Her research has focused on the history of the Modern Movement and on contemporary architectural theory, examining issues concerning the connections between architecture and ideology. She is co-editor of *Architecture, Criticism, Ideology* (Princeton Architectural Press, 1985) and *Architecture Reproduction* (Princeton Architectural Press, 1988), and is editor and contributor to the book *Charlotte Perriand: An Art of Living* (Abrams, 2003).

MICHAEL EDWARDS studied planning at University College London (UCL) from 1964. He then worked in Nathaniel Lichfield's practice, doing most of the economic inputs to the Plan for Milton Keynes and learning the joys and hazards of working in a multidisciplinary team. He became a lecturer at UCL in 1969, where he has enjoyed working ever since. He blogs at michaeledwards. org.uk

MURRAY FRASER is Professor of Architecture & Global Culture at the Bartlett School of Architecture at University College London, and also Vice-Dean of Research. He has published extensively on design, architectural history & theory, urbanism, and cultural studies, including the award-winning book *Architecture and the 'Special Relationship': The American Influence on Post-War British Architecture* (Routledge, 2008). He is a founding member of the Palestine Regeneration Team (PART).

PEG RAWES is Senior Lecturer at the Bartlett School of Architecture, University College London. Her research examines the material, aesthetic and political constructions of architecture, nature and the built environment. Publications include: *Poetic Biopolitics* (IB Tauris, forthcoming – co-editor), *Relational Architectural Ecologies: Architecture, Nature and Subjectivity* (Routledge, 2013 – editor); *Space, Geometry and Aesthetics: Through Kant and Towards Deleuze* (Palgrave Macmillan, 2008) and *Irigaray for Architects* (Routledge, 2007).

PENNY SPARKE is Professor of Design History at Kingston University, London. She has taught the History of Design at Brighton Polytechnic and the Royal College of Art. Her books include *As Long as It's Pink: The Sexual Politics of Taste* (Pandora, 1995), *Elsie de Wolfe: The Birth of Modern Interior Decoration* (Acanthus Press, 2005) and *The Modern Interior* (Reaktion, 2008).

SIR PETER HALL is Professor of Planning & Regeneration at The Bartlett, University College London, and President of the Town & Country Planning Association (TCPA). He is the author, co-author or editor of over 40 books on urban and regional planning and related topics, including *Good Cities, Better Lives: How Europe Discovered the Lost Art of Urbanism* (Routledge, 2013).

SARAH WIGGLESWORTH heads her own London-based architectural practice pioneering an approach using low-energy principles and economical materials in a highly innovative way. She is Professor of Architecture at University of Sheffield and is co-author of several books. She was awarded an MBE in 2003, appointed a CABE Commissioner in 2010, and made a Royal Designer for Industry in 2012.

TANIA SENGUPTA is Lecturer in Architectural History & Theory at the Bartlett School of Architecture, University College London. Prior to this, she practised and taught architecture and urban design in India. Her interests lie in postcolonial and transcultural studies in architecture and urbanism – specifically in spatial cultures of governance and domesticity, everyday and 'minor' architecture, provinciality and urban–rural relationships.

THOMAS WEAVER works at the Architectural Association School of Architecture in London where he edits the journal *AA Files*, is managing editor of all of the AA's other publications and teaches architectural history and theory within the school's MA and PhD programmes.

TOM DYCKHOFF is a writer and broadcaster about architecture, places and cities. Architecture critic for the BBC's *The Culture Show*, he has presented many documentaries for British television and radio. He has written a weekly column for *The Guardian* since 2000, and, from 2003 to 2011, was architecture critic at *The Times* newspaper.

TONY FRETTON is Principal of Tony Fretton Architects and a Professor at the Faculty of Architecture, TU Delft, the Netherlands. Works by his practice include the British Embassy in Warsaw, Fuglsang Art Museum in Denmark (shortlisted for the RIBA Stirling Prize in 2009), the Red House in London's Chelsea and the Lisson Gallery, also in London. Fretton's books include *Buildings and their Territories* (2013).

VICTORIA PERRY trained as an architect at The Bartlett, University College London, where she completed a PhD which won the RIBA President's Award in 2010. She contributed to the English Heritage book *Slavery and the British Country House* (2013) and to *The Oxford Companion to Black British History* (Oxford University Press, 2007), and is completing a monograph for Ashgate provisionally titled *Slavery, the Atlantic Trade and British Architecture, Art and Landscape 1740–1840* (due 2015). She is Senior Historic Building Advisor at Donald Insall Associates.

WILLIAM MENKING is the co-founder and editor of *The Architect's Newspaper* in the United States. He has organised, curated and written catalogues for exhibitions including *Archigram: Experimental Architecture 1961–1974* (PIE Books, 2005); *Superstudio: Life Without Objects* (Skira, 2003); *Architectures Experimentales 1950–2000* (FRAC Orléans, 2005); *The Vienna Model* (Austrian Cultural Forum, 2012); and *Shrinking Cities* (Van Alen Institute/ Pratt Manhattan Gallery, 2007). He is a tenured Professor at the Pratt Institute in New York.

YAT MING LOO, an architect and architectural historian, is the author of *Architecture and Urban Form in Kuala Lumpur* (Ashgate, 2013). His research explores intercultural cities and postcolonial urbanism. He is currently writing a book on London's Chinese East End for English Heritage. Having taught at University College London and the University of Brighton, he is now teaching Architecture at the University of Nottingham, Ningbo, China.

Index

Photo Credits